PERSONS OF THE MARKET

PERSONS OF THE MARKET

Conservatism, Corporate Personhood, and Economic Theology

KEVIN MUSGRAVE

MICHIGAN STATE UNIVERSITY PRESS | *East Lansing*

Copyright © 2022 by Kevin Musgrave

Michigan State University Press
East Lansing, Michigan 48823-5245

Library of Congress Cataloging-in-Publication Data
Names: Musgrave, Kevin, author.
Title: Persons of the market : conservatism, corporate personhood, and economic theology / Kevin Musgrave.
Description: East Lansing, Michigan : Michigan State University Press, [2022] | Includes bibliographical references and index.
Identifiers: LCCN 2021052850 | ISBN 9781611864335 (paperback) | ISBN 9781609177034 (pdf) | ISBN 9781628954715 (epub) | ISBN 9781628964653 (kindle)
Subjects: LCSH: Capitalism—Religious aspects—Christianity. | Liberalism.
Classification: LCC BR115.C3 M87 2022 | DDC 261.8/5—dc23/eng/20211228
LC record available at https://lccn.loc.gov/2021052850

Cover art and design by David Drummond, Salamander Design, www.salamanderhill.com

Visit Michigan State University Press at *www.msupress.org*

To Lydia, Cece, and Leo. With lots of love.

Contents

ix   Acknowledgments

xiii   Introduction

1   CHAPTER ONE. Genealogies of the Person

23   CHAPTER TWO. Body

55   CHAPTER THREE. Soul

95   CHAPTER FOUR. Voice

137   CHAPTER FIVE. Conscience

175   Conclusion

189   Notes

229   Bibliography

251   Index

Acknowledgments

I would like to acknowledge and thank the many individuals who made this project possible. Though it is a trite statement to claim that much like raising a child, writing a book takes a village, after writing a book—and currently raising two children—I can attest that the statement is true in both cases.

First, I would like to thank my graduate advisors—Lisa Foster and Robert Asen. Without Lisa I would never have ventured into, and ultimately found a home within, rhetorical studies, nor would I have gone on to attend the University of Wisconsin, where I got to work closely with Rob. It was under the tutelage of Rob—and so many other brilliant and kind faculty members at Wisconsin, including Karma Chavez, Robert Howard, Jenell Johnson, Stephen Lucas, and Sara McKinnon—that I truly began to understand the historical, theoretical, and practical significance of the rhetorical arts. It was also here that I learned to write and craft arguments. The learning curve was steep. I stumbled along the way. But Rob was always patient with me as I explored the field and tested ideas. He was quick to offer praise and guidance. He was also there to offer solace when needed. I would not be the scholar I am today without the help of Lisa and Rob. Thank you.

Second, I would like to thank the peers and friends I've made in the field who have contributed not only to this book, but to my work as a whole. Specifically, I need to thank Jeffrey Tischauser. Jeff and I came into the University of Wisconsin at the same time—though in different departments—taught the basic course together, took graduate seminars together, and now have published together. Jeff's friendship and willingness to discuss ideas—often over a beer—has been invaluable. I would also like to thank Trevor Aufderheide, Olivia Conti, KC Councilor, Marissa Fernholz, Brooks Gallman, Kelly Jakes, Jennie Keohane, Hana Masri, Andrew Peck, Meg Rooney, and Megan Zahay for their contributions to my thinking on many of the ideas presented in this book.

At Southeast Missouri State, I would like to thank Pete Soland, first and foremost, for his friendship and also for reading a draft of chapter 3. Pete was always willing to bounce ideas off of one another, but was also quick to go hiking, play basketball, and share tequila when the tireless work of writing a book got to be too much. I would also like to thank Brooke Clubbs for chatting about the book with me over coffee, Lesli Pace for her guidance and mentorship, and the entire department of Communication Studies and Modern Languages for helping create such a nice place to work.

A big thank-you is also in order to those who have helped me work through my ideas on economic theology and conservatism. Namely, I would like to thank Catherine Chaput, Crystal Colombini, Ronald Greene, and Joshua Hanan for their insights during a panel on rhetoric and economic theology at the 2019 meeting of the National Communication Association (NCA) in Baltimore. Further, I would like to thank Leslie Hahner, Casey Kelly, and Mike Lee for their thoughts on the relationship between conservative and far-right rhetoric during a panel devoted to those topics at the 2020 NCA virtual conference. Both panels have proven formative for the arguments present in these pages—thank you.

Third, I would like to thank my editor at Michigan State University Press, Catherine Cocks. Catherine was a joy to work with and made the publication process clear and manageable. Her comments, as well as those of two anonymous reviewers, greatly improved the tone and force of argument in my writing. Thanks, too, to Bonnie Cobb, Anastasia Wraight, and the editorial team at MSU Press for their careful proofreading of the text. This book is all the better for their concise, generative feedback. It goes without saying that any and all errors in the text are mine, not theirs.

Finally, I want to thank my family. To my parents, Scott and Kim, thank you for all your love and support. To my brother, Kyle, thank you for encouraging me to go to graduate school in the first place. As we've often said, even if we weren't related, we would be best friends. To my wife Lydia, thank you for providing me the space—physically and intellectually—to complete this book. Throughout the process you have been my rock, my confidant, and my perpetual interlocutor. To be sure, you have heard me talk about conservatism, corporate personhood, and so many other topics far more than you would have liked. Sorry for always talking your ear off and thank you for your willingness to entertain me, nonetheless. Your partnership means the world to me.

Introduction

At their core, Christianity and the science of political economy provide comprehensive visions of the person and its relationship to other bodies—human, social, political, and divine. One is theological, the other secular. One is concerned with the transcendent components of being, the other with the immanent. One is antiquated, the other modern. Indeed, in typical accounts of the history of Western thought, we are offered a narrative of secularization in which mankind gradually but progressively breaks free of the unreason of religion and the despotism of the so-called Dark Ages, entering an era of Enlightenment in which humanity becomes its own sovereign. In this narrative, political economy becomes the primary means by which the people are able to supplant the sovereign right of kings, establishing a social order based on the autonomous, contractual activities of market actors. This new idea of the human is unmoored from the fetters of religion and state. This human is rational, autonomous, and is self-possessed. This person stands in stark contrast to that envisioned by early Christian theology, who was neither autonomous nor a rational owner of the self, but rather a product of God's divine will. Likewise, the liberal

xiii

individual stands in contrast to the person of medieval political theory, rife with its language of organicism and natural social inequality. At long last, this new science had made every man a king. Or so the story goes.

The story of secularization, I contend, is much more complicated than this traditional view. Far from a simple loss or decline of religion, secularization should be understood as the gradual process of the emergence of a new social imaginary that occurs in and through theological grammars, not against them. Likewise, I argue that we should understand the process of Western secularization as emerging from within particular forms of Christian thought, rather than from the structural shifts of modernity itself.[1] From this perspective, I understand political economy as, in many regards, a product and extension of Christian thought rather than its negation.

The person of political economy and the person of Christian theology are thus not as different as they may first appear, sharing points of complementarity and affinity with one another.[2] Indeed, Christianity inaugurates an economic understanding of law, government, and personhood that has continued to be modified and adapted through the process of secularization in the Western world.[3] For example, whereas in ancient Christian theology human freedom and value were found in the economic relationship of credit and debt between the human person and the person of Christ, and in the medieval period freedom and value were created in the contractual relationship between the human person and the person of the state, embodied by the king—under U.S. liberal political economy the relationship between human and corporation is where freedom and value are constructed.

This is to say, in part, that the rise of liberalism has ushered in significant shifts in theories and locations of sovereignty, pushing it ever downward from the heavens to earthly, human terrain—that is, from the transcendent to the immanent plane. Yet, the movement of sovereignty does not mean that the transcendent plane is no longer active within contemporary economic theory and practice. Rather, it has been displaced and dispersed. According to a growing body of literature of what I will later outline as economic theology, it is this theological inheritance of political economy, as well as the tensions between transcendent, sovereign power and immanent, economic government that we must reckon with to reach a fuller understanding of power in Western society and, I contend, to more fully understand our current moment.[4]

Taking corporate personhood as my starting point, I observe the complex and entangled nature of Christian theology and liberal capitalism to shed new light on the historical relationship between the two and to better comprehend their seemingly odd marriage in contemporary politics. Doing so, I highlight how theories of corporate and human personhood historically have been and contemporarily remain bound together. Further, I trace a rhetorical history of the extension and attribution of personhood to the corporate form, which illustrates how, in this process, the corporation has increasingly become a normative model or ideal to which human persons should aspire. Finally, I conclude the book by offering preliminary ideas about how we might reimagine the relationship between corporate and human persons, economics, and theology, by fashioning a more democratic and humane understanding of what it means to be a person.

Such insights are of scholarly significance yet are also crucial to more fully comprehend the constant barrage of front-page stories regarding claims to corporate personhood in American politics—from *Citizens United* to *Hobby Lobby*, from Mitt Romney to Donald Trump. Thus, while I hope to demonstrate the utility of economic theology to scholars of rhetorical theory, I also hope to demonstrate its utility as a way of understanding our complex history and the maladies of our contemporary moment. Before I begin this project, however, I must first outline my approach to criticism, define key terms, elucidate my understanding of economic theology, and preview in greater detail the arguments to come.

A Note on Method and Theory

Broaching topics as diverse as rhetorical theory, personhood, the corporation, political and economic theory, and theology, a few caveats are required up front. First, this book adopts an inherently interdisciplinary approach to the study of the rhetoric of corporate personhood. This interdisciplinary grounding affects my orientation to and understanding of rhetorical criticism as method. In many regards, my perspective is deeply rooted in Edwin Black's elucidation of rhetorical criticism insofar as I find criticism to be too personal a task of exposition to be systematized.[5] Indeed, the critic as the instrument of observation—that is, as the method—should bring all that they can to a text in order to say something insightful and generative. And much as Kenneth Burke suggested so many decades ago, I believe that part of this critical task is to be aware of the *theological function* of rhetorical discourse, even within contexts that may on their face seem devoid of such ideas.[6]

Yet, while I share an interest in Burke's socioanagogical approach to rhetoric—that is, noting the continued importance of anagogical readings of contemporary social texts—my perspective toward and understanding of economic theology is not reducible to such a mode of critique. An economic-theological genealogy of political economy and of the corporate person cannot stop at the anagogical level but must take into account larger questions of synchronic and diachronic permutations in rhetorical meaning. Theology is one register within which this meaning-making occurs. In this sense, my perspective on method is also influenced by more recent work in rhetorical theory and historiography that engages in genealogical critique à la Friedrich Nietzsche and Michel Foucault.[7]

Such an approach to historiographical method reverses the traditional humanist relationships between will and power, agency and structure, cause and effect, emphasizing the role of discourse in shaping the subject and its possibilities for action in history. A genealogy of the corporate person would thus not look for a unified and clear development of its conceptual basis in the teleological or dialectical unfolding of capitalist logic or in the concerted efforts of a unified bourgeois stratum, but would instead observe, at the level of human and linguistic practice, the ways in which individuals respond to "haphazard conflicts" by repurposing the discursive constraints and tools of the contexts in which they find themselves. In this sense, as Foucault argues, the unfolding of history occurs not in "a decision, a treaty, a reign, or a battle, but the reversal of a relationship of forces, the usurpation of power, the appropriation of a vocabulary turned against those who once used it."[8] As I approach it, such a perspective pushes history into the terrain of rhetoric and rhetorical theory in a double sense.

In the first sense, genealogical histories are rhetorical insofar as they call our attention to the role of the languages of power and the power of language as primary objects of critical inquiry. Recognizing and critiquing the language of power is to practice history with an eye toward the ways in which rhetorical discourses both create and suppress possibilities for action, as well as how such discourses create and suppress opportunities to enact social change in positive terms. Likewise, to recognize the inherent power of language in history is not simply to observe it as an instrumental force of persuasion, though doubtless it is, but also to attend to the constitutive nature of rhetorical interaction. As James Jasinski insists, such a perspective toward rhetorical history notes "the ways specific discursive strategies and textual dynamics shape and reshape the contours of political concepts and ideas."[9] From this perspective, rhetoric not only moves individuals to act, but actively shapes the normative, cultural, and ideational contexts in which they act. To adopt such a perspective to the study of corporate personhood, for instance, would not look simply at how particular actors persuaded others either for or against the idea of the corporate person, but how such rhetorical interaction actively shaped the very idea of corporate personhood and simultaneously shaped the normative grounds upon which such debates occurred.

In the second sense, genealogical histories are rhetorical as they demonstrate the inherently rhetorical nature of historiography itself. This is to say that genealogical history calls attention to the narrative form of historiographical method, moving toward a literary, cultural, and indeed rhetorical perspective toward history that is attuned to the intimate relationships between language and truth. In other words, a rhetorical genealogical perspective challenges the epistemological grounds of Truth, calling attention to the always partial, always incomplete, always pragmatic, and always constructed nature of any telling of historical time.[10] While this perspective toward history notes the always partial and interested nature of historical narration, I should be clear that this does not reduce history to mere fiction. To borrow from E. Culpepper Clark and Raymie McKerrow, what separates the two is "the historian's determination to authenticate the record" they provide.[11]

As Michelle Ballif has argued, such a form of historical narration is not focused on "historicizing what indeed 'happened,'" but instead performs the rhetorical task of "historicizing the so called 'present.'"[12] Drawing from the work of Jacques Derrida, for Ballif history is figured not as a constative act, but rather as a performative one that creates history as much as it describes a record of preexisting historical facts. Adopting such a genealogical approach, I do not attempt to offer a discrete chronology of the historiographical development of the corporation. Nor do I pretend that I have offered the only story about the history of corporate personhood. Rather, I highlight four moments in U.S. political economic history on which to focus my attention as I chart the rhetorical permutations of corporate personhood. In this way, I do not hope to capture a synoptic view of history, but rather to collect a series of snapshots that might put the present into starker relief.

The second caveat I should note is that while corporate personhood—and the notion of personhood more generally—are certainly by no means unique to the United States, or to the West more generally, it is here that I focus my scholarly attention.[13] I do so for multiple reasons, chief among them being that this is where my academic training and expertise lie, that this is where corporate personhood is most significant and developed in its political consequences, and relatedly, that by attending to the economic and theological underpinnings of corporate personhood in the United States we might not only better understand power and politics in the modern West, but may be more fully equipped to criticize it and imagine possible alternatives to it. In this sense, my work is in conversation with theories of new materialism, Black feminist theory, and decolonial scholarship that trouble the overly economistic Western figure of Man, but I am committed to reworking the Western tradition largely from within.[14] Indeed, my primary task here resonates with that of William Connolly in his 2008 *Capitalism and Christianity, American Style* as I view the modern assemblage of economics and Christian theology in the United States both as hegemonic and as "distinctive and fateful in the dangers that it presents."[15] Better understanding the role of the corporation and of personhood in this assemblage is thus a central task of this book, as is pointing to possible alternatives.

Finally, the inherent danger and latent possibilities of such an interdisciplinary approach stem from the fact that it demands much of the author (and doubtless the reader, too). Likewise, it can be rather tough going once you've entered into these adjacent conversations and extant bodies of literature, replete with differing academic histories, concepts, vocabularies, methods, concerns, and so on. The rewards of these efforts, however, are nonetheless worth it and I believe offer much for rhetorical critics who desire to gain a more complete understanding of a text's complex history and function in the world. With this said, however, I should note that I do not claim to be an economist, a historian, or a theologian—I am first and foremost a scholar of rhetoric and communication. As such, I approach economics, history, theology, and other areas of inquiry in terms of what they offer rhetorical theory and use these insights to better understand the function of rhetorical discourses regarding economics and corporate personhood.

As I approach this diverse literature please allow me, up front, to define some of my key terms. First, I have chosen to use the term theology—as opposed to religion—as theology connotes a more systematic and intellectually rigorous study of the relationship between the transcendent and the immanent, the divine and the worldly, the sacred and the profane, while religion connotes specific manifestations and cultural practices of particular theological commitments.[16] Christianity, in the example of this book, can be studied both theologically in terms of the evolution of its doctrine and also in its various religious and denominational manifestations through time. Yet, religious practices are epiphenomenal and are indicative of larger theological commitments and differences.

Second, I have chosen to use personhood—as opposed to identity or subjectivity—as personhood rests at a deeper, ontological level of analysis than do these other terms and as such gets to the heart of the questions that guide this book. For instance, if we think of identity as a point of contact between subject positions and the self, personhood interrogates the very notion of "self" by asking who or what is legible—legally and culturally—to be a person.[17] Yes, both Christian theology and political economy create identities and subject positions for individuals, yet at a deeper level both also construct normative visions of what it means to be a person—that is, to be able to possess an identifiable self in the first place.

Third, and finally, the term conservatism is central to my analysis. Conservatism, no less than theology or personhood, is an elusive term, particularly in the U.S. context. Absent a feudal past, conservatism in the United States has always looked different than in its European counterparts, possessing a distinctly liberal flavor.[18] In this sense, the differences between conservatism and liberalism in U.S. politics are at times difficult to discern in any conventional sense, leading to some difficulties historically and conceptually. For instance, are libertarians conservative? Are so-called neoliberals conservative? Some libertarians claim to be conservatives, others not.[19] Likewise, some neoliberals may claim the mantle of conservative while others ardently reject it.[20] However, in today's political culture, many in each camp get labeled conservative as both are political positions that took an embattled stance against the reshaping of political liberalism from FDR to Johnson and beyond, and insofar as both defend liberalism as a system of market order from the vicissitudes of democratic life.[21]

Attempting to deal with these difficulties, I rely upon Michael Lee's definition of conservatism as a political language—replete with different dialects—for understanding, describing, and creating the world.[22] Points of unity among competing forms of conservatism are tenuous but can coalesce, and historically have done so, on a few key issues: the sanctity of the individual, the need to protect and enshrine the private realm, and a staunch anti-Communism. But I digress. More to come on these terms later. For now, allow me to elucidate my theoretical perspective—that of economic theology—which synthesizes these key terms into a framework of analysis.

Complicating Political Economy, Complicating Secularity

Initially sketched by Michel Foucault in the closing remarks of his *History of Sexuality*, Vol. 1, the rise of biopolitics was made possible by the circumstances of the shift to an era of political modernity.[23] Providing a more complete genealogy of the concept in his series of lectures *The Birth of Biopolitics*, here Foucault demonstrates the ways in which biopolitics is a particular political rationality that regulates life not by sovereign mandate but through statistical norms. Refashioning the relationship between life and law, biopolitics exercises power not on the individual body but on the life and body of the population.[24] Further, such statistical knowledge of the population and the simultaneous self-limitation of sovereign power are dependent upon liberal theories of government, the development of civil society, and the science of political economy.[25] A correlative to the state, civil society is thus the province of government, a site of political management in the production of economic freedom and order. Following Miguel Vatter, we can claim that for Foucault "biopolitics is what allows liberalism to replace politics by police government, rule of law by governance, action by normalized conduct."[26] When viewed as a political rationality of liberal government, biopolitics provides a historical and theoretical lens to understand the complex relationships between state, society, and market in classical liberalism.

However, we might also fruitfully understand biopolitics not simply as a political rationality and mode of governance, but also as offering a rich hermeneutic framework for unsettling and rethinking the discourse of liberal government. In this way, even as biopolitics as a political rationality emerges from and makes possible liberal theories of state and economy, it also provides a theoretical vocabulary—and a useful supplement to genealogical method—capable of destabilizing and challenging the taken-for-granted assumptions of traditional theories of political liberalism from within. Writing on these tendencies, Thomas Lemke argues that the importance of biopolitics "lies in its ability to make visible the always contingent, always precarious difference between politics and life, culture and nature, between the realm of the intangible and unquestioned, on the one hand, and the sphere of moral and legal action, on the other."[27] Thus, as a hermeneutic, biopolitics provides a powerful way of interrogating the complex and power-laden articulations of the structures and practices that govern social life.

Indeed, what Foucault's penetrating work demonstrates is that liberalism as a mode governing social life through the logics of capital—or, rather, governing life by and for capital—becomes the primary focus of historical analysis and critique. Thus, rather than treating capitalism as the wellspring of our discontents, a focus on liberalism and liberal governance illustrates the shifting relations of law, state form, and technology that articulate capitalism's institutional shape and praxis at various historical moments. As opposed to a transhistorical force that produces the terrain of social and discursive action, then, capitalism is produced in and through the rhetorical workings of civil society.

This point also helps illuminate Foucault's critique of socialism and the demand for a new governmentality of the left, as most historical forms of socialism—including the utilitarian socialism of J. S. Mill and various strands of Marxism—remain, in one way or another, committed to underlying principles of political liberalism.[28] Simultaneously, however, as Foucault notes in his later works, we cannot simply step outside of or beyond liberalism but must challenge and destabilize its discursive logics on its own terms, turning its conceptions of the sovereign, rational, and self-possessing individual against itself. This critical task is broached in Foucault's treatment of neoliberalism, as well as his later writings on the practices of the self.

Consequently, it is also in Foucault's turn to neoliberalism where we see the extension of his work on the genealogy of governmentality and the early rumblings of economic theology as a critical project. Bringing his discussion of the origins of modern practices of government from the Christian pastorate to the twentieth-century emergence of neoliberalism, Foucault's lectures on neoliberalism begin to trace the theological inheritances of neoliberalism from its more classical variants. However, as Mitchell Dean and Kaspar Villadsen argue, Foucault's work, while originally offering an extension of the insights of Max Weber, Carl Schmitt, and others on the theological inheritances of politics and economy, culminates in something approaching a narrative of secularization in which neoliberalism exorcises its theological ghosts and ushers in an atheistic, immanent set of governmental practices at odds with conceptions of a centralized sovereign power.[29] This sentiment is captured in Foucault's proclamation near the end of his lectures that "Economics is an atheistic discipline; economics is a discipline without God; economics is a discipline without totality; economics is a discipline that begins to demonstrate not only the pointlessness, but also the impossibility of a sovereign point of view over the totality of the state that he has to govern."[30] Indeed, this point is indexed by Foucault—perhaps counterintuitively—with reference to Adam Smith's notion of the invisible hand as a marked repudiation of sovereign power in economic science.

Taking up, extending, and challenging Foucault's insights on the Christian inheritances of modern political economy, Giorgio Agamben's 2011 *The Kingdom and the Glory* seeks to offer a corrective to Foucault's seeming misdiagnosis of both the origins of economic rationality in the history of the West, and his proclamation regarding the secularity of political economy. Locating the emergence of economic thought not in the rise of the Christian pastorate but rather in early articulations of Trinitarian theology, Agamben's work understands political economy not as a secular, atheistic science but instead as arising from theological and political theories of sovereignty.

Indeed, it is in Trinitarian thought, Agamben argues, that the notion of *oikonomia* emerges and "makes possible a reconciliation in which a transcendent God, who is both one and triune at the same time, can—while remaining transcendent—take charge of the world and found an immanent praxis of government whose supermundane mystery coincides with the history of humanity." Put differently, the formation of Christ's economy of being made possible a theory of government that reconciled divine, transcendent reign and mundane, immanent governance as two sides of a providential order. This ontological split maps onto modern political economy as well, with the seeming opposition of sovereign power and economic governance in fact rendering each other possible, as they "refer back to each other for the solution of their aporias."[31] To truly understand power in the modern West, then, we must understand the dynamic relationship between sovereign reign (state power) and economic government (market order).

Since the publication of Agamben's book, disciplines across the humanities and social sciences have begun to expand upon his insights in the development of economic theology as a critical approach to the history of political thought.[32] Though differing in their historical scope, objects of inquiry, and methodological perspectives, I contend that each of these authors converges upon a central premise: the idea that in order to better understand the history, theory, and contemporary praxis of political economy, we must understand its relationship to theology.

Understanding the relationship of political economy to specifically Christian theology provides a different understanding of its history, theory, and contemporary power. Indeed, I argue that what the perspective of economic theology provides is (1) a different hermeneutical framework for reading the history of political economy (and the place of the corporation in this history); (2) a more robust understanding of power in Western society; (3) a more nuanced understanding of the rhetorical force of economic discourse; and (4) a different way of understanding opposition to neoliberalism.

For example, my project takes economic theology as a framework to read the history of political economy and of corporate personhood in the United States as inherently intertwined with theological and cultural understandings of personhood; to understand how centralized state power and the diffused power of the market economy require one another and work in tandem to produce and govern civil society; that the rhetorical force of economic discourse is not simply from its appeals to rational self-interest but also from theological notions regarding human nature; and that resisting or opposing neoliberalism requires that we begin at these existential, theological levels, fashioning an alternative vision of personhood and relationality.

In this way, I see economic theology as offering important extensions of and contributions to extant literature in the rhetoric of economics. For instance, the work of Robert Asen, Catherine Chaput, Joshua Hanan, and Ned O'Gorman—albeit in different ways—call attention to the power of neoliberalism as not simply one of rational argumentation and subject formation but also of a latent materiality, one that structures modes of stranger relationality, orders our social world, directs and orients our bodily rhythms, and provides its own cosmology of how the world works.[33] Though these authors may disagree as to the nature of this materiality, what these authors concur on is an insistence on rethinking neoliberal capitalism's rhetorical force and thus how we resist and oppose it. Chaput's work is most incisive here, as she argues that anti-capitalist rhetorics cannot simply focus on increased calls for rationalism and deliberation alone—indeed, she argues that this has been a common mistake of figures on the left, including Thorstein Veblen and John Kenneth Galbraith. Instead, opposition to capitalist rhetoric must attune itself to affective, ontological, infrastructural, and even existential registers.[34]

Likewise, I see economic theology as offering important contributions to extant literature in rhetorical studies and critical organizational communication regarding the corporation and corporate personhood. Here, too, scholars in the discipline are broaching conversations regarding materiality in what Dennis Mumby calls the "post-linguistic turn" toward new materialisms, including renewed understandings of autopoiesis, ritual, and narrative to investigate the materiality of organizational discourse.[35] The work of Timothy Kuhn, Karen Ashcraft, and Francois Cooren is illustrative here, as their synthesis of the literature on new materialisms under the banner of the communicative constitution of organizations (CCO) indicates the significance of the ontological turn in organizational communication studies. Specifically, they note the possibilities opened by various approaches, including post-humanist performativity, economic performativity, sociomateriality, affect theory, and actor-network theory (ANT).[36] Here, communication can be reimagined as simultaneously constitutive and instrumental, as transmission and practice, to better understand the force and power of communication beyond rational deliberation and persuasion.

When applied to corporate rhetoric, for instance, Nicholas Paliewicz—utilizing ANT to better understand the granting of constitutional personhood to corporations in 1886—observes the immanent frame in which the Southern Pacific Railroad Co. was able to craft a larger, networked rhetorical culture in which the idea of corporate personhood became almost commonsensical. As he argues, from this perspective, "corporate personhood was not a historical necessity shaped by premeditated critical-rational debate or formalistic interpretations of the law; it occurred by force, without metaphysical origin, or even disputation."[37] Though we should be careful not to ignore the efforts to rationalize corporate personhood within an existing framework of law and legal precedent, the need to understand corporate personhood beyond the confines of legal formalism and instrumental persuasion is well-taken, and one that these divergent bodies of literature concur on.

Significantly, I maintain that economic theology offers another entry point into these conversations, as it examines the rhetorical force of economic discourse and corporate rhetoric not only through rational appeals to human nature, but also as a kind of secular faith. The notion of political economy as a secular faith operates here as both metaphor and historical phenomenon. This is because for many committed neoliberal acolytes, even in the face of global recessions and pandemics, the market will providentially secure salvation for all so long as we submit to its imperatives. Yet also, the development of political economy occurs in and through the development of Christian theology. This theological lineage remains alive and well in contemporary economic theory and praxis and, I argue, informs not only our understandings of markets and of power in the modern West, but also our very understandings of personhood. To resist neoliberalism thus requires that we engage not only at the level of rational persuasion, but at the existential level of our theological commitments to, and investments in, our understandings of what it means to be a human person.

It is in this theoretical conversation—at the nexus of biopolitics and economic theology—that *Persons of the Market* situates itself. The contribution I seek to make is twofold: First, by bringing rhetorical theory and criticism into conversation with economic theology, I offer a new narrative of the historical development of the corporation that paints a clearer picture of the nature of economic power—one that highlights the entangled nature of Christian theology and liberal capitalism. Second, in doing so, I hope to set our collective understanding of our contemporary culture in a clearer light while offering alternatives to the visions of personhood offered by late neoliberalism. Ultimately, it is my position that if we want to understand the economic theological problem of sovereign power and immanent governance that structures our political economy, we must start with the corporation—an institutional form that stands as a limit figure between the two.[38] Significantly, however, the corporation straddles not only the binary of sovereign and economic power, but also that of private and public, state and society, and most significantly for our purposes, *person and non-person*.

Preview of Argument and Outline of Chapters

As I undertake this theoretical and historical argument, the text unfolds in five central chapters, the first of which takes a slight detour from U.S. history and offers a genealogy of notions of personhood—corporate and corporeal—in the West. Using the work of Roberto Esposito as a way of approaching this history, I understand personhood not in terms of a neo-Kantian category but rather as a *dispositif*.[39] Such a perspective demonstrates how personhood has always functioned as a legal and cultural instrument of power—one that is inherently wed to economic and theological discourses throughout history. This brief excursus will chart the development of personhood in ancient Roman law and culture, its transmutation and metaphysical status in early Christian theology, its extension in the shift to medieval liturgical kingship, its secularization in the development of the early modern state, its eventual transformation under Enlightenment theories of liberalism and the social contract, and the adoption of these theoretical principles in the United States.

The remaining four chapters develop chronologically and thematically, tracing the attribution of key metaphorical attributes of personhood to the corporation at four critical junctures in U.S. political economic history—Body, Soul, Voice, and Conscience. Likewise, I argue that at each juncture the corporation is not only rhetorically attributed markers of personhood but also increasingly becomes a normative model of personhood to which corporeal persons should aspire.

For instance, in chapter 2, "Body," I observe arguments regarding the corporate personhood and the corporate body in the decades surrounding the infamous pronouncement in *Santa Clara* in 1886 that corporations were constitutional persons under the Fourteenth Amendment. Specifically, this chapter interrogates larger debates regarding incorporation and the body that occurred at multiple cultural registers: the incorporation of recently freed slaves into the republic, the incorporation of Chinese laborers into the ever-expanding Western territory, and the incorporation of capital in the creation of large railroad companies in Supreme Court justice Stephen J. Field's expansive Ninth Circuit. These debates, I contend, focused on the body of the nation, the body of the corporation, and the body of the laborer, figuring each in a metonymic relationship to the other, wherein all were meant to protect an idealized white, masculine, able body that underwrote the producerism of classical political economy as well as the theological and economic doctrine of manifest destiny.

Chapter 3, "Soul," follows the shifting theological, political, and economic discourses that accompany the transition from producer economics to a nascent consumer culture in the Progressive Era. Having already secured their status as legal persons, corporations now had to defend the legitimacy of this status in a cultural era marked by religious zeal and anti-corporate sentiment. For many progressive reformers, if the corporation was indeed a person, it was one who lacked a soul or its secular counterpart—a discernable personality. Following the work of Roland Marchand, this chapter argues that early advertising and public-relations practitioners—specifically Quaker Oats's Henry Parsons Crowell, and Batten, Barton, Durstine, and Osborn's (BBDO) Bruce Barton—responded to this spiritual crisis by adapting to and rearticulating the very critiques levied against them through what I call a discourse of evangelical capitalism that was capable of crafting a corporate soul.[40]

In chapter 4, "Voice," I chart the debates between the transcendent vision of society offered by conservative traditionalists and the immanent market-based society proffered by the libertarians, which gave rise to a fusion of religion and markets in the development of a new public faith. In the process, arguments for a corporate voice emerged, with words becoming weapons for the defense of Western civilization in the Cold War. For many, a new fusion of faith and markets was required to win the struggle against global Communism, one in which corporation and state were not mere allies in the fight for the spiritual health of the West, but in which the corporation led the charge and the state followed. In other words, the corporation needed to find its voice.

Luckily, it found a champion in the likes of Supreme Court Justice Lewis F. Powell Jr., who in his infamous 1971 letter to the Chamber of Commerce, "The Attack on American Free Enterprise System"—now simply referred to as the Powell Memo—and his later decisions in *Buckley v. Valeo* (1976) and *First National Bank v. Bellotti* (1978) mobilized the business community to lead the charge in the struggle for America. Despite expressing concerns for individual freedoms and rights, however, the corporate voice was prioritized over all others as it became the archetypal Cold Warrior, upholding the virtues of the market amid an ideological war for Western civilization. In the process, the neoliberal viewpoints were given a strong legal and political legitimacy—a legitimacy that would maturate under Ronald Reagan's tutelage throughout the 1980s.

Chapter 5, "Conscience," focuses on the trials and tribulations of the conservative movement during and after Reagan-era neoliberalism, including the fracturing of the long-standing and contentious fusion of conservative traditionalists and libertarians. With this fracturing came a lack of cohesion and identity among conservatives, including the resurgence of debates between traditionalists—now under the moniker of paleoconservatism—and committed free-market conservatives. In this chapter I argue that Trump himself—and Trumpism, more broadly—offers a new admixture of neoliberalism and far-right evangelicalism, one that is inherently distinct from that of Reaganomics. While Adam Kotsko calls this a heretical variant of neoliberalism—one that distorts it from any recognizable form of neoliberalism yet claims to purify it—it may also be viewed as a heretical conservative traditionalism: one that turns populism into oligarchy, transcendent ideals into vulgar political ploys, and Christianity into a stronghold of state power.[41] Somewhere, Russell Kirk is rolling over in his grave.

To help make sense of this fact, I draw from and extend Luke Winslow's theorization of the catastrophic homology that explains formal rhetorical correspondences between fundamentalism and Trumpism.[42] As I argue, we can use the homology to understand not simply such points of correspondence but how, for many evangelicals, Trumpism is part and parcel of their theological worldview—that is, Trumpism is its own (economic) theology. In a political world in which traditional evangelical and neoliberal understandings of personhood and white masculine supremacy are supposedly under assault by "attacks" on religious freedom and a doctrine of political correctness that work in tandem to abridge freedom of conscience, Trump emerges as the embodiment of this vision of personhood and conscience as well as its redeemer. Here, the convergence of markets and faith work in tandem to sustain a culture of political nihilism and existential resentment for the fragility and inherent vulnerability of human personhood, and a fascist promise to restore a white masculine ideal of possessive individualism. How to combat this nihilism and articulate possible alternatives to our present moment is thus the task to which I turn in my conclusion.

In the conclusion, I argue that the challenge of our moment requires a rethinking of the relationship between the transcendent and the immanent in political economy. Unlike various thinkers of the left and right, however, I argue that we must avoid the urge to collapse these competing polarities. While one advocates a governmental atheism that subsumes politics within pure immanence, and the other insists upon the preservation of transcendental truths that must anchor political life, I maintain that the dirty work of politics, and thus of rhetoric, lies in the constant negotiation of transcendence and immanence. In this regard, I am more closely in line with the thought of Mitchell Dean, who argues that "attempts at the decapitation, mutilation, and burial of the king are part and parcel of the very 'economy' of power" that such a move seeks to dismantle. Indeed, as he notes, "were we to drag the decapitated body off and bury it, we would still have an 'empty throne'" to contend with—that is, the power of economic government without its sovereign lord.[43] From this perspective, the attempt to escape power in the political realm is a futile one. Rather, we should see power and sovereignty as a political negotiation—part and parcel of the rhetorical workings of democratic politics. Indeed, such a recognition eschews eschatological promises of salvation from above or below and commits us to democratic action in this world while not precluding the possibility of reimagining it.[44]

Taking rhetorical lessons from those moments and actors studied in the preceding chapters, I argue that in order to move beyond our current economic theological system, we cannot begin immediately from the outside—for there is no clear outside of power nor of the U.S. Christian capitalist assemblage—but must instead turn its language in on itself, recognizing the latent possibilities of its organizing grammars, utilizing the rhetoric of (neo)liberalism to move beyond it. Rather than beginning with arguments of policy, however, I argue that we must begin at the existential register of our political realities.

This means troubling (neo)liberal notions of possessive individualism and its attendant ideas of rights, responsibilities, and property while simultaneously rearticulating them in a way that refashions and secularizes ideas of personhood as gift.[45] Indeed, if personhood is always at once economic and theological—and one because it is the other—any alternative vision of the person is tethered in some regard to these logics. Reimagining personhood as a divine gift, however, challenges the idea of the sovereign individual, calls attention to the embodied and social nature of human personhood, demands a sense of collective responsibility for the world, and finds the value of life not in the ability of persons to create, produce, or consume in the market, but in the fragility of human life itself.[46] Configuring life as gift in this way thus offers an alternative rhetorical economy of the person, one that operates both prior to and beyond the art of political rhetoric and the science of political economy, but also within and through them such that we may utilize economic and theological logics to practice them otherwise.[47] For even as personhood is an insufficient concept in its own right, I maintain that it is necessary if we are to insist upon the inherent value and dignity of human life and to preserve the promise of democratic government.

CHAPTER 1

Genealogies of the Person

One of the earliest and most insightful attempts by modern social science to grapple with the concept of personhood as a question of social and cultural significance is Marcel Mauss's 1938 lecture "A Category of the Human Mind: The Notion of Person; the Notion of Self." Drawing from and extending the work of his uncle, the great French sociologist Emile Durkheim, in this lecture Mauss argued that personhood, far from a stable signifier, was a dynamic concept that evolved throughout the progression of Western history—from classical antiquity to the advent of Roman law, from the metaphysics of Christian theology to the emergence of Enlightenment notions of individualism. In Mauss's particular account, the social history of the concept is traced evolutionarily in a manner that leads, as Martin Hollis claims, from "pure role without self to a finish in pure self without role."[1] This is, of course, but one story we might tell about the history of personhood, and one that in fact leads Mauss toward an orientalizing account that fetishizes modern, Western notions of individualism. Yet, as Steven Lukes argues, for all these problems and confusions, Mauss's work is nevertheless significant as it "expand[s] the category of the person in another direction, seeing it rather as a structure of beliefs."[2] Not simply a social fact, the person, for Mauss, is something that

1

emerges from the interaction of self and society and is articulated according to the larger social structures and norms of a given culture.

While Mauss's work offers a crucial step toward understanding the person, his work carries with it many pitfalls, including an inability to speak to personhood's broader cultural functions outside the figure of the human. From our perspective, his account is incapable of satisfactorily speaking to the historical rise and contemporary problems of corporate personhood, even as it may offer some insights along the way. The contemporary biopolitical theory of Italian theorist Roberto Esposito, however, offers a more robust account of personhood and its role as a technique of government. Understanding personhood not in the neo-Kantian terms of a category but rather as a *dispositif*, for Esposito personhood is a contingent figure that is historically produced at the nexus of law, politics, economy, and theology.

A term popularized by a particular strain of post-structural Continental theorists including Giorgio Agamben, Gilles Deleuze, and Michel Foucault, the concept of the *dispositif* lacks a unified consensus on its precise meaning and origin.[3] As I understand it, however, the *dispositif* is an ordering power that displays discursive force both centripetally and centrifugally as it pulls together disparate elements into a cohesive, unified whole.[4] Standing opposed to theories of sovereign power, the ordering power of the *dispositif* does not operate from a transcendent vantage over the social field, but rather arises immanently from civil society itself. As such, it is an economic form of power and governance that stands opposite to that of sovereignty—a point that Foucault makes clear in his lectures on the rise of biopolitics.[5]

As Catherine Chaput and Joshua Hanan argue, from within the parlance of rhetorical theory, the *dispositif* combines the constitutive and deliberative functions of rhetorical discourse, creating, ordering, and rationally governing the social world.[6] Notably, in their rendering of the concept, they draw from Foucault and Agamben to note the inherent linkage between rhetoric and economics in Trinitarian theology. For Esposito, too, the notion of economic governance premised upon an immanent rhetorical and legal ordering power emerges in Christian theology—namely, in its reworking of the relationship between personhood and the law.[7]

Indeed, for Esposito, personhood is not simply a legal status but is representative of a regime of politics that categorizes, divides, and ascribes value to human and nonhuman bodies, prioritizing particular modes of life over others.[8] Inherited from the ancient Roman *persona*, designating a mask or social role embodied or performed in society, personhood can be understood in a like manner, for as the mask never fully adheres to the face that wears it, personhood cannot be reduced to the body it is ascribed to.[9] Thus, the person begins with the human body but does not end with it. In this way, personhood becomes a rhetorical technique for demarcating and placing particular bodies into a system of biopolitical governance that ranges from nonpersons or things on one end of the spectrum, to full persons and citizens on the other.[10]

The concept of the person thus not only classifies and defines but stands as a circuit of relations that governs the norm and the exception, creating limits and exemptions to full legal and moral standing. Historically, those rendered outside of legal personhood were often constituted as its opposite—the thing. A central and organizing fault line of the Western political tradition, the distinction between persons and things is an effect of the political structures and discourses that govern society. Esposito contends that, as opposed to a natural bipolarity, the relationship between persons and things should rather be seen as one "fitted together in a sort of *chiasmus* structure, a reversed crosswise arrangement, that projects the profile of one onto the other."[11] In other words, the person and thing, when pushed to their limits, reach a point of indistinction with one another, such that a person can become a thing and a thing may become a person. This is the case in slavery, when a person becomes a mere legal and economic instrumentality, and when a corporation becomes a person—when a thing becomes a legal and economic person.

Understood in this way, personhood becomes inherently intertwined with questions of value. That is, personhood is a cultural and legal technology that determines which lives come to matter and which do not.[12] This is the point reached by Lisa Marie Cacho, who argues that the assignation of value marks the condition of possibility for the legal exclusion of particular populations from crossing the threshold of full personhood.[13] However, as I argue, the problem of personhood does not lie in what Cacho describes as the inherent, ontologically determined tyranny of value, and the answer does not necessarily lie outside of or beyond value.[14] Rather, this problematic demands a reworking and rethinking of value—and thus, of personhood—in terms other than accumulation, appropriation, and exploitation. In this

Chapter One

sense, I follow Chaput and Hanan in advocating what they term a "post-humanist humanism" that is attuned to articulating "an alternative political rationality of value."[15] Put differently, I argue that we must think value and personhood outside of and beyond the dominant grammar of capital and liberal notions of possessive individualism.

To do so requires that we develop a deep understanding of the historical relationships among theology, economy, and political thought, in order to think them otherwise. The figure of the corporation again becomes crucial here, with its legal personhood standing as a prime example of the artificial and ideologically laden nature of personhood, as well as its complex and shifting relationship to economic and theological thought. Indeed, even a cursory look at the historical development of personhood and the corporate form is telling of the ways in which liberalism alters earlier theological understandings of personhood as a divine gift into understandings of personhood as a natural, contractual right of self-ownership.[16]

Pre-Christian Understandings of Personhood and Economy

Reflecting on pre-Christian understandings of *oikonomia*, Dotan Leshem offers a brief but illuminating narrative of *oikonomia*'s shifting nature from the classical period to its imperial formation. Intimately bound up with this narrative is the figure of the person. Outlining what he refers to as the human trinity of economy, politics, and philosophy, Leshem details that "Most philosophical schools in Greek-speaking antiquity (with the exception of the cynics) defined the economic sphere as one in which man, when faced with excessive means, acquires a theoretical and practical prudent disposition in order to comply with his needs and generate surplus that appears outside its boundaries."[17] Here, *oikonomia* was identified as the sum total of one's property, slaves, servants, wife, and children, and consisted of the wise usage, management, and administration of these goods to create prosperity and satisfy one's needs.[18] Writing similarly, Angela Mitropoulos argues that for classical thinkers such as Aristotle and Xenophon, the *oikos* was figured not simply as the "physical structures of the house," but more broadly of estate management and household governance of persons, things, and property according to logics of utility for material prosperity.[19]

Central here is the idea of excess, which, as Leshem notes, "was seen by ancient Greek writers as a human condition that forms part of the ontology of abundance capable of satisfying all of man's needs and beyond." Existing outside of and beyond the human, yet simultaneously constituting its very ontology, excess was to be turned to surplus, in turn enabling man to enter into the political and philosophical realms as detailed in Hannah Arendt's account of Greek life in *The Human Condition*. Yet, as Leshem observes, missing from Arendt's account—as well as others—is the figure of the matron, even as she is the first "to live a one-dimensional economic life as a freeborn person, and the first to experience happiness and demonstrate virtue restricted from a political or philosophical life."[20] This is not to pine for an imagined Athenian golden age of democracy, however, but rather to point to earlier rumblings of economic theories of personhood, their inherently limited notion of what it means to be human, and what Mitropoulos calls the domopolitics (as in domicile politics) of classical *oikonomia*. The economic government of the *oikos* necessitated the rule of both master and matron, each enabling and serving the other, albeit with the matron never capable of leaving the privacy of the home or attaining the total fulfillment of the human trinity and legal personhood.

The relationships among economics, politics, and philosophy would shift with the rise of the Roman Empire, with economics no longer confined to prudent household management as the arts and sciences themselves were subject to an "economic colonization."[21] Of critical importance here is the art of rhetoric and its various formulations, first by Plato and Aristotle, and later their uptake by Cicero and Quintilian. Forgoing a nuanced discussion of the similarities and differences of these thinkers on the nature, functions, and scope of rhetoric, suffice it to say that by the imperial era, rhetoric had been separated into both order (*taxis*) and style (*lexis*).[22] Fashioning rhetoric as an art of economizing thought, rhetoric was an ordering power that made a message suitable for public consumption and the moral suasion of the masses.[23] In other words, rhetoric was the immanent means (human speech) by which transcendent ends (truth) could be packaged to various audiences. *Oikonomia* thus began to take on a public function, moving beyond the walls of the home into the political realm of public address. In the process, human relations and personhood itself became economized, as rhetoric was a means of economizing not only thought but social interaction and speech itself.

Another significant shift occurred in early Roman law, as it is here that personhood came to connote a concrete legal status. Indeed, personhood here becomes a legal category that is defined by an ontological and instrumental hierarchy between person (*persona*) and thing (*res*). Part and parcel of the economic ordering power of rhetoric in the imperial age, this strict legal demarcation between persons and things is a central component in the development of personhood. As Esposito powerfully argues, it is the lasting Roman inheritance of the West and provides the political-theological basis of even contemporary understandings of personhood.[24]

However, even as the distinction between person and thing seems firm, the boundaries between the two is and has always been porous, such that one may easily slip into the other. And, Esposito demonstrates, this slippage is often performed on and through the body, for the body is at once a precondition of personhood and simultaneously an object or thing to be mastered and owned. The body thus emerges as a kind of third term that mitigates the relationship between person and thing, for "the body was often the channel through which the person was transformed into a thing," and at the same time ownership and mastery of one's own body was how one became a subject of legal right.[25]

We may observe this fact by quickly turning to Roman ideas of slavery. As Orlando Patterson has noted, Roman slavery was a product of the fiction of absolute ownership—of dominium. It was not the case, however, that because the slave was rendered property that he was in fact a slave. In fact, becoming a legal subject required that we own ourselves as well. Rather, as Patterson explains, "the slave was not a slave because he was the *object* of property, but because he could not be the *subject* of property."[26] In other words, the slave was denied legal personhood as he was incapable of owning himself, and thus of being granted the rights to full ownership and participation in Roman political culture. The slave was thus a slave as he was subjected to the absolute ownership and dominium of another. Patterson is worth quoting at length here, for as he explains:

More than just a relation between a person and a thing, dominium was absolute power. And this absolute power involved not simply the capacity to derive the full economic value of a thing, to use (*usus*) and enjoy its fruits (*fructus*), as well as "to use it up" (*ab-usus*), to alienate it, but perhaps most significantly, as the Dutch legal historian C. W. Westrop notes, it has the psychological meaning "of inner power over a thing beyond mere control."[27]

The true force of slavery, and thus of the Roman ideas of the person that upheld this legal economy, was that it justified not simply the power to own human beings, but that its power reached an interior, psychic level upon which the slave was entirely dependent upon the master for any kind of social existence or value. This "natal alienation," as Patterson terms it, renders the slave socially dead, as the slave has "ceased to belong in his own right to any legitimate social order."[28] The slave was thus not capable of owning one's self or of belonging to society as such. This liminal position of being both inside and outside of society, of being both person and nonperson, exemplifies the rhetorical workings of personhood as a legal technique of governing and administering life according to logics of ownership and value.[29]

The Economy of Christ and Personhood's Christian Economy

Yet, if the *dispositif* of the person emerges in Roman law, it undergoes a series of important and significant shifts with the emergence of patristic legal and theological thought regarding Trinitarian doctrine as well as with the miracle of the Incarnation. As Mauss notes, it is in Christianity that we see an important shift in Western conceptions of the person, as it is here that personhood is provided a firm metaphysical basis in which persona comes to denote not a social role but rather a *substantia rationalis individua*. Thus, it is in Christian thought that the person becomes "a rational substance, indivisible and individual."[30] This metaphysical formula provides a way of reconciling unity and plurality—providing unity despite division; for even as the human as such is a unified rational substance, she is divided

Chapter One

between body and soul, rationality and animality, sacrality and profanity. Thus the economy of Christ is a way of theorizing human personhood, and subsequently comes to bear upon Roman conceptions of the person, such that, as Esposito argues, whereas "in Roman law this cleavage affected the entire human species," in early Christian thought "the same division cut through the identity of the individual, causing a differentiation within it."[31] Christianity thus marks an interiorization of the Roman legal demarcation of person and thing, pressing this split inward into the very constitution of the subject.

Extending this argument, Mauss's student Louis Dumont likewise places the roots of modern personhood and individualism in early Christianity, arguing that its gradual development, culminating in Luther, leads to a Christian articulation of a wholly "inworldly individualism."[32] Elettra Stimilli likewise argues that Christian theology economizes personhood, as through its liquidation of the Hebrew legal tradition, Christianity becomes a "*dispositif* that feeds on the ability of human beings to shape and value their lives as 'being in debt'" to Christ the redeemer.[33] Leshem stakes a similar claim, noting the economistic logics of Trinitarian doctrine and of patristic thought, for as he writes: "Whereas in the classical moment the needs of the life process itself, common to all human and all other living beings, are economized, in the Christian moment the divine within humans—that which humans and God hold in common—is economized."[34] That which is economized here is personhood itself—the divine trace of a creator God in humanity, which is said to separate the human from all other forms of biological life.

The economization of personhood under Christian thought bore important lessons for early corporational doctrines as well, for as the mystery of Christ's economy provided a formula for conceiving of human personality, so too did it help deal with the metaphysical complexities of organizational and corporate personality. Take for example the distinction made between natural and artificial persons in the Roman Canon. While natural persons denoted the corporeal, biological human person, artificial persons were civil bodies, such as the corporation, that served the ends of the state. Tracing the history of natural and artificial persons, the great medievalist Ernst Kantorowicz argues that the corporate form descends from a political theology that replicated and secularized ancient Christian doctrines of the unified yet plural nature of Christ. Originating in the twelfth century as a mode of fashioning a Christ-centered kingship, the metaphysics of Christian theology were slowly adapted by secular apparatuses, fashioning the body of the king as ontologically bifurcated, being both "human by nature and divine by grace."[35] An earthly extension of the natural divine law of Christ, the king was granted perpetual life beyond the bounds of corporeal embodiment via the divine and eternal powers of his office.[36]

Yet, in the shift from the legal system of a medieval liturgical kingship to the rise of the modern state, this metaphysically doubled nature of the sovereign body was fundamentally altered to denote not a split between human and divine bodies, but rather bodies individual and collective. Here, the corporational doctrines of the Church as a *corpus mysticum* were transferred and extended to the collective body of the state and its administrative corporate bodies. As Kantorowicz details, "The notion of *corpus mysticum* signified, in the first place, the totality of Christian society in its organological aspects: a body composed of head and members."[37] This mystical body of the Church took the legal form of a *persona ficta*, a fictitious or artificial legal person, which became applied to various civil bodies in medieval political life.[38]

Yet, just as the shift to secular kingship made use of medieval corporational doctrine of the *persona ficta* of the Church to theorize and explain the personality of the state, the continued secularization of the state also brought about a legal and theoretical shift away from the corporation as an intermediary political body. This is because the move away from organic theories of society and its gradual replacement with a contract theory saw politics refashioned as a rational economic exchange between the state and its people. As German legal theorist Otto Von Gierke writes, "The Sovereignty of the State and the Sovereignty of the Individual were steadily on their way towards becoming the two central axioms from which all theories of social structure would proceed, and whose relationship to each other would be the focus of all theoretical controversy."[39] In other words, what we see is a gradual eradication of intermediary political bodies, as these are absorbed either into the will of the individual or the power of the state. The legal personality of the corporation thus was rendered fictional, with

Early Modern and Liberal Theories of Corporate Persons

This legal move toward the absorption of the corporation into the sovereign state is perhaps given its most definitive account by Thomas Hobbes in his *Leviathan*. Moving away from a universal and eternal conception of a sovereign God toward a secular sovereign in the form of the state, corporate bodies provided a crucial means to realize perpetual sovereignty grounded in juridical rather than divine right, while simultaneously granting the state a sacred, theological foundation. In a secular rendition of the body of Christ, individuals were to surrender themselves to the "Mortal God" of the state in the promise of security and salvation in return.[41]

In this work, Hobbes takes great care to distinguish between artificial and natural persons. Indeed, Hobbes declares that "a person is he whose words or actions are considered either as his own, or as representing the words or actions of another man, or any other thing to whom they are attributed, whether truly or by fiction." Those who are capable of speaking and acting for themselves are deemed natural persons, and those who do not own their words or actions are said to be a "feigned or artificial person."[42] The key factor distinguishing the two lay in the author function, such that a natural person is an author whereas artificial persons act through a granted authority. Such a category is flexible enough to encompass on one end, as Hobbes claims, "children, fools, and madmen that have no use of reason," but also the corporate bodies of churches, hospitals, or states.[43]

In this sense, Hobbes's theory of personhood marks a crucial point in the development of personhood as a larger political concept, and of corporate personhood more specifically. Standing at a critical juncture between the sovereignty of the European feudal state on the one hand and the emergence of liberal theories of civil society on the other, we can see in Hobbes's thought early efforts to craft the person outside of its theological inheritance. Utilizing naturalistic and organic metaphors of the body to describe and legitimize state power, the proper relationship between the corporation and the sovereign state was fashioned in the biological idiom of health and disease.

Not yet private commercial enterprises, the corporation was granted its existence via corporate charters intended to help serve the general interest of the commonwealth. A technique of governance, corporate charters enabled the monarchy to, as Joshua Barkan claims, govern "indirectly in a liberal and decentralized way not confined to the state's territory."[44] Yet, while corporate bodies were crucial to efficient government and the proper functioning of the body politic, greed, monopolies, and the corporate form also represented central threats of bodily revolt. Here, Hobbes refers to these dangers as diseases of the commonwealth, equating them to blood disease, pleurisy, and worms, respectively.[45]

Of most concern here is Hobbes's professed concern regarding the potential of corporations to usurp the sovereign powers of the state. Essentially smaller commonwealths within the entrails of the state, corporations, if unchecked, stood as parasites capable of disturbing the natural functions of the body politic through a kind of weakening of the sovereign immune system. In this sense, non-state corporations, standing as smaller, collective bodies within the body of the commonwealth, were capable of distributing popular will and sovereignty such that they might undermine the unified power of the sovereign.[46]

Standing as neither exclusively public or private, the personhood of the early modern corporation rendered the corporate form simultaneously a gift granted by sovereign charter and a capacity that granted it limited sovereign powers of its own as an agent of civil society. Ontologically linking state and society, transcendent sovereignty and immanent economic praxis, corporate bodies existed in a liminal space rife with tensions and potential antagonisms between the imperatives of the state and the interests of the corporation.[47] Significantly, however, it is in the work of Hobbes that we can begin to see a marked shift away from earlier, medieval theories of the person and toward early rumblings of what C. B. MacPherson has called a possessive market model of the person.[48] This shift would not become complete, however, until the advent of market liberalization policies and the subsequent rise of political economy as a rationality of governing the state. Writing on liberalism's power to alter the metaphysics of personhood initially offered by Roman law, Esposito articulates a change from personhood as a sovereign gift to an object of property and self-ownership. Such a shift marks a significant rearticulation of personhood's economic theology.

The culmination of such liberalization can be seen in the work of John Locke, for it is with Locke that we first receive a theory of social contract without the assumption of an all-powerful sovereign. For whereas Hobbes theorized the state as a necessary bulwark for maintaining peaceful economic competition and enforcing institutionalized rules and standards for civil society, Locke maintained that humans were rational enough to ensure this harmonious stability of their own accord. As MacPherson writes, this enables Locke to "assume that neither money nor contracts owe their validity to the state; they are an emanation of the natural purposes of men and owe their validity to man's natural reason."[49] Money, property, inequality, and the like thus emerge from a state of nature that exists prior to the instantiation of a sovereign state, and as such it is civil society that (self-)regulates human affairs through the rationality of self-possessed economic actors. Further still, such a perspective enables a new vision of the person, which—like money, property, and contracts—becomes untethered from the yoke of a sovereign power. The person becomes, then, a radically autonomous, self-possessed, semi-sovereign subject that exists a priori to community, society, and state.

Locke was not influenced only by the secular impulses of modern political theory, however, but also by shifts in theological understandings of human nature, agency, and divine grace. Further to the point, the secular and theological developments of the era were inherently intertwined as the very distinction between the secular and the theological or religious is the creation of modernity itself. As Benjamin Friedman meticulously demonstrates, the challenges to and ultimate eclipse of orthodox Calvinism would pave the way for a cultural, political, and religious climate in which arguments about individual freedom and agency that undergirded classical political economy could emerge. Crucial here are both the Jansenist and Arminian heresies, one that—in the works of Pierre Nicole—presaged Mandeville and Smith on the notion of the beneficial and unintended consequences of self-interest, and the other that argued against Calvinist doctrine of human depravity and predestination.[50] Indeed, both Jansenism and Arminianism would prove in differing ways amenable to the bourgeois liberalism of Locke and his notion of the rational, sovereign, economic individual.

Yet, the Lockean assumption of the sovereign individual provides liberalism with a cracked foundation upon which it theorizes the social world, for it not only provides a narrow view of human nature and rationality, but in the process produces a chasm between those worthy of full personhood and those deemed unworthy. Indeed, those subjects incapable of or unwilling to embrace such an economic rationality were rendered outside of full individuality and personhood, including women, children, peoples of color, and those with physical or mental disabilities. This promise of the free, rational, sovereign individual was thus the crux of liberalism's blessings and curses, for as MacPherson argues, "full individuality for some was produced by consuming the individuality of others."[51] The human of liberal humanism has therefore never been human enough.

This consuming force of liberal personhood is due in large part to its heavy emphasis on formal rationalism. Of course, Locke was not the sole author of this idea, as Descartes before him had stressed the disembodied nature of reason, and Kant thereafter would proclaim its moral universality. Indeed, as Armond Towns argues, it was Kant who would stabilize the subject/object dualism of form and matter, person and thing along racial, gendered, sexual, and classed restrictions.[52] What emerges from various strands of Enlightenment liberalism, then, is a theory of disembodied, universal reason that became codified in law in the development of legal subjectivity and modern liberal individualism. Despite claims to a disembodied universality capable of overcoming the particularities of bodily difference, as Anna Grear argues, there is "a body smuggled into Western disembodied rationalism."[53] This body is the white, male, able body, whose capacity for labor underwrote theories not only of legal subjectivity but also of modern political economy.

Indeed, the economic man of classical political economy championed its universal mode of reasoning even as it imagined a particular white, male subject. Thus, as Grear argues, the disembodied nature of Western rationalism might better be described as a kind of *"quasi-disembodiment,"* a term better equipped to identify and critique the paradoxical nature and impossibility of a truly disembodied vision of the human person. Rather

14 | Chapter One

than entirely absent, then, "The body is used in liberalism as that which defines the boundaries of rights-holder. But beyond that, the body is devalued and objectified—a mere container or outer limit for the rational subject."[54] This quasi-disembodiment that underwrote British and Scottish legal thought traveled to the United States in the likes of both Locke and Adam Smith, informing early debates regarding political economy in the burgeoning republic.

Smithian political economy, in particular, had a large influence on many Revolutionary figures.[55] Considered the father of modern political economy, Smith had a treatise, *An Inquiry into the Nature and Causes of the Wealth of Nations*, published in 1776, the very same year of the American Revolution. In a climate in which the disputes between Catholicism and Protestantism had already hardened into a religiously divided continent, and in which the Church of England, after the Glorious Revolution, had already become largely Arminian in orientation, Smith's writings could take theological notions of human freedom, happiness, and self-interest as given.

Trained as a Scottish moral philosopher and political economist, Smith championed a laissez-faire vision of economy by separating the market from state and society, in the process creating a private realm of economic activity and self-interest distinct from the political fetters of social life. A professor at the University of Glasgow when he wrote his *Theory of Moral Sentiments* and his magnum opus *Wealth of Nations*, Smith was in close contact with Francis Hutcheson, whose work in theology directly influenced his own writings. As Friedman argues of Smith and his contemporaries in eighteenth-century Scotland, the young moral philosophers were "secularizing the essential substance of their friends' theological principles."[56] Theological and economic values found common ground in Smith's theory of the private world of political economy as opposed to the public world of political life.

This split at the heart of classical political economy is representative of the founding fallacy of modern economics and the blind faith it engenders. Economic historian Duncan Foley highlights that stemming from this fallacy is a deep question of moral philosophy and theology that lies at the heart of Smith's competitive market mechanism: namely, the position that "urges us to accept direct and concrete evil in order that indirect and abstract good may come of it."[57] More than simply a logical or moral fallacy, however, this idea demonstrates the element of theodicy that lies at the core of classical political economy. Political economy for Smith—and the invisible hand of the market itself—illustrates the providential vindication of God's divine will. The market turns vice into virtue, self-interest into collective benefit, evil into good. The question of how an all-powerful God would allow human suffering is given an answer here by Smith—a free market turns individual suffering into a social good, which contributes to the economic health of the nation. Importantly for Smith, a free market means a market safe not only from governmental intervention—or at least too much of it—but also from corporate bodies. Indeed, corporations were figured by Smith as artificial impediments to a realm of free economic exchange.

U.S. political economists borrowed both from the Scottish liberalism of Smith and the English liberalism of Locke in their arguments for a new liberal state, to the extent that Friedman argues that religion and economics were in nearly full harmony in the late eighteenth- and early nineteenth-century United States.[58] Though liberalism was originally a good that was imported to the United States, it was also shaped to comport with uniquely American conditions.[59] Not simply an amalgam of Smithian and Lockean liberalism, then, U.S. liberalism also spoke back to these influences, crafting them to the exigencies of U.S. life. Chief among the notable characteristics of U.S. liberalism are commitments to Protestant values of self-determination, hard work, and religious freedom; an understanding of material progress as synonymous with constant expansion; and a sharpening, legally and politically, of the distinctions between the public and private realms.[60]

The finer details of such an American flavor of liberalism were worked out in the early years of the republic, through a rhetorical admixture of the political economy of Smith and Locke and an emphasis on biblical moral authority. Indeed, many of the early political economists of the United States were trained theologians.[61] What emerged was a vision of a republic of proprietary individuals who understood property ownership as the basic unit of society at large, as well as of popular sovereignty. As Jeffrey Sklansky explains, "Unlike in England, where ownership of real property was the privilege of a dwindling minority, in the American colonies ownership of the land as well as the family labor needed to support a household was the norm rather than the exception."[62] The American ideal of self-sufficiency, then, was premised upon a household economy that was freed from the fetters of a feudal lord and made sovereign in its own right.

16 | Chapter One

As the central unit of the early U.S. market, the domestic *oikos* of the household, however, was not entirely subject to the science of political economy. Here, as Sklansky notes, "The classical distinction between household and polity informed the Enlightenment assumption that family relations were essentially apolitical, governed by different laws than those of free will and voluntary association."[63] This stark distinction justified the existence of patriarchal familial authority within the home, while championing Enlightenment values of egalitarianism outside of those four walls. This seeming contradiction is reconciled by the fact that—as explained above—the requisite mental faculties of Enlightenment reason, those of the self-interested, virtuous actor capable of mastering their passions, were always already identified with masculinity as such. In other words, this dichotomy of domestic and political economy was justified by liberal visions of personhood, and its attendant racialized and gendered logics of quasi-disembodiment. In this way, Christian notions of mastery and of *pater familias* on the one hand and economic notions of a realm of egalitarian exchange on the other, worked hand in glove to facilitate a moral and social order premised upon patriarchal rule.

A question left largely unanswered in these debates in the early republic was that of the corporation. Breaking with the mercantilism of the British monarchy and its commercial arm, the British East India Company, the very model of the plebeian household economy outlined above was meant to supplant the special privileges afforded by both king and company. Yet, the question of the corporation and corporate property quickly became central to U.S. law, for what was the United States to do with British companies, contracts, and property in their young republic? Despite a deep suspicion of the corporation—and a silence regarding them in the Constitution—early justices were tasked with reconciling the existence of the corporate form to the new U.S. economy. Here, the notion of corporate personality was central. As Scott Bowman notes, the corporation "could not have secured its extraordinary legal privileges or achieved ideological acceptance so readily without assuming the guise of personhood in a market economy." A collective institutional form, modern American jurisprudence transformed the corporation into a legal person that fit within the rhetorical strictures of liberal individualism.

The doctrine of Smith, an outspoken critic of the corporation, thus became a means for reimagining the corporation as a mere tool of monopoly power to a "modern, anthropomorphic conception of the corporation suited to the individualistic premises of liberalism." Through what Bowman refers to as an "ideological trick of mirrors," the jurisprudence of the early nineteenth-century republic granted the corporation constitutional rights to property and contract under the guise of "corporate individualism."[64]

These protections were originally established in the case of *Terrett v. Taylor* in 1815 and more fully developed four years later in *Dartmouth v. Woodward*. These early cases faced the difficulties of how to treat British corporations and their property in America post-revolution. At a time when corporations were not yet viewed as inherently public or private, but as a hybrid formed through governmental action, utilized in private commerce, and geared toward public infrastructural works, *Terrett* established an early distinction between private and public corporations.[65] Additionally, the case maintained that property acquired by corporations prior to the Revolution did not transfer to the state, protecting civil rights to property and upholding British common law post-revolution. Focusing on property belonging to the Episcopal Church of Alexandria, Virginia, these decisions were penned in the majority opinion by Justice Joseph Story on the basis that the church, chartered as a private corporation under British law, was a "persona ecclesia," a legal person with its own contractual individuality and the ability to transmit its property to its successors.[66] The decision ultimately established the legislature's power over public as opposed to private corporations, respecting the authority of the charter and the rights to private property it was meant to protect.[67]

These logics would be extended in the *Dartmouth* case, which, as Bowman observes, "translated the higher law principles of *Terrett* into constitutional doctrine."[68] The case arose following a struggle for internal control of the board of Dartmouth College, established by the British under a private charter as an eleemosynary corporation for the education of Native Americans in Christian values in 1769, in which the legislature of New Hampshire attempted to amend the charter to gain power over the board. The case had to deal with the primary considerations of whether or not the contract of the charter was protected under the U.S. Constitution. Derived from this issue was the distinction between public and private corporations addressed in *Terrett*. Drawing implicitly from *Terrett*'s doctrine, Justice John Marshall delivered the lead opinion claiming that the original charter of 1769 must be upheld as a private contract protected by article 1, section 10 of the Constitution, "which declares that no state shall make any law impairing the obligation of contracts."[69] For Justice Marshall, the property of a corporation is protected by the Constitution as it is a legal person.

Though its personhood for Marshall was a legal fiction, corporate property and contracts required legal protection. In large part, this is because, for Marshall, the corporation was primarily a tool "of clothing bodies of men" in an individualized legal personality. Concurring with this opinion was Justice Story, who wrote that the corporation is "in short, an artificial person, existing in contemplation of law and endowed with certain powers and franchises . . . exercised through its natural members."[70] In the cases of *Terrett* and *Dartmouth*, then, we see the early jurisprudential work of fitting the corporation within liberal contract law, understanding the personhood of the corporation as a product of those natural persons gathered together in its name. The personhood of the corporation was thus artificial and remained politically and economically subservient to human and public needs.

The corporate form was not only of vital legal concern but became a politically divisive issue in the young republic—specifically in the attack on the Second National Bank that emerged under Andrew Jackson's first term. Entering the political arena in Tennessee shortly following the Panic of 1819, Jackson had maintained that the bank was largely responsible for the depression and other national troubles through its paper-money policies and the corrupt politicians that supported them. The Second National Bank amounted to a centralization of economic privilege that threatened to erode the promise of mass white male democracy that Jackson embodied. Under the tutelage of Nicholas Biddle, however, the bank had been able to regain its social standing after the panic. Yet, for the Jacksonians, Biddle and his bank were "living symbol[s] of aristocratic disdain for the people and their representatives."[71] Indeed, as Robert Remini explains, for Jackson the bank was a "'hydra-headed monster' whose powers and potential were so enormous that it threatened the safety of the Republic."[72] Eventually destroying the bank and vetoing its rechartering, Jackson defended a republic of common white male laborers against the artificial forces of economic privilege.

The age of Jackson would concurrently see a rapid liberalization of corporate law. Indeed, throughout the mid-nineteenth century the corporation would acquire an increasingly private function under the law. It was during this time period that the power of charter and incorporation was shifted from a special privilege of legislative mandate to the creation of laws at the state level regarding general acts of incorporation. Intended to democratize commerce by making charters of incorporation more readily available to entrepreneurs, this development marked a rapid growth in the corporate form in the United States.[73] With the rise of manufacturing, mining, and railroad companies, the United States saw a fundamental shift in its political economy. As Thorstein Veblen notes, this new political economy was premised not primarily upon industry, the production of material goods, but rather on business, the making of money for free on property assets through capitalization.[74] This shift is represented for Veblen by the rise of finance capital and the joint stock company in the creation of an economy premised on credit.

Prior to the 1840s, technological and communicative limitations in the institutional structures of production prohibited the facilitation of large-scale, multi-unit corporations in the United States. During this time, business enterprise was owned and operated primarily in the form of individual or partnership contracts, foregoing a need for hierarchical systems of management. Additionally, while the economy was becoming more specialized in the early nineteenth century, streamlining and routinizing business transactions, production and distribution were still primarily carried out through traditional technological means of wind and animal power.[75] Yet, as the nation saw growth in its population and expansion into new territories, trade and commerce across the nation increased.

The increase in trade necessitated an increase in production and labor. For most companies prior to the 1840s, however, centralization of production and specialization of labor forces were not yet required.[76] Indeed, it was not until the rise of coal power, railroads, and telegraphy that production and distribution processes were revolutionized. These advances in transportation and communication technologies afforded the rise of the large, multi-unit corporate enterprise, found first and primarily within the railroad companies themselves.

As Mansel Blackford and Austin Kerr explain, the realization by railroad executives of the need for "firm, exact, human control over the new railroad technology" saw the development, experimentation, and pioneering of new methods to meet their growing managerial needs.[77] The speed, regularity, and volume of trade made capable with the development of rail technology led to the creation of new organizational structures and internal methods of communication premised on a new class of business managers capable of co-ordinating trade. Thus, as business itself became decentralized, management took on a hierarchical and stratified structure, seeing middle management positions increase among a diverse set of departments established to ensure the smooth and efficient coordination of business operations.[78]

The rise of this new managerial class was premised first and foremost on the fundamental break of management from ownership in the modern corporation. As enterprise grew in scope and scale, so too did the capital required for the foundation of new business ventures. This need was largely met in structural changes in corporate ownership as individual, family, and partnership contracts gave way to the quasi-public, joint-stock corporation under the newly liberalized laws of incorporation. Indeed, the continued development of the railroad industry helped to bring about the central-ization of capital markets in New York City.[79] The burgeoning reliance on outside capital and the internal organizational changes of managerial methods mutually reinforced one another and helped solidify the separation of ownership that transformed the nature of the U.S. economy in the rise of the quasi-public corporation.

The rapid rise in material prosperity and the continued westward expansion of the United States in the age of Jackson were also inherently entangled with the shifting theological attitudes of the day. Indeed, Charles Sellers reads the cultural struggle over the American ethos during the market revolution as one between two competing theological strands of Protestantism—the democratically minded Antinomianism of the yeoman farmer and the Arminianism of the investor/entrepreneur. What emerges from this struggle, for Sellers, is not the triumph of one over the other, however, but rather a fusion of the two in which capitalism parasitically fed on and co-opted the democratic spirit.[80] The end result of this fusion, for Sellers, was a culture of bourgeois democracy and liberal capitalism that has been embedded in the American spirit ever since. Though we may take issue with Sellers's claims to a kind of *gemeinschaft/gesellschaft* split between the more humane, authentic, and democratic virtues of yeoman culture as opposed to the inhumane, inauthentic, and debased virtues of bourgeois life, we may find here a new synthesis of faith and markets that is unique to the American notion of a middle-class society.[81]

It is also during this period of meteoric rises in standards of living, the subsequent rise of technological progress, and geographic expansion that arguments for a millennial mission for the United States began to emerge. From essayist Ralph Waldo Emerson to historian George Bancroft, an optimistic sense of America as a divinely ordained nation became increasingly common and would come to its muscular, nationalist culmination in the doctrine of manifest destiny. Though this line of thought was already nascent in Jeffersonian Anglo-Saxonism, it was here that it would come to maturity as manifest destiny took on new economic and theological significance given the unique exigencies of the era of Jackson. How these new insights would be understood and applied in the decades to come, particularly in an era marked by the spread of large, quasi-public corporate bodies, would become a key question for many, including Supreme Court justice Stephen J. Field.

CHAPTER 2

Body

Incorporation invokes the body. Perhaps more aptly, it invokes multiple bodies. Incorporation can be defined as "the action of incorporating two or more things, or one thing with (in, into, to) another; the process or condition of being so incorporated; union in or into one body."[1] Thus, as a cultural as well as an industrial process, incorporation signifies the internalization and unification of foreign elements into the body. It is a process of amalgamation, of assimilation, of making others the same through combination. As such, incorporation is a technique of power—a political process—enacted on and through the body. When viewed in this way, incorporation becomes a useful hermeneutic with which to read and understand power and politics—one that makes the body visible for critique in important ways.

This is significant, for as Karma Chavez pointedly notes, the body has always been an implicit concern in rhetorical studies. As an implicit concern, however, the body has remained largely unintelligible to rhetorical analysis. When it has been made explicit in more recent theorizing, however, Chavez avers that there has been too strict a focus on abstract notions of the body and embodiment as opposed to the actual body or bodies that become material markers of Otherness. As she states clearly, "with rare exception,

23

only when actual bodies are *not* white, cisgender, able-bodied, heterosexual, and male do they come into view as sites of inquiry."[2] Demanding that rhetorical scholars pay attention to the actual bodies and how they come to matter, Chavez's work both articulates a disciplinary history of the body in rhetorical studies and calls for renewed attention to it as an object of study.

Approaching incorporation as a way of making the body and its mattering visible, this chapter interrogates the ways in which the body became the primary and ordering metaphor for understanding personhood in the mid–late nineteenth century. During this time period, the United States underwent a series of complex debates regarding incorporation and the body that traversed multiple rhetorical registers—political, economic, cultural, and theological. Primarily, these debates focused upon the issues of expansion, immigration, and industrial capital, along with their inherent entanglements. Indeed, for many in the populist movement the rise of the large business corporation, the growth of metropolitan urban centers, continued westward expansion, and increased immigration shared a common cause, leading to the erosion of a so-called traditional yeoman lifestyle of rural America. The continued expansion of the nation, of urban life, and of capital were thus perceived as inimical to republican values of free land and labor in general, and to classical political economy's ideal of the white male producer more specifically. Following Alan Trachtenburg, I argue that incorporation as a rhetorical and material process represented a larger cultural clash over the very idea of America.[3] These debates regarding Americanness throughout the nineteenth century played out most forcefully in the new western territory of California.

A symbol of the very processes of westward expansion, industrial and racial incorporation, and laissez-faire economics that marked the era, California is also where eventual Supreme Court justice Stephen J. Field and labor agitator Denis Kearney would debate the meaning of personhood with regard to the Fourteenth Amendment. These debates would play out over the question of Chinese labor and the large railroad companies who employed them, as well as the attendant contract rights of each to operate within a free market economy. What emerges is a complex set of debates regarding personhood and the body that plays out in economic, racial, and theological terms. Debates over incorporation and the body thus were debates about the body of the nation itself in an era when traditional notions of economic liberty were being upended.

In order to trace the complexities of these debates, I will first provide an overview of Justice Field and his Jacksonian persuasion. Though these debates regarding corporate personhood occurred after the so-called age of Jackson, the principles of Jacksonian democracy nonetheless are crucial to understanding Field's arguments. Indeed, I argue, following Field's biographer Paul Kens, that Field's jurisprudence is largely an attempt to apply Jacksonian principles to a post–Civil War era marked by the rise of large corporate actors.[4] Jacksonian democracy provides a particular marriage of theology and economics for Field to make sense of the new West—particularly through the ideas of a providential free market, a civilizing mission of industrial capital, a millennial understanding of the United States in world history, strict notions of white male superiority, and the virtue of manly labor that emerge in the doctrines of manifest destiny and popular sovereignty. Here, personhood is reduced to the body of the laboring producer, with all of its racial and theological baggage.

Next, I turn to a closer look at the development of Field's jurisprudence, and his extension and adaptation of Jacksonian principles in the embrace of the large corporation. This jurisprudential history, too, is where Field meets Kearney, as Kearney and his Workingmen's Party of California (WPC) rise to power in opposition to Field's seeming embrace of industrial interests and Chinese labor. These disputes ultimately lead me to my analysis of two primary legal cases in which Chinese labor and corporate personhood are evoked together to challenge the narrow, originalist understanding of the Fourteenth Amendment's Equal Protection Clause—*In re Tiburcio Parrott* (1880) and *San Mateo County v. Southern Pacific Railroad* (1882). It is in these cases that the rhetorical work of crafting corporate personhood and equal protection is done, using the Chinese laborer as a crucial tool to gain legal footing for the corporation. I contend that these cases and the ultimate declaration by the Waite Court in 1886 that corporations were in fact persons under the Fourteenth Amendment culminated in the creation of a hierarchy of personhood. Atop this hierarchy was the corporation as it came to embody the principles and virtues of a republic of white male laborers.[5]

26 | Chapter Two

Justice Field's Jacksonian Persuasion

Keeping alive and redirecting the Jeffersonian impulse in an age of industrialization, Jacksonian culture was marked by a mass politics that harbored a deep distrust of political privilege, an assault on class divisions among white men, and a liberal critique of economic concentration.[6] These mutually reinforcing positions led many Jacksonians to advocate the cause of hard money and attack the large corporation, exemplified at the time by vast banking monopolies. For these individuals, the corporation was anathema to the revolutionary spirit of Jefferson and created fears of the return of aristocracy in the form of an oligarchical, moneyed elite. This led Jacksonians to launch an assault on their more conservative Federalist and Whig counterparts, advancing instead a liberal democratic anti-monopoly position that opposed a centralized financial system. The corporation was thus seen by many Jacksonians as an alien and monstrous other to be excluded from the body of the nation. Indeed, it is in Jackson's veto message that we are offered a unified vision of Jackson's constitutional and democratic ideals.[7]

This anti-monopoly sentiment is true of other prominent Jacksonians as well, as the bank proved a defining issue for the Democratic Party. In his tract *What Is a Monopoly?*, for instance, radical democrat Theodore Sedgwick argued that the corporation was a product of aristocratic privilege and an alien entity brought to the shores of America by British colonial rule. Corrosive of the egalitarian aspirations of the U.S. republic, corporations threatened both political equality and the promises of an open and free market of exchange for individual producers.[8] Significantly, these arguments were at once political, economic, racial, and theological, for as Alex Zakaras has argued, for many radical democrats "the market seemed a natural phenomenon, a pure embodiment of the laws of God and nature, which promised to every man the fruits of his own toil."[9] Here, Sellers's arguments regarding the Arminian/Antinomian split during the Jacksonian era are worth revisiting. Specifically, he argues that Arminian theology clothed "the market cosmology in the forms of puritan tradition," ultimately comporting traditional rural values to "the market's Newtonian/Lockean myth."[10] In other words, the market was given theological and scientific standing as the representation of God's natural law.

Corporations, most notoriously the Second Bank of the United States, however, were imagined by many Democrats as artificial impediments to the natural, providential functions of an unfettered free market of white laborers. As Sean Wilentz notes, Jackson's vision was to "liberate democratic government from the corruptions of men and institutions of great property with political connections," utilizing federal power to intervene in the market to eradicate artificial impediments to a naturally free market rather than to erect them.[11]

It was into a Jacksonian culture and family that Stephen J. Field was born in November 1816 in Haddam, Connecticut. The sixth child of David Dudley Field and Submit Dickinson Field, David was a congregationalist minister who quickly moved the family to Stockbridge, Massachusetts, where Stephen spent his early years. A family of great prominence, Stephen's brother Cyrus was a businessman and telegraphy pioneer, and his brother David II was a prominent lawyer and legal reformer. Stephen and his brothers would grow up to be committed members of the democracy, translating its precepts into legal doctrine. As Arthur Schlesinger Jr. has chronicled, the Fields quickly became one of the most distinguished families of northeastern Jacksonianism, with Stephen's brother David's efforts to reconstruct, simplify, and improve legal codes "represent[ing] the culmination of the Jacksonian demands for legal reform."[12] Yet, for all of David's efforts, it was perhaps Stephen who would go on to have an even greater impact on U.S. law later in his life as a justice on the Supreme Court.

Before his appointment to the Court, however, Stephen was among those who quickly settled in the new territory of California, leaving Massachusetts to seek the promises of freedom, liberty, land, and wealth that the so-called Golden State came to represent in the American mind in 1849. The forty-niners—or Argonauts as they were sometimes called—came from around the globe to build a new life and attain the elusive American dream of economic liberty in the foothills of the Sierra Nevada Mountains. Indeed, as legal historian and biographer Paul Kens argues, Field's experiences in the Gold Rush would be formative, shaping his radically individualist understanding of Jacksonian politics, which would later take form in his legal theories of labor and personhood.[13]

The very prospect of life in California seemed to bring Jacksonian principles to life. It was acquired after the Mexican American War, a war that was waged upon the Jacksonian principles of manifest destiny—a political, economic, and racial theology that rhetorically sutures a providential vision of laissez-faire political economy and national prosperity through continued geographic expansion. Originally coined by radical democrat Locofoco and publisher John O'Sullivan in his *Democratic Review*, manifest destiny provided divine reasoning for continued U.S. expansion in Texas, Oregon, and California.[14] Somewhat paradoxically, then, manifest destiny, while dependent upon the move away from orthodox Calvinist notions of individual predestination, clings to notions of predestination and attaches them to the nation itself.[15] Individuals were free to act and choose as moral and economic agents, but the United States was preordained with a messianic role in world history. Though manifest destiny was given its popular flavor by the radical democrats, however, the historical origins of its ideological positions on issues of race, economy, and nation date back much further.

As Reginald Horsman argues, manifest destiny emerges from a longer history of racial Anglo-Saxonism and American exceptionalism that vivified the revolutionaries, particularly Thomas Jefferson. Viewing the Revolution as both a return to an ancestral Germanic tradition of liberty and as an embodiment of the new Enlightenment theories of liberalism, Jefferson understood the birth of the United States as the culmination of cultural, if not racial providence. Just fifty years later, Jacksonian culture, as the successor of Jeffersonianism, was able to recast this myth within the mutually reinforcing American Romanticism of the age and the rise of racial pseudo-science that brought empirical weight to the supposed natural racial distinctions among peoples. Manifest destiny became the rhetorical packaging for this racial mythology, providing "a sense of national racial destiny" for the United States to bring Christianity and republican government to the world.[16]

The supposed proof of this providential destiny was provided for many by the continued economic growth and prosperity of the republic itself. A continent of vast expanse, comprised of a seemingly endless bounty of natural material goods, the United States appeared a veritable Garden of Eden for God's chosen people. As Adam Gomez argues, for O'Sullivan and his ilk, the nation itself was chosen and pure, as he "locates sin exclusively outside the borders of the United States and understands America as a purely virtuous entity obligated to work as a missionary of democracy throughout the world."[17] Continued westward expansion and economic penetration of foreign markets became the primary ways in which the United States performed the civilizing mission God had ordained.[18]

Yet, expansion also raised the difficult question of incorporation. The complexities of this problem became evident in the debate regarding the annexation of Texas. The disputes that led to the Mexican American War in the first place were used by many radical democrats, including O'Sullivan and Romantic historian George Bancroft, to argue for the divine right of the United States to the territory. As Lyon Rathbun explains, Bancroft's *History of the United States* "revealed how the Divine Will was enfolded within the historical development of the American nation."[19] Indeed, the nation was impervious to outside forces and could not be stopped in this mission, as, for Bancroft, the nation was "steaming, infallibly, toward the millennium."[20] However, after annexation, the question of what was to be done with the Mexican peoples gave pause to many Democrats. Once hopeful of civilizing the supposed heathen and savage peoples of the continent, many became convinced of the unassimilable nature of peoples of color. As Horsman notes, by the 1840s, "The conflict was no longer viewed as that of civilization against savagery," but rather was becoming "the white race against the colored races."[21]

This declamation of inherent racial inferiority caused problems for manifest destiny's political theology. If the nation was civilized, Christian, prosperous, and pure—that is to say, white, in all of its coded language—how could it incorporate a people that was deemed biologically incapable of reaching these statuses? For O'Sullivan and others, the answer came in the crafting of democracy as a personal faith, a secularized theology that largely wrote out peoples of color yet left space for their conversion.[22] This political theology played out in a more practical, policy-oriented way in a platform of state's rights, individualism, and laissez-faire economics, buttressed by a strong sense of racial absolutism that protected the white male worker. Thus, as historian Joshua Lynn has argued, Jacksonian Democracy was a persuasion bent upon preserving the white man's republic at all costs. Indeed, the body of the white male producer and the body of the nation stood in for one another, so that to protect and preserve one was to protect and preserve the other.[23]

This fact was particularly true of the party as its antislavery factions splintered from the democracy in the 1850s in the aftermath of the

30 | Chapter Two

Kansas-Nebraska Act. Seeing many of its rank and file leave to form the short-lived Free Soil Party and eventually the Republican Party in Ripon, Wisconsin, in 1858, the party of Jefferson and Jackson was fundamentally altered. Yet, while some, following the work of Schlesinger, have argued that a unified Jacksonian party was torn asunder with its more committed antislavery members' exit from its ranks, and was further weakened in the adaptation of a "neo-Jeffersonian" conservatism by the withering Federalists, Lynn's recent work demonstrates a doubling-down on core Jacksonian principles among those who stayed in the party as it, too, adopted a more conservative position.[24] These principles included a seemingly odd cocktail of "majoritarian democracy, racial absolutism, the limited state, and liberal individualism."[25] Culminating in the principle of popular sovereignty, Democrats utilized the language of social contract and liberal democracy in order to espouse a new form of conservative politics that saw the individual of Enlightenment liberalism as representative of both liberty and order, economic progress, and the social preservation of the white body of the nation.

This admixture of liberalism and conservatism in the body of the white male worker is illustrative of Jacksonianism's particular politics of personhood. In an assemblage of theological, economic, political, and racial ideologies packaged together in the mutually reinforcing ideals of manifest destiny and popular sovereignty, the white male citizen alone was considered capable of the burdens of self-government. The white male citizen alone was capable of acting as the sovereign of popular sovereignty, as he alone was thought to possess the requisite moral, rational, and economic character that made republican government possible. This particular ideal of personhood thus also created what Lynn has called "parallel regimes of rights," wherein "Egalitarianism and liberal individualism conditioned white men's interactions in public, while conservative organicism shaped household relations" for white men and for their gendered and racialized others.[26] Liberal political economy thus required a gendered and racialized division of labor to sustain itself. White male autonomy was conditioned by a presumed natural mastery of domestic others.

Popular sovereignty was thus the rhetorical and policy tool utilized to fortify and conserve the white man's republic within the grammar of liberal democracy. As Lynn explains, "Devolving decision making, Democrats promised, would exert a conservative influence, as white men could be trusted to use democracy to preserve the racial and gender order from which they benefitted."[27] Racial and gender essentialism was the rhetorical glue that bound together Jacksonians across sectional and political differences, and popular sovereignty became the platform used to conserve this hierarchy.

The racialized and gendered subject of Jacksonian Democracy became synonymous with the rule of natural law, political order, and economic progress, all of which were providentially ordained by God. To interfere with the natural order of things, as Democrats would accuse their new enemy "fanaticism" (a hodge-podge of abolitionism, nativism, Catholicism, and temperance movements) of doing, would be to use the moral power of the state to create injustice and sow disorder. Much as with political aristocracy, economic concentration, and other older Jacksonian foes, to use the state in this way would erect artificial privileges in an otherwise organic meritocracy.[28] Thus, even if its constituency had changed, as had its primary foe, there remained a commitment among Democrats to anti-statism, laissez-faire, and white male supremacy. This was just as true of Field's California when he came of legal fame in the young territory as it was of the South.

Appointed to the State Supreme Court in 1857, Field was faced with the challenge of melding a consistent system of law from disparate and competing elements of extant Mexican law, U.S. custom, and his own laissez-faire principles. Facing such a challenge made his impact on the state and its legal system immense and gained him national notoriety both as a sharp legal mind and committed Democrat. Indeed, decades later, Field would run as the Democratic candidate for president, campaigning on a platform of laissez-faire and states' rights.[29] This vision of states' rights would be unmoored from the language of popular sovereignty and tied instead to his reading of economic liberty, as the doctrine proved incapable of fending off the looming moral reckoning with slavery that culminated in the Civil War and the end of the age of Jackson.[30]

It was Field's notoriety as a sharp legal mind and vocal Democrat that led to his appointment by Abraham Lincoln to the U.S. Supreme Court as the tenth justice in 1863. When the Court returned to nine justices in 1869, Field remained on the bench, overseeing the Ninth Circuit of the Pacific Coast.[31] This position, accompanied with Field's staunch ideological commitments and his tendency to utilize the courts to implement his personal politics, figured Field as a key agent in the fashioning of the concept of liberty and personhood after the Civil War. As many of his critics would note, Field was as much a politician as he was a judge, giving "weight to principles that were political, or economic, or moral, or religious, or all of these," as well as legal matters.[32] This was particularly true with Field's economic interpretations of due process and corporate equal protection under the Fourteenth Amendment.

Though at first glance it may seem that Field's embrace of the large corporation was a move away from his Jacksonian upbringing, it is in fact an intensification and radicalization of his Jacksonian beliefs. This is in part because the Jacksonian stance against corporations was somewhat more complicated than it may appear at first glance. It is indeed true that for many, including the aforementioned Theodore Sedgwick, the corporation led naturally to monopoly and thus to special privilege; yet the problem here was not with the corporation per se but rather with laws of incorporation. In other words, the issue was that corporate charters were special privileges granted exclusively by the state, creating special legal immunities only when the state deemed it beneficial to its own power. The answer thus lay not in abolishing the corporate form but in liberalizing laws of incorporation to create a free market environment in which incorporation was available to any and all laboring men. By liberalizing incorporation, the corporate body was no longer to be seen as an artificial creation of the state but a product of the spontaneous order of a market of free laboring men.

Of course, the result of such efforts proved in time to lead to the opposite of what they had hoped for. Rather than ushering in a democratic market system, the liberalization of corporate law, as Schlesinger argues, "sprinkled holy water on corporations, cleansing them of the legal status of monopoly and sending them forth as the benevolent agencies of competition."[33] Indeed, this conclusion seems apparent in Field's jurisprudence wherein a radically laissez-faire approach to the corporation enshrined it as a cornerstone of a free market system, particularly through the idea of corporate personhood.

Whereas earlier Jacksonians saw the corporation as an artificial impediment to the providential workings of a free market of white producers, for Field the corporation became, to borrow from critical legal theorist Carey Federman, "the normal understanding of the new American man, the bodily expression of male power, the individual self liberated from the constraints of the past and 'the molestations of society and state.'" This was in large part due to the fact that the corporation was understood as a "construct of a well-placed, self-interested enterprising group of persons willing to stake their lives and livelihood for economic success. As such, the corporation meets the requirements of the 'balanced character,' that psychological trait necessary (and applied only to elite males) for the emerging commercial economy of the late nineteenth century."[34] The corporate body was thus placed in a metonymic relationship with the body of the nation and of the white male worker, and as such the legal personhood and rights of the corporation were merely extensions of the persons gathered in its name. Rather than a tool of economic injustice, the corporation was the embodiment of the white male laborer and the primary means through which the nation would enact its civilizing mission. To explain how Field arrived at such a position, I now turn to a more nuanced view of his jurisprudence.

Field and Kearney on Economic Liberty, Corporate Personhood, and the Chinese Question

Field's particular understandings of liberty of contract, due process, and equal protection can be traced to his dissenting opinion in the *Slaughter-House Cases* of 1873. Indeed, as Jay Howard Graham argues, the whole "modern interpretation of the Fourteenth Amendment rests upon his [Field's] dissenting opinions in the *Slaughter-House* and *Granger* cases," as well as upon "opinions at circuit holding that corporations are 'persons' within the meaning of the equal protection and due process clauses."[35] The first case to reach the Supreme Court under the Fourteenth Amendment, the *Slaughter-House Cases* dealt primarily with a Louisiana law seeking to centralize and regulate the slaughtering industry in order to protect the health and safety of its consuming public.[36] Opponents of the measure argued that the centralization of industry power represented governmental interference in service of corporate special privilege, with this argument coming primarily from independent butchers in the area. Despite such contestation, the majority opinion upheld the establishment of a centralized,

34 | Chapter Two

regulated slaughtering industry. In his dissent, Field laid the groundwork for what would become his theory of liberty of contract into the 1880s—a jurisprudential theory that was a vital component of his conceptions of corporate equal protection and corporate personhood.[37]

Arguing against the centralization of the industry, Field held that the Fourteenth Amendment fundamentally altered state police powers, including granting the federal government the ability to intervene in industry to protect the New Orleans butchers' rights to pursue a trade. The right to pursue a trade, Field posited, was an inviolable and natural right of all citizens, an ideal "reflected in the desire of the Declaration of Independence to guarantee the pursuit of happiness." If, however, Field's economic interpretation of the Fourteenth Amendment in the *Slaughter-House Cases* came in support of free labor, his later opinions and adoption of liberty of contract would find him abandoning this issue in the protection of private property and corporate privilege from governmental regulation.[38]

This shift from pro-labor to liberty of contract positions on the Fourteenth Amendment would prove complex and ultimately damning for Chinese migrants. For while these arguments ultimately provided a way of expanding the purview of the Equal Protection Clause of the Fourteenth Amendment to include all legal persons, Field was more concerned with consecrating the rights of corporations than Chinese workers. It was the slipperiness of the term "persons" used by the primary drafters of the Equal Protection Clause, Roscoe Conkling and John A. Bingham, that enabled Field's rhetorical usage of the Chinese worker to argue for the rights of the corporation. The polysemy of the term, alongside the complicated history of corporate legal personality, made the Fourteenth Amendment a legal stronghold of corporate power. As Monroe Berger notes, the fervor with which corporate lawyers argued for protection can be seen by assessing the number of Supreme Court cases tried under the Fourteenth Amendment from the years 1868–1911. During this time frame the Court "handed down 604 decisions in cases involving the Fourteenth Amendment, but only twenty-eight of them affected Negro rights," leading scholars to claim that the amendment afforded "more protection to industrial capital than to minorities."[39] The Reconstruction amendments, offered primarily as a way to republicanize the South and create a culture of racial parity after the war, rather offered a way of reconstructing corporations as persons and elevating them as legal models of personhood. This point is equally significant when we understand the ultimate failure of Reconstruction in what Benjamin Quarles has called the decades of disappointment following the passage of these amendments.[40] Indeed, we may say that the corporate takeover of the Fourteenth Amendment is a key component of this disappointment.

This fact of corporate abuse of the Fourteenth Amendment would ultimately lead many to ask the question: why use the term "person" as opposed to "human" or "citizen" in the Equal Protection Clause? Perhaps most notably, decades later Progressive historians Charles and Mary Beard would argue that Roscoe Conkling, a close friend of Stephen Field and former corporate lawyer turned Republican senator of New York, intentionally smuggled the term into the Equal Protection Clause to empower the great railroad trusts.[41] The close circles of political, judicial, and economic clout that surrounded key figures in the creation of corporate personhood no doubt stood out to the Beards as a prime example of the corruption that undergirded the economic and moral maladies at the turn of the century in Gilded Age politics. Adding fuel to the fire, Conkling would later argue in the State Supreme Court of California, before his friend Justice Field in the case of *San Mateo* in 1882, that he and Bingham did in fact mean for the term "persons" to include the corporate form. Despite these and other damning pieces of evidence, the Beards' claims to a corporate conspiracy falls apart upon closer historical scrutiny.[42] In place of such a conspiracy, what we see is a confluence of historical forces—the most powerful of these the political, social, and economic exigencies of the Civil War itself—that culminated in a mixture of idealist and economic strains in constitutional theory that enabled corporate interests to exploit efforts to grant Black Americans the constitutional protections so long denied them.[43]

Prior to Conkling's arguments in *San Mateo*, an argument to which I will return later, Justice Field utilized the question regarding Chinese immigration to expand the purview of equal protection. Throughout the 1870s Field saw the Chinese question as a powerful political tool to help him leverage his jurisprudence throughout the state of California and eventually nationally. Described as an archetype for the modern activist judge, Field took these cases as a chance to legislate from the bench, using unappealable decisions of several habeas corpus cases to cement his interpretation of the Fourteenth Amendment into his Ninth Circuit.[44] Most notable among these cases, Field's decision in *In re Ah Fong* (1874) cited the Equal Protection Clause of the Fourteenth Amendment to shut down attempts by the state of California to prohibit the entrance of twenty-one women deemed to be "lewd and debauched."[45] The state claimed to be exercising its police powers to exclude these women for the protection of public health, for fear of racial miscegenation and disease of the twenty-one women deemed to be prostitutes aboard the steamship *Japan*.[46] A subject of the emperor of China appealed the case, and Justice Field ruled that to exclude these women violated the 1868 most-favored nation status given Chinese immigrants under the Burlingame Treaty, as well as the Fourteenth Amendment.

Decisions such as *In re Ah Fong* earned Justice Field a reputation among the white working class in California as a protector of the Chinese. Labor organizations such as the Knights of Labor and Kearney's WPC ridiculed Field as using the law to protect corporations and the Chinese. A socialist, nativist, non-Marxist, and anti-union labor party, the WPC maintained that the industrial woes of California were not born of class conflict but of a series of historical events particular to the politics of the state.[47] The uniqueness of Kearney's understanding of the problems facing the workingman in California led him to four usual targets of his vitriol: "contempt for the press, contempt for capitalists, contempt for politicians, and contempt for the Chinese," all of whom conspired against the white male worker.[48] Indeed, this ire was manifested within their party platform. Detailing the guiding principles of the WPC, Larry Shumsky explains that

> Simply put, the WPC wanted to restore the Union. It considered itself a movement dedicated to destroying the nefarious plot of land-grabbers and the Chinese. It intended to maintain traditional American institutions and to revitalize the American republic itself. . . . The WPC considered itself a holy crusade dedicated to preserving and reinvigorating the Republic of the founding fathers.[49]

The body of the Chinese laborer thus became a signifier of a host of anxieties regarding a perceived loss of agency, autonomy, and liberty brought on by significant industrial shifts and a perceived erosion of the true American republic.[50] As Alexander Saxton explains, "the heart of the indictment was that Chinese labor accentuated the trend toward monopoly," and were pawns of the industrial giants of the new corporate economy.[51] The natural answer, for Kearney, was that both had to be expunged from the body politic—corporations and the Chinese were unassimilable to the American way of life. Assimilation, for Kearney, was an a priori condition of whiteness and attendant notions of Christian civilization. The corporation, then, for Kearney, was understood as nonwhite, an alien from abroad to be feared and attacked.

Yet if Kearney and contemporary historians have seen Field as a protector of the Chinese, this is a gross misunderstanding.[52] Field's decision in *Ah Fong* was more a defense of his understanding of natural rights and the altered state powers following the passage of the Fourteenth Amendment, as for Field, the issue of exclusion was a matter of constitutional law rather than states' rights. As Kens notes, "He [Field] maintained that the Fourteenth Amendment was proscriptive only. It did not impose on the states any duty to guarantee rights; it simply prohibited states from passing and enforcing laws that were designed to accomplish the ends forbidden by the amendment."[53] Rather than acting in defense of the Chinese, Field simply maintained that any decision on Chinese exclusion must be marshaled at the federal rather than state level. As he argues in *Ah Fong*,

> I am aware of the very general feeling prevailing in this State against the Chinese, and in opposition to the extension of any encouragement to their immigration hither. It is felt that the dissimilarity in physical characteristics, in language, in manners, religion, and habits, will always prevent any possible assimilation of them with our people. *Admitting that there is ground for this feeling*, it does not justify any legislation for their exclusion, which might not be adopted against the inhabitants of the most favored nations of the Caucasian race, and of Christian faith. *If their further immigration is to be stopped, recourse must be had to the Federal Government, where the whole power over this subject lies.*[54]

A more accurate description of Field's political position on the Chinese question would be that he maintained a paternalistic stance that granted them protection in cases held at the state level and sought to exclude them

Chapter Two

at the federal level. As Edlie Wong argues, Field often resorted to "yellow peril" imagery, and in the federal case of *Chae Chan Ping* adopted Chinese exclusion as a "kind of 'war measure'" necessary to protect the American way of life.[55] Field's legal opinions regarding the complexities of Chinese immigration are better captured by Carl Swisher, who describes his opinion as following "a jagged seam," which perhaps had more to do with his political commitments and short-lived run for the presidential nomination on the Democratic Party ticket in 1880.[56]

Yet, his underlying belief in the superiority of the white race never wavered. This can be documented in an 1882 letter written to his friend Professor John Norton Pomeroy of Stanford University, claiming that "even if they [the Chinese] could assimilate, assimilation would not be desirable." Adding to this claim, Field writes, "You know I belong to the class, who repudiate the doctrine that this country was made for the people of *all* races. On the contrary, I think it is for our race—the Caucasian race."[57] Though these facts are doubtless clearer in the hindsight of historical investigation than for men like Denis Kearney, they bear emphasis. While many saw Field as supporting the rights of the Chinese, this supposed ally saw them more as a means of expanding and concretizing his laissez-faire constitutionalism, capitalizing on labor's demonization of the Chinese and corporations to expand corporate equal protection. While at the state level the Chinese proved a useful tool in this regard, at the federal level Field supported Chinese exclusion and the abrogation of the Burlingame Treaty and the Equal Protection Clause in the name of national security.

Regardless of these positions, Kearney and many white laborers in California lamented Field's power and perceived support for the Chinese and helped rally laborers into an organized political force. The party flexed its political muscle in 1878, as it utilized a network of anti-coolie clubs to try to gain control of the Democratic Party's political machine in San Francisco. Winning ten senatorial seats in San Francisco's 1878 elections, the Workingmen influenced California's 1879 constitutional convention and, as Saxton notes, "took the lead in writing a set of bristling anti-Chinese clauses."[58] Most notable of these clauses was Article 19, section 9, which "prohibited corporations from employing in any capacity any 'Chinese or Mongolian.'"[59] However, the party ultimately fell short of attaining any true labor reforms in the state.[60] Perhaps what the party was most successful at was propping up the power of corporations despite their intent to do just the opposite, for as Graham writes, anti-Chinese bigotry "relit and held the candle for the American corporate bar."[61] Reciting Henry George's arguments, Saxton reaches a similar conclusion, stating that "the use of the Chinese issue in politics must also serve monopoly since it would tend to distract and immobilize potentially radial segments of the population," ultimately standing in the way of any meaningful instance of labor reform.[62]

This phenomenon became evident in the case of *In re Tiburcio Parrott*. Coming in response to the new California state constitution of 1879, specifically Article 19, section 9, Mr. Tiburcio Parrott was president and director of the Sulfur Springs Quicksilver Mining Company. After being jailed for violating this new article in the state constitution for hiring Chinese workers, Parrott filed a writ of habeas corpus claiming that "both the statute and the state constitution were unconstitutional." Parrott was represented by Delos Lake, a close friend of Justice Field's, and T I. Bergin, with the case presided over by Judges Sawyer and Hoffmann of the State Supreme Court in San Francisco. Underlying the argument of Lake and Bergin was the "inalienable" right to labor.[63] Sawyer and Hoffmann turned to Field's dissents in the *Slaughter-House Cases* to uphold this argument, using the Equal Protection Clause to argue that the right to property depended upon a right to pursue a calling. Additionally, the clause was found to violate the freedom of contract of both corporations and Chinese laborers, violating both groups' liberty of contract. These arguments chipped away at the narrow understanding of the Fourteenth Amendment set in motion by the *Slaughter-House Cases*, which would be given its final blow in the railroad tax cases of *San Mateo* in 1882 and *Santa Clara* in 1886, both of which saw Justice Field on the bench.

The Southern Pacific Railroad Company, perhaps the largest and most powerful in California, faced several lawsuits, including those from the counties of San Mateo and Santa Clara. The *San Mateo* case began at the county level in April 1882, in order to collect taxes not paid by the Southern Pacific Co.[64] On its face, the case was about the California state tax law of 1879, which stated that property taxes were based upon the actual value of said property, minus the amount of any mortgages held against this property, with railroads and other quasi-public corporations being an exception. These tax cases caught the eye of Justice Field, who

Chapter Two

heard them at the state level with Judge Sawyer, who presided over *Tiburcio Parrott*. Calling upon the power of the Fourteenth Amendment, the railroad argued that the taxes levied against it were discriminatory, based not upon different forms of property but instead upon an unfavorable stance toward the corporate form. The railroads were represented by former congressman Roscoe Conkling himself. As a congressman, Conkling sat on the Joint Committee on Reconstruction and helped write the Fourteenth Amendment that he evoked in his defense of the Southern Pacific Railroad.[65] Just twenty years after the passage of the Fourteenth Amendment, Conkling's arguments in *San Mateo* that corporations were denied equal protection under the Fourteenth Amendment, coupled with the opinions of Field and Sawyer, helped sound the "death knell of the narrow 'Negro-race theory' of the Fourteenth Amendment."[66]

In re Tiburcio Parrott and Corporate Personhood in the Ninth Circuit

The case of *In re Tiburcio Parrott* marks a turning point in discourse surrounding the corporate person. Under siege from the Workingmen's Party and their clauses in the new State Constitution of California, corporate lawyers and pro-corporate judges portrayed the corporate person as "an innocent abroad" that was unfairly persecuted and oppressed by organized labor and the state.[67] Whereas Kearney rhetorically linked the Chinese laborer and the corporation together as aliens that threatened the moral industrial order, pro-corporate voices often invoked the Chinese as kindred souls, suffering a similar fate. As I argue, however, these lawyers and judges more often than not saw the Chinese problem as a solution, exploiting the oppression of the Chinese body to expand the purview of the Equal Protection Clause of the Fourteenth Amendment to include corporations. Indeed, the *Parrott* case offers an important instance of this rhetorical work, linking together the unequal protection levied against the Chinese and the corporation, and paving the way for the arguments in the *Railroad Cases*.

Falling short of ruling that corporations are persons under the Fourteenth Amendment, Judges Ogden Hoffman and Lorenzo Sawyer nonetheless argue for the protection of corporate property against the state, embracing Justice Field's theory of liberty of contract and his laissez-faire doctrine in the process. By this point, through other cases heard in courts throughout the expansive Ninth Circuit, Field's conservative jurisprudence had been widely adopted and implemented, especially in San Francisco.[68] Thus, though the *Parrott* case was on Field's radar, he decided to not head to San Francisco to hear the case, trusting that his colleagues would articulate an opinion in line with his own legal thought.[69] Correct in this assumption, the two judges often invoked Field's opinions, including his dissent in the *Slaughter-House Cases*, arguing for an expanded interpretation of the Equal Protection Clause of the Fourteenth Amendment. Holding that section 2 of article 19 of the Constitution of California, which forbade the employment of Chinese and Mongolian laborers by corporations, was in violation of the Burlingame Treaty and the Fourteenth Amendment, Hoffman and Sawyer ruled that Chinese laborers were persons under the Fourteenth Amendment whose natural rights to property and contract must be protected from state overreach.

Additionally, the clause was found unconstitutional as it also violated the rights of corporate property, forbidding the ability to enter freely into legally formed contracts. The clause in question not only would have forbidden corporations from entering into employment contracts with whom they deemed fit, but also would have, it was argued, granted the state the power to fundamentally alter, restrict, and revoke corporate charters, representing an abuse of state power. Citing the decision of *Dartmouth v. Woodward* that established that corporate charters were legal contracts between a corporation and the state, Hoffman claimed that any ability for the state to alter or revoke such a contract would amount to an illegal voiding of the founding contract and illegitimate seizure of private property.

Indeed, as Judge Hoffman begins his line of argumentation, he portrays the case as a violation of the rights to property and contract of the corporation and moves on to sanctify these rights of the corporation as natural rights as sacred in their purview as the natural rights to life and property of natural persons. This line of reasoning holds that the clause in question violates the natural right of contract of corporations, writing that "when a contract has been made, or property acquired; by a lawful exercise of the granted powers, the contract is as inviolable, and the right of property, with everything incidental to that right, as sacred, as in the case of natural persons."[70] Maintaining that rights to contract held by the corporation are as sacred as those held by natural persons, he equates artificial legal personality with corporeal personhood, while simultaneously rendering each a sovereign body immune from unlawful state power and seizure.

Defending the right to labor of Chinese residents of the United States, Hoffman states that to restrict employment flies in the face of the "privileges, immunities, and exemptions of the most favored nation," bestowed by treaty. Chief among these privileges is that of the "right to labor for a living," which stands as "inviolable as the right of the property, for property is the offspring of labor."[71] To restrict the rights of Chinese labor, in this sense, is to rob many Chinese immigrants of the only forms of property they may own, their bodily capacity for work and production in a capitalist economy. Judge Sawyer levies a similar opinion to that of Ogden Hoffman, writing that "As to by far the greater portion of the Chinese, as well as other foreigners who land upon our shores, their labor is the only exchangeable commodity they possess. To deprive them of the right to labor is to consign them to starvation."[72] Such a shirking of the sovereign's responsibilities to its population was to mark the Chinese for starvation or death. The denial of the right to labor and self-ownership was thus tantamount to a denial of life itself.

What may on its face appear a defense or recognition of the inherent value of the humanity and personhood of the Chinese peoples and a reading of the Chinese laborer within the logic of possessive individualism is in fact anything but. Indeed, their personhood is granted only in a limited sense, acting as a kind of inclusionary exclusion that forbids the Chinese from fully crossing the threshold to legal personhood. This is to say that in his extension of natural rights to corporations, Hoffman simultaneously draws limits and exceptions to the universal extension of natural rights to Chinese laborers.

While their rights to labor must be protected according to federal treaty, thus rendering the clause in the state constitution illegal, Hoffman pleads for efforts for Chinese exclusion at the federal level via the abrogation of the Burlingame Treaty. This liminal position as both person but not represents the biopolitical power of race to apportion personhood, extending the *Herrenvolk* democracy of the Jacksonian age—preaching egalitarianism, universal rights, and equal protection while maintaining a strict racial hierarchy of persons.[73] Such a rhetorical move placed the Chinese within the position of what Giorgio Agamben describes as the sovereign ban—an inclusionary exclusion that subjected them to the threat of violence and social death along the lines of racial difference.[74] Not fully things and not full legal persons, the Chinese body became legible only within the interstices between these categories.

We can see this partial apportionment of personhood to the Chinese even more clearly if we understand the claims to their right to labor in relation to the first portion of Hoffman's opinion on the rights of the corporation. This line of argument states that to deprive the Chinese of their productive capacities also deprived the corporation of more plentiful sources of labor and production, and by extension adversely affected the property of those corporators gathered together to form the corporation. Indeed, the central thrust of his argument is that to deprive the Chinese of labor is to deny the right of the corporation to enter freely into contract with whom it pleases. To deny the rights to labor of the Chinese was to restrict the full rights and privileges of the private property of those white laborers that lay behind the corporate veil. Relying upon the rhetoric of the labor theory of value, allowing a free market for labor enables entrepreneurial actors to purchase labor at the lowest price possible, in turn providing the most efficient production of goods. This free market for labor is thus presumed to ensure the natural prosperity of all market actors.

Describing this line of reasoning as the quasi-logical appeal of the rhetoric of the labor theory of value, William Herring and Mark Longaker argue that its rhetorical force stems from the claim for the ultimate justice of a capitalist society despite evidence to the contrary. According to such logic "the free market for labor and commodities most generously rewards all its participants, workers and capitalists alike."[75] Such appeals to universal justice, however, miss the realities of market relations and power under a corporate economy, as well as belie the latent racial and gender antagonisms that undergird the producerism of classical political economy and the very notion of the white man's republic.

As Hoffman concludes his arguments, he offers a candid and concise statement on the problem of Chinese immigration:

> That the unrestricted immigration of the Chinese to this country is a great and growing evil, that it presses with much severity on the laboring classes,

Chapter Two

and that, if allowed to continue in numbers bearing any considerable proportion to that of the teeming population of the Chinese Empire, it will be a menace to our peace and even to our civilization, is an opinion entertained by most thoughtful persons. The demand, therefore, that the treaty be rescinded or modified is reasonable and legitimate. But while that treaty exists the Chinese have the same rights of immigration and residence as are possessed by any other foreigners.[76]

In many regards echoing the yellow peril rhetoric and invasion narratives of Kearney and those within the WPC, the rhetoric of the judges actively decoupled Chinese immigration from monopoly capitalism, rendering the corporation a hapless victim of working-class ire while shifting concerns regarding national dissolution entirely on the threat of a nonwhite, non-Christian nation. Though the Chinese were persons to be included and protected by the U.S. government so long as it was engaged in treaty with China, the Chinese were ultimately not persons worthy or capable of inclusion within the body politic. Viewed as a dangerous threat to the bodily integrity of the nation, continued Chinese immigration was to be stopped at the federal level.[77]

Fears regarding the collapse, demise, and eventual devouring of a white Christian nation offered in narratives of yellow peril legitimated claims to Chinese exclusion. Indeed, as K. C. Councilor has argued, fears of Chinese immigration were figured in the rhetorical framework of consumption and digestion, with the body of the nation consuming more than it could readily assimilate. Part of the fear was thus that overconsumption would lead to a kind of national indigestion, which "expressed a fear of debility, and also a fear of becoming foreign, of being consumed by the consumed."[78] Importantly, as I hope to demonstrate in my turn to the case of *San Mateo*, similar logics warranted the inclusion of the corporation within the Fourteenth Amendment's purview. Perhaps tellingly, the fear of intestinal disease and consumption by the consumed was once also a powerful rhetorical appeal against the proliferation and empowerment of the corporation. For Thomas Hobbes the corporation was figured as an intestinal parasite that threatened the sovereign nation. Indeed, corporations were akin to "many lesser commonwealths in the bowels of a greater, like worms in the entrails of a natural man."[79] To allow these political bodies to grow and proliferate compromised the integrity of the sovereign, much as the incorporation of large numbers of Chinese migrants threatened the promises of a Christian nation.

Yet, if the corporation went from parasite to person, the path of the Chinese mirrored this development. The corporation, then, once understood as a monster of capital, an alien, and even a worm in the entrails of the nation, became worthy of legal personhood while full claims to such status were denied to racialized others to preserve the fictional ideal of the White Man's Republic. Moving to the *San Mateo* case, I argue that corporate inclusion was premised upon its racialization as white, representing and embodying ideals of industrial modernism, Christian society, and the normative position of the white, masculine, bourgeois subject.

Justice Field on the Corporate Body in the *San Mateo Railroad Case*

An opinion delivered on September 25, 1882, just months after the Chinese Exclusion Act was ratified by Congress and signed into law by then president Chester A. Arthur, *San Mateo* is the first of three in a series of suits commonly referred to as the *Railroad Tax Cases*. These cases, filed by the counties of San Mateo and Santa Clara against the Southern Pacific Railroad Co., were, on their face, a series of dry arguments regarding taxation rates for quasi-public corporations operating in multiple counties in the State of California. However, the cases were taken as an opportunity to further the cause of corporate inclusion and equal protection under the Fourteenth Amendment. Heard at the Circuit Court for the District of California, the defense of the Southern Pacific was argued by Roscoe Conkling, co-drafter with John Bingham of the Equal Protection Clause of the Fourteenth Amendment, who claimed that to tax the corporation at a different rate due to its legal status was a violation of the Fourteenth Amendment.[80]

The case was heard by Judge Lorenzo Sawyer and Justice Field himself. Two years after the decision in *Parrott* and just months following the passage of the Chinese Exclusion Act, the *San Mateo* decision would mark the

46 | Chapter Two

"death knell" of the Negro-only doctrine, and the eventual inclusion of the corporate person in the Fourteenth Amendment just four years later in *Santa Clara*.[81] Standing as a crucial moment in corporate inclusion and Chinese exclusion, then, the *San Mateo* case marks a point in which to examine the racialization of the corporate person.

In his opinion, Justice Field establishes that the different rates of taxation levied by the state constitution of California are unconstitutional, as the statute imposes "discrimination too palpable and gross to be questioned."[82] The discriminatory nature of the law in question stems from its targeting of the corporate form. Rather than levying different rates of taxation on the basis of a classification of types of *property* held by the corporation, it was argued that the unequal taxation faced by the Southern Pacific was the product of an unjust classification of *persons*. In other words, seeking to tax corporations at a different rate than other so-called natural persons violated the Equal Protection Clause of the Fourteenth Amendment, subjecting the corporate person to state power so severe and uncompromising as to render it defenseless against state violence. Indeed, citing Justice Marshall, Field proclaims that "the power to tax is the power to destroy," and goes on to compare the unequal taxation of corporations as akin to "eminent domain" and "confiscation" at the whims of the state.[83] To tax the corporation differently, then, was to exempt them from the legal protections afforded residents of the United States.

Comporting with his radical individualist understanding of liberty, Field's jurisprudence largely figured the corporation in a bottom-up manner that drew its personality from the real persons and citizens gathered together in its name. Such an associational theory of the corporation originally emerged as a liberal inversion of the so-called concession theory that holds that the corporation owes its existence to the sovereign gift of the state charter.[84] Rather than owing its rights, privileges, and immunities to the state, the corporation gathers its legal standing from the sovereign individuals whose market activity constitutes the very fabric of civil society.

Part of the strength, yet ultimate fragility, of Field's argument, however, is that he seemingly waffles between the associational theory and a natural entity theory of the corporation's person. In other words, Field at times appears to argue that the corporation is simply an aggregate of the natural persons behind it, while at others that the corporation possesses its own discrete legal person. This complicates things both legally and philosophically. Where, thus, does the body of the corporation lie? Is it the body of the corporators that the law must ultimately protect, or does the corporation possess a fictitious body of its own—one that would allow it to be a subject of property rights? The metaphysical complexities of these questions have a long history in Western thought.

The difficulty in both of these formulations, however, is an inability to recognize the distinct personality of a corporation that enables it to hold rights and duties apart from the state on the one hand, and apart from those individuals gathered in the corporate name on the other hand. Both a creature of the state and a collective body constituted by its members, the corporation also stands as a distinct legal person apart from both. In the parlance of economic theology, then, the corporate form—and its attendant legal personhood—straddles the binary of sovereign power and immanent economic government. It is at once sovereign and the subject of state power. It is both an individual and a collection of individual persons. The corporate legal person emerges somehow between sovereignty and economy without ever fully resolving the paradoxical nature of its being.[85]

These tensions in locating the personality of the corporation emerge in Field's opinion, as he at times oscillates between locating the rights of property and personality of the corporation in its members and in the corporation itself. The interplay between the two, however, played strategically to obscure the tensions inherent in Field's argument, providing important space for rhetorical maneuvering. According to Justice Field in his opinion in *San Mateo*, the property of the corporation is in reality the property of the corporators, and an unequal tax levied against the corporation is an unjust taxation of the property of citizens of the State of California. In this sense, contractual rights of the corporation regarding the acquisition and usage of its rights to property lie in the individuals associated behind the corporate body. Yet, if the property of the corporation is reducible to the natural persons that collectively constitute it, it is said by Field that "the lives and liberties of the individual corporators are not the life and liberty of the corporation."[86] Belying claims to a strict associational theory of the corporation, Field here seems to grant the corporation a life distinct from that of its members, as well as a set of liberties and rights apart from its corporators, noting the power of the state in granting the corporate form special legal privileges and immunities.

We see here the difficulties of applying a liberal, individualist jurisprudence to the collective body of the corporation.[87] One must recognize the distinct personality of the corporation that holds certain rights and liberties, chief among them a contractual individuality and perpetual life only capable of being granted by the state. One must also, however, attempt to find the locus of personality with regard to property. Here, liberty of contract penetrates the cloak of the corporate form and is to be found in those who comprise it. Though corporations are not citizens, a point Field is careful to note, the property rights of corporations are those of the enterprising citizens behind the corporation. Any attempt to tax the property of the corporation differently due to its status as a corporation is taken as an act of discrimination, a violation of the Fourteenth Amendment rights against the citizens behind the corporations simply because they chose to associate for a more efficient and prudent management of their private property.

This central point is represented in Justice Field's assertion that "whenever it is necessary for the protection of contract or property rights, the Courts will look through the ideal entity and name of the corporation to the persons who comprise it and protect them, though the process be in its name." Judge Sawyer echoes this sentiment, writing that "The fact that the corporators are united into an ideal legal entity, called a corporation, does not prevent them from having a right of property in the assets of the corporation, which is entitled to the protection of this clause of the Constitution."[88] Claiming corporate equal protection here reduces the corporate person to those behind the corporation, locating its personality in those property-holding citizens of the United States.

These property-holding citizens represented the enterprising and industrial values of modernity under a system of corporate capitalism. The powers of combination and aggregation in the new capital markets of the day were capable of fulfilling the promises of liberal modernism. A civilizing force, the corporation was capable of uplifting the nation morally, spiritually, and economically—to carry on the manifest destiny of the republic of white men. As Justice Field explains, "there is nothing lawful to be done to feed and clothe our people, to beautify and adorn their dwellings, to relieve the sick, to help the needy, and to enrich and ennoble humanity, which is not to a great extent done through the instrumentalities of the corporation."[89] This aligning of the corporate person with a moral mission of cultural enrichment and material prosperity stands in stark contrast to the understandings of the Chinese as barbarous and savage that was utilized to justify their exclusion from the United States. While the Chinese were read outside the bounds of legal whiteness and personhood, the corporation came to represent the civilizing capacities of white society and capitalist production.[90] Comporting with the tropological construction of the person under liberalism, the corporate person as the driver of a modern, Christian civilization rhetorically positions the corporation as an ideal liberal subject. Entailing its own dominant and hegemonic modality of being, what Nikolas Rose calls a "regime of personhood," liberalism molds subjects through principles of rationality, privacy, autonomy, self-governance, and an enterprising spirit.[91]

Rendering the corporate person within this framework, the corporation came to signify values of a supposedly universal utilitarian rationality, self-calculation, and an entrepreneurial spirit. The disembodied nature of the corporate person helps it fit within this conceptual space. By placing the body and racial identity outside of culture, liberalism relegates race to the private realm, normalizes white masculinity, and presumes the essence of being to be in rational thought detached from the sensuous body. This Cartesian duality of mind and body becomes reified in the corporation, recognizing the ontological being of personhood not as an attribute of corporeal or phenomenological embodiment, but rather in the *cogito*, the capacity for rational calculation and a proprietary relationality with the self.[92]

Indeed, the corporation represents the culmination of the utilitarian rationality and self- calculation in a market economy under a liberal economic system. A collective body organized for the purposes of capital aggregation, efficient management of labor and resources, and wealth generation, the corporation exists first and foremost to maximize profits and returns for itself and its members. As Field and Sawyer argue, the property of the corporation, while said to be owned by the natural persons gathered in its name, is held by the corporate person in their trust and solely for their benefit. In a court of law, then, it is these property-owning citizens for whom the corporate person stands. Thus, while the metaphysical person of the corporation fits within the supposedly neutral position of the self-governing, self-calculating, and universally rational logics that shape the liberal subject, the materiality of the corporate body was figured as reducible to the natural persons and property-owning citizens congregated together in its name.

In the words of Judge Sawyer, the Fourteenth Amendment, in protecting the property rights of the corporate person, grants it the right to be "subject to like . . . taxes, licenses, and exactions of every kind, and to no other, as 'white citizens.'"[93] Subjecting the corporation to a different rate of taxation amounted to unequal exaction of private funds and property that violated the rights of the corporate person. To deny and revoke the rights of the corporation, then, stood as a sign of state power subverting the tenets of equality and liberty, and indeed of a justly and naturally ordered free market. To this point, Judge Sawyer concludes by writing:

> If the life, liberty, property, and happiness of all the people are to be preserved, then it is of the utmost importance to every man, woman, and child of this broad land, that every guaranty of our National Constitution, whatever temporary inconvenience may be felt, be firmly and rigorously maintained at all times and under all circumstances.[94]

Here, the rights and interests of the corporation stand in for the rights and interests of society as a whole. The very promise of American liberal democracy and its millennial aspirations stand under threat when corporate property is subject to differential taxation as it signifies the ability of the state to unjustly exercise its monopoly on the legitimate means of force to confiscate, steal, and destroy the rights to property of any and all of its citizens. These rights to corporate property must be defended at all costs, even if this struggle creates negative consequences for the citizenry. In this sense, the struggle for the rights of one is a struggle for the rights of all (white men), in which short-term pain and suffering are warranted for the maintenance and protection of democratic rights.

Standing not as a universal space of utilitarian reason but rather as a form of legal protection for the interests of white property owners, the corporate person was a metaphysical extension of whiteness in its rational capacities for economic governance and efficiency, as well as a body of white natural persons gathered to protect their economic interests from the powers of the state.[95] The attendant whiteness of the corporation granted it the legal protections of full personhood under the law and rendered it worthy of inclusion within the nation while reading the Chinese outside the bounds of the body politic.

Mapping the space of corporate privilege and legal protection becomes easier when reading the case of *San Mateo* against cases regarding the rights of Chinese laborers, specifically *In re Tiburcio Parrott*. Demonstrating the different ways in which the notion of the person was constructed for the corporation and the Chinese, we can see how a process of racialization was at play in each instance, creating a legal and cultural taxonomy of personhood. The Chinese stood as the racial other of the corporation, signifying a heathen, savage, uncivilized, and thus unassimilable people, whereas the corporation stood for the powers of white Western civilization, its calculated rationality and efficiency, the modernizing forces of industrialism, and the capacities of a rights-based democracy to ensure prosperity and equality through a procedural system of justice. These conflicting images ultimately legitimated Chinese exclusion from and corporate inclusion within, the body politic.

Conclusion

The fruits of Field's labors would eventually come four years later in the infamous 1886 case now simply referred to as *Santa Clara*. The final of the numerous *Railroad Cases*, at this point the Court had spent years listening back and forth to arguments regarding the nature of corporate personhood. Presumably weary of the abstractions of such arguments from the more concrete and pragmatic issues of taxation, Chief Justice Morrison Remick Waite announced before the Court began its opinion:

> The Court does not wish to hear argument on the question whether the provision in the Fourteenth Amendment to the Constitution which forbids a state to deny any person within its jurisdiction the equal protection of the laws applies to these corporations. We are all of the opinion that it does.[96]

52 | Chapter Two

Not technically part of the opinion, but rather recorded merely as a footnote, the constitutional personhood of the corporation would nevertheless be taken from here on out as legal doctrine. This fact leads Federman to argue that "The *Santa Clara* decision anchored the modern self in the highest legal concept the nation (prejudicially and parsimoniously) had to offer, thereby creating a struggle for national recognition among various other kinds of persons."[97] Though it should be clear from the arguments offered here that I agree with Federman's position that the corporation was granted a legal position atop the hierarchy of persons, it should also be evident from the historical argument offered here that the rhetorical work required to wed the modern, white laborer and the corporation was done years before.

Led primarily by Field and his vast Ninth Circuit, these efforts should be seen within the larger context of Field's Jacksonian upbringing and his adaptation of these principles to a post–Civil War era in which questions of liberty, incorporation, and personhood were paramount. Field utilized his laissez-faire jurisprudence to make sense of the shifting nature of the times, and to provide legal order by crafting the corporation as a normative model of personhood. Here, the body of the white male worker, the body of the nation, the body of the Chinese laborer, and the body of the corporation were constructed together, creating a taxonomy of persons in the process. This taxonomy was simultaneously political, economic, and theological, as the white male laborer and ultimately the corporation represented the virtues of white Christian society.

Significantly, these arguments are indicative of the rise of a unique brand of U.S. conservatism, one that does not actively resist liberalism but uses its language to defend social order. What emerges is a conservative laissez-faire and a racially essentialized social order premised upon libertarian values. Thus, as Lynn suggests, "Scholars of conservatism have not pushed the long history of libertarianism back far enough."[98] The early groundwork of this position was established by those faithful to the party of Jackson in the 1850s and was later extended and applied to a corporate economy by Justice Field in the 1880s. As opposed to an artificial impediment to a free market of white laboring men, this new conservatism rhetorically sutured the corporate person to a laissez-faire society, as it was argued to be an extension and creation of the body of the white male laborer. In this way, the legal codification of corporate personhood consecrated this body as the standard-bearer of personhood. Yet, the corporation would ultimately unsettle it as the continued ascendancy of the large corporation threatened to displace labor itself. This was, of course, the tenet of Jacksonianism that was lost in its adaptation to the corporate form, and perhaps the one kernel of truth in Kearney's nativist pro-labor arguments—the corporation was, more often than not, no friend to labor, but rather its enemy.

This fact became clearer to many in the growing inequality of the Gilded Age and the long, conservative reign of the Lochner era of the Court from the mid-1890s to the 1930s. Populist and socialist reformers such as William Jennings Bryan and Eugene Victor Debs would rail against the great money-power and argue for a more humane economy. Workers would rally and strike against abuses of corporate and industrial power. Journalists would uncover the darker side of the supposedly civilized corporate person in long exposés of poor working conditions and child labor. The Progressive Era was on its way and would make the corporate person its primary target.

Yet, moral defenses of the corporation were not bound to libertarian dogmas. As the nation entered into the Progressive Era, the language of liberalism would shift to challenge the now more conservative notions of social contract and classical individualism.[99] Conservatism, too, adapts to changing social custom and in the process is able to find rhetorical space within the discourse of Progressivism. In turn, conservatives were also able to adapt and offer a moral defense of the corporation not within the more materialist, immanent defense of free markets and national prosperity, but in the creation of a socially responsible, Christian industry.

CHAPTER 3

Soul

As the nation entered the twentieth century, the corporation was in need of saving. With a wave of Progressive reformers critiquing the crass materialism, scientism, and turn from traditional Protestant value systems that facilitated the rise of the large corporation, the industrial community was facing a spiritual crisis. Having already earned significant legal standing and legitimacy, the corporate person now faced new challenges. Viewing corporations as inversions of traditional democratic value systems, Progressive reformers demanded a moral reform of social norms and institutions.[1] If, as historian T. J. Jackson Lears has argued, the period between Appomattox and the First World War was a time of national rebirth, so too was this time period one of rebirth for the large, quasi-public corporation.[2] Indeed, the exigencies of the day demanded the corporation be reborn, saving the corporate soul while aligning an emergent modernism with traditional Protestant values.

The Progressive movement, growing from and changing the face of the agrarian populism of the mid-nineteenth century, was a largely white, middle class, and urban movement bent on eradicating the corrupting and

55

56 | Chapter Three

corrosive influence of the modern corporation through Protestant and democratic moralizing. Described by Robert Crunden as "ministers of reform," Progressives championed ideals of experimentation, personal responsibility, and strong moral character as a means of righting the path of U.S. culture.[3] In an era in which the strength of institutions such as "the family, the church, and the local community suddenly seemed dwarfed by the sway of giant corporations," Progressives attempted to reign in the ever-expanding corporate form to maintain the strength of traditional social institutions.[4]

Seeking to rehabilitate individualism, economic freedom, and a Protestant value system in a society that was becoming increasingly large and impersonal, the Progressive critique of the corporation was thus twofold. First, there was a moral critique of concentrated wealth and unprecedented political corruption that demanded a spiritual remedy, and second, there was an economic criticism of the decreasing competition and opportunity once seemingly available in a market of diffuse ownership. Importantly, these two lines of criticism were inherently intertwined as they focused on the impersonality of scale that accompanied the modern, quasi-public corporation.

The split of ownership from management in the modern corporation, a key component of the managerial revolution in business enterprise, abstracted the corporate entity from its consumers. In an age of entrepreneurial capitalism, a business was often owned and operated by an individual entrepreneur, family, or partners who owned the majority of company stock and executed management decisions regarding the firm.[5] However, the rise of finance capital and joint stock companies scattered ownership across the country to thousands of individuals in absentia, creating what Thorstein Veblen termed a process of "absentee ownership."[6] Thus, as Adolf Berle and Gardiner Means wrote in their treatise on the modern corporation, the dispersion of stock ownership abstracted "the spiritual values that formerly went with ownership" from business, creating a lack of a readily identifiable corporate personality.[7]

These changes in U.S. industry led to a crisis of moral legitimacy for the large corporation at the turn of the century. The inability of the corporate community to project a personifying image coupled with the fact that many in the general public viewed the corporation as being driven solely by money and greed led to cries that corporations were soulless.[8] In this sense, the corporation was a body without a soul, a kind of monster created in the name of economic efficiency. Fearful of the size and increasing power of the corporation, the public attacked its character, or lack thereof. Recognizing a need to address these criticisms, many in the business community sought to humanize the corporation by utilizing new techniques and technologies of mass communication. Crucial to these efforts to sway the public were the burgeoning professions of advertising and public relations.

The Rise of Corporate Communications: Advertising, Public Relations, and the Corporate Soul

Both advertising and public relations emerged as techniques of marketing communications within the nineteenth century. While modern advertising emerged around the time of the Civil War, public relations did not emerge in its modern form until closer to the turn of the century. With modern advertising coming of age as a technique of bridging the growing chasm between producer and consumer in an economy of scale, public relations was a means of managing public opinion regarding both consumer products and free enterprise itself.[9] Though related, each mode of communication arose to address different political exigencies and to address different marketing problems. Thus, while advertising is attuned to and driven toward the monetary fortunes of corporations, public relations efforts are attuned to its political fortunes.[10] Despite these differences, however, both proved important tools for the large corporation to defend and humanize itself in the public sphere.

While individual merchants experimented with advertising methods in the eighteenth century, national advertising of branded consumer products was largely a product of the late nineteenth century.[11] The demand for advertising at a national scale was the product of recent developments in communications and transportation technologies that expanded markets and created new consumer needs, especially in the burgeoning urban areas.[12] Advances in production, increasing corporate concentration, and the influx of large amounts of capital into industry in the late nineteenth century

58 | Chapter Three

fueled these trends and created the need for many in the business community to communicate with the consumer more directly. Thus, modern advertising arose as a problem of marketing and business strategy concerned with product recognition in an economy of abundance.

Among the first to attempt to reach consumers directly were large manufacturing companies. Given their power and market share, companies such as Dodge, Eastman Kodak, Campbell Soup, B. F. Goodrich, and Quaker Oats viewed advertising as a means to hold onto this power and centralize control in a crowded market.[13] As manufacturing companies gradually began to take on the cause of advertising and product marketing in an economy of scale, the production of advertising messages became specialized and modernized. Whereas advertising prior to roughly 1880 was largely handled by owner-managers of business firms, the later decades of the nineteenth century saw the rise of a specialized class of advertising professionals that were either taken in-house by producers of consumer goods or formed their own specialized agencies to meet the advertising needs of businesses at the turn of the century.[14]

Whether undertaken by manufacturers or specialized agencies such as N. W. Ayer & Son, J. Walter Thompson Company, or the Batten Company, national advertising was part of a larger cultural and industrial struggle over distribution and control in the late nineteenth and early twentieth centuries. As a method of managing the changing relationships among wholesalers, manufacturers, and retailers in the new corporate economy, advertising was often viewed as a more efficient means of controlling distribution than the potentially monetarily and politically costly and invasive measures of vertical integration. Seen in relation to larger business and marketing strategies and techniques, advertising met the twin needs of convincing consumers to purchase a given manufacturer's products and also convincing retailers to keep these products on their shelves, maintaining market power in a fundamentally altered economy.[15]

Yet, advertising, of course, was not only an institutional response to new business needs, as it served manifold cultural purposes as well. Indeed, the cultural functions of advertising often operated to legitimize the new industrial realities of the U.S. market and to counter the attacks of Progressive activists against the corporate economy. Accomplishing these tasks required a diverse array of rhetorical strategies. One such strategy was an attempt to justify the industrial shifts of the time and the accompanying sociocultural grievances voiced by many in the population by attaching consumer goods to notions of material progress. As Pamela Walker Laird notes, advertisers were quick to identify their business goals with a larger "ideology of progress" through visual representations and associations of industry with abundance, personal prosperity, and motifs of electrical imagery that stimulated the national imagination and evoked a "technological sublime" that promised better living through consumption and technological advancement.[16] Painting industrial growth as a necessary component of national progress attached industry to deeply entrenched values of classical liberalism in the United States and justified any social ills that arose, as consequences of the new corporate economy, as necessary and natural costs of the continued march of progress and development.

It is important to note here that those in the advertising profession did not simply allow public discontent to fall on deaf ears. Rather than actively shaping the industrial system to the demands of consumers, however, advertising agents sought to shape consumers to the demands of industry. Addressing the anxieties that accompanied what Walter Lippmann described as a state of drift in the transition to modernity, Marchand has observed that advertisers performed the important cultural work of creating a new language of urbanity and a new logic of living appropriate to the complexities of life in a modernized, corporate economy of scale and speed.[17] In this capacity, advertisers acted as a kind of spiritual adviser that could actively "console, befriend, and reassure the public" of the benefits of industrial progress.[18] It was the task of advertisers as "apostles of modernity" to not simply mirror the social realities of the age but to assuage public anxieties and actively shape the cultural mores and norms of a complex corporate culture.

As advertisers provided a new language and logic of living in a corporate society, they also attempted to address the growing desire for connection, personality, and humanization in an increasingly large and complex social world. Progressive reformers had portrayed the corporation as a faceless bureaucratic person that lacked a moral character and identifiable personality. Through branding and trademarks, advertising professionals were

60 | Chapter Three

able to fight these assertions by personifying companies and their products. Trademarks and brands were able to act as a kind of buffer, an intermediary between consumers and the large corporation. In point of fact, it is with the rise of the "trifecta of trademark, package, and promotion" that historian Timothy Gloege identifies the modernization of advertising as a profession.[19] In this sense, trademarks and brands placed a face upon impersonal corporate bureaucracies, humanizing them for consumers, as well as helping to legitimize advertising as a business function of large corporations.[20]

Additionally, such strategies met the desire for personalized products, and the consumption of "personalities" crafted by advertising professionals. As Marchand argues, at its extreme, advertising attempted to "re-personalize" public life through a "tacit recognition of an unvanquished public propensity for animism." It was in this propensity for animism among a consumer public that individuals, through the attribution of personality, sought to "emancipate the product from its association with a complex and obscure process of mass production and imbue it with 'human meaning' once again."[21] One crucial function of advertising was thus to humanize and personalize the impersonalities of scale that accompanied the rise of corporate capitalism.

Also seeking to humanize the large corporation, public relations emerged in its modern form at the turn of the century. A response to anti-corporate activism and reporting from Progressive reformers, activists, intellectuals, and muckraking journalists, public relations professionals sought to sell free enterprise to the public. Yet, while advertising was concerned primarily with effectively managing distribution and consumption in a complex marketplace, public relations as a field was concerned primarily with managing corporate image and public opinion. As Richard Tedlow succinctly states, public relations arose "as an institutional response to the problem of managing the business reputation," and as an attempt to craft a method of scientific management of public opinion.[22] The perceived need in the business community to craft a science of managing public opinion reflected larger feelings of social unrest and a search for control in a time of social drift. Indeed, many began to see the social sciences as holding the key to engineer democracy in the creation of a solid foundation for democracy in a corporate economy.[23]

This larger politics of administration that emerged around the turn of the century was the product of the growing social authority of science, stemming from, and at times conflicting with, philosophical pragmatism's conceptions of epistemology and social action. Indeed, the rise of science's authority was due to the impacts of Darwinism, the role of science in industrial progress, and the Progressive faith in science to harmonize democracy and scientific truth.[24] It is primarily this final hope—the hope that the application of technical reason to political affairs could lead to social control—that legitimized the rationalization of the press in the rise of public relations. Drawing from the social and group psychology of thinkers as diverse as Otto Von Gierke, Auguste Comte, Gustave LeBon, and Gabriel Tarde, among others, many pragmatist philosophers provided the epistemological basis of corporate rationalization.[25]

While internally corporate managers relied on the managerial insights and techniques of Frederick Winslow Taylor to condition, plan, and control the workplace, externally men such as Ivy Lee, Theodore Vail, and Edward Bernays were relying on social psychology in attempts to scientifically condition and manufacture public opinion. Fashioning himself a "doctor of publicity," Ivy Lee was among the first practitioners of public relations to view publicity as a science. This science, for Lee, was one in which the press agent negotiated public interest and corporate policy in a two-way process of interpretation between corporation and public.[26] Working for the Anthracite Coal Operator's Committee of Seven, the Rockefeller family, and other well-known clients, Lee handled scandal and crisis, and argued for an imperative that business manage the irrationality of the crowd in the creation of a shared set of interests between publics and corporations.

These interests, no doubt, were envisioned as serving corporate ends. President of AT&T Theodore Vail articulated a sentiment similar to Lee's, believing that corporations had a duty to combat the false, utopian promises of academics and social reformers. Indeed, Vail held the opinion that publicity was a means to "educate the public" regarding the nature of free enterprise and to provide an "alternative truth" regarding the social circumstances of the day. As Edward Bernays, the double nephew of Sigmund Freud and so-called father of modern public relations, might argue, the task of public relations was akin to that of "an applied social scientist who advises

62 | Chapter Three

a client or employer on the social attitudes and actions to take to win the support of the publics upon whom his or her or its viability depends."[27] In other words, the corporation needed to be able to speak the language of the people in order to advise, influence, and persuade them as to the benevolence of big business. This process of publicity required corporations to take communication seriously in order to create an image of public opinion able to be interpreted and appealed to by corporate communications professionals.

The need to take communication seriously, however, was met with resistance. Though some in the industrial community were quick to see the merit of public relations, others were hesitant to adopt such measures. Indeed, business leaders viewed public relations as a softer side of the business corporation, both in that it was difficult to prove the monetary benefits of such practices and because of an assumption that communications and publicity were "feminine" endeavors.[28] As Deirdre McCloskey has well argued, talk has been long associated with femininity, and the shift toward an economy premised upon service and speech as opposed to the seemingly more masculine work of production brought about anxieties of feminization and emasculation.[29]

This perceived femininity of publicity work stood in stark contrast to the more "masculine" functions of mass production. This split in attitudes regarding the femininity of publicity work and masculinity of production was also reflected by a disdain by industry leaders for the seemingly superfluous nature of words as opposed to action.[30] Thus, while men such as Henry Ford argued that continued production was the best way to demonstrate responsibility for the public, others, such as Owen D. Young of General Electric, recognized the need of corporations to appeal to a broader sense of social obligation in the adoption of a statesman-like orientation to consumer publics. Efforts to sell corporate communications to the business community were thus also attempts to masculinize these endeavors.

This skirmish regarding production and publicity was indicative of a larger friction between those still largely committed to a producer-oriented industrial ethos and a new generation of business leaders committed to linking industrial progress to consumerism and service.[31] It is in this skirmish that advertising and public relations professionals found common purpose. Both modes of corporate communications saw the future of industrial and national progress in a consumer society. While advertising was able to meet the increasing demands placed upon manufacturers and distributors in an economy of scale and to provide consumers with a reassuring, therapeutic image of modernity, public relations was able to counter the political demands placed upon corporations by Progressive agitators through the creation of counter-narratives in the press in an attempt to educate the public on the benefits of free enterprise and adjust their attitudes accordingly. In this sense, both advertising and public relations operated to create a sense of moral legitimacy for the corporation during a time in which this legitimacy was in question.

This struggle for legitimacy was a struggle for a sense of moral obligation and personality. Through brands, trademarks, institutional advertisements, and public-image campaigns, advertising and public relations proved essential tools for projecting and disseminating a personified image of the corporation. Through images of company founders, factories, skyscrapers, and more, advertising and public relations professionals sought to place a face on the corporate person. Though the modernization of these industries brought about the innovation of many mass communication strategies for the corporation, perhaps none were as innovative as Henry Parsons Crowell of Quaker Oats and Bruce Barton of the advertising giant Batten, Barton, Durstine, and Osborne (BBDO). Both Crowell and Barton not only were early advocates of the shift from producerism to consumerism, but also saw in corporate communications a means to marry their ideological commitments to free enterprise and evangelical Protestantism.

The shift to consumer culture that saw the rise of corporate communications placed a premium on service as the primary product and justification of business bigness, and this notion of service provided a means with which to rearticulate the relationship between discourses of corporate capitalism and Protestantism in the creation of a corporate soul. In what follows I will provide a theoretical explanation of the discourse of evangelical capitalism, as well as both Crowell's and Barton's unique articulations of this discourse through rhetorics of stewardship and service. Both of these rhetorics proved crucial to the larger effort to mount a moral defense of business to a skeptical public through the co-optation of Progressive rhetorical strategies and, I argue, portrayed the corporation as a benevolent shepherd capable of guiding a bewildered public to material salvation.

64 | Chapter Three

Corporate Shepherds and Public Flocks: The Discourse of Evangelical Capitalism

As we have seen, advertising arose amongst a period of cultural, industrial, and spiritual change. The growth of urban centers, the emergence of new technologies of communication and travel, the rise of the quasi-public corporation, and the decline of religious authority that occurred simultaneously near the turn of the century challenged core tenets of liberalism's conception of rational individual autonomy and selfhood. This decline of autonomous selfhood created a longing for personality and a renewed sense of self that could combat the anomie and emptiness that accompanied the luxuries of modernity. The cultural anxieties that accompanied the rise of the large corporation were largely met by the therapeutic ethos of the budding consumer culture. Promising self-fulfillment and actualization, consumerism offered the promise of reversing the rationalization of society through the self-actualizing powers of consumption. However, advertisers largely replaced one set of social controls with a different, subtler means of directing human behavior.[32] Indeed, I argue that this new form of social control is premised on a particular articulation of the relationship between Protestantism and consumer culture by advertising and public relations professionals—what I refer to as a discourse of evangelical capitalism.

As a discourse, evangelical capitalism derives its power and cultural authority from what Michel Foucault has called pastoral power. Originally theorized as a form of power tied to the Christian Church in the seventeenth and eighteenth centuries, Foucault has noted that since the rise of the modern state and structures of governmentality, pastoral power has remained a potent force in modern culture. Indeed, rather than disappearing with the birth of the state, the pastorate was reformulated and absorbed into the modern political economy. This new pastorate is a form of religious power that promises not otherworldly salvation but a salvation of this world—a salvation through material well-being.[33]

Operating on a logic of submission, pastoral power is premised upon a relationship of shepherd and flock. The power of the shepherd over its flock is one of benevolence. As Foucault notes, pastoral power is fundamentally beneficent and operates "as a power of care" that manifests in a duty to protect the flock.[34] Extending this formulation, Brian Kaylor argues that the role of the shepherd "is to protect, direct, and nurture the people under their authority."[35] The leadership of the shepherd, then, is a "self-sacrificial leadership where the shepherd-leader acts in the best interest of the people." Yet, in order to act in the interest of the people the shepherd must know his flock, as pastoral power "implies knowledge of the conscious and an ability to direct it."[36] This knowledge of one's flock is gathered through the therapeutic act of confession. As a rhetorical act, confession operates constitutively to formulate subjects capable of being led. The act of confession is thus also an act of submission to the shepherd, and an admission of need to be guided to redemption.

Yet, this submission does not forego the capacity for agency. The subject position of the sheep requires an acceptance of the message and a desire for personal transformation. In the discourse of evangelical capitalism, then, agency is figured not as a collective or deliberative endeavor but rather as an act of individual volition and choice. Understanding agency not as speech but as choice is due to evangelical capitalism's understanding of communication as dissemination. As John Durham Peters notes, the parable of the sower in the synoptic Gospels offers a conception of communication that "celebrates broadcasting as an equitable mode of communication," capable of spreading the good news far and wide."[37] Communication here is figured as an inherently public and asymmetrical act concerned less with the capacity for dialogue and exchange and more so with the capacity to distribute the message to all those with ears to hear it. Agency is figured as hearing the good news and choosing to follow it. Thus, agency lies in the self-reflective and hermeneutic act of decoding and "harvesting" the message, not in the more egalitarian exchange of dialogue. To engage in dialogue would in fact jeopardize the shepherd-flock relationship, for as Kaylor reminds us, it's the shepherd who knows best.[38]

Within the discourse of evangelical capitalism, it is my contention that corporate communications professionals figured the corporation as a shepherd capable of guiding a lost, adrift, and bewildered public flock to salvation through the saving forces of consumption. As apostles of modernity, advertisers and public relations practitioners crafted an evangelical corporate framework by modernizing Protestant Christianity and crafting a faith in consumption as a means to economic and spiritual renewal. The preaching of the gospel of modernity was done largely through what Marchand has

66 | Chapter Three

called the great parables of advertising. As rhetorical devices, these common tropes intimated the benevolence of corporate society to its audiences, seeking a kind of tacit consent to and reinforcement of their messages.[39]

For instance, the parable of the Democracy of Goods promised egalitarianism and a harmonized relationship among laborers, consumers, and industrialists, not through redistribution of wealth but through the equalizing forces of cheap consumer goods in an economy of scale. At a deeper level, Marchand notes that the Democracy of Goods provides a "secularized version of the traditional Christian assurances of ultimate human equality," materializing the spiritual promises of common humanity. Similarly, the parable of Civilization Redeemed sought to persuade audiences that modernity could purge its own excesses, and that consumer goods offered the way of doing so. In this sense, the parable taught audiences that "the advance of civilization, temporary afflictions notwithstanding, need never exact any real losses. Civilization had become its own redeemer."[40] As these two examples illustrate, though the messages offered varied from parable to parable, taken as a whole the larger claim was that all social ills could be ameliorated through consuming advertised products. As the great parables of advertising illustrated, the corporation was not something to be feared. Rather, the good news offered by modernity's missionaries was the redeeming and benevolent power of the large corporation.

The relationship with the faceless corporation, then, was fashioned as one akin to a relationship to an unknowable God, understanding each relationship as a submission to a transactional stance with a faceless "person" that guaranteed freedom, safety, and salvation as both God and the corporation were seen to be "assuring from afar, satisfying, and empowering."[41] Yet, despite claims to a kind of universal agape for its flock, the image of the Promised Land of material abundance portrayed by advertisers was one that reinforced existing gender, race, and class hierarchies. The corporation was assuring and empowering to some and a more malevolent force for others. This unequal promise of wealth, power, and self-actualization is due largely to the fact that advertisements, as many scholars have noted, mirror the desire and anxieties of those who create them more than the audiences that these messages are oriented to.[42]

Thus, the great parables brought with them their own paradoxes and excesses incapable of being resolved by their own rhetorical force. While the notion of a "democracy of goods" was premised upon an egalitarian ethos, this democracy left many of its citizens disenfranchised and subordinate to its consuming elite. As M. M. Manring has noted, national consumer goods such as Maxwell House coffee and Aunt Jemima pancake mix peddled their goods through narratives that romanticized plantation life and the myth of racial harmony in the Old South by depicting a normative vision of race, class, and gender relations that saw black laborers as affording the white man a life of leisure and abundance. Advertisements for these prominent brands made the argument that their products, and by extension the rise of consumer capitalism, provided a means to reunite and reconcile the North and South in a harmonized social order. This vision of social harmony, however, was largely a product of the predominantly white and male composition of the advertising industry itself, promoting a social order that understood "black women in service to their families black and white; white women directing the social affairs of the household but free of the hard work associated with cooking and cleaning; [and] white men atop the whole structure, protecting it but often aloof, worried about more important things."[43]

These racist and sexist ideologies were not only a reflection of the cultural assumptions of white male advertisers; these visions of social order were also projected onto very real political and economic shifts brought about by factory life that saw capitalism penetrate the privacy of the home. Reconfiguring domestic relations, consumer capitalism was premised on the construction of the single-family home as the heart of political and economic life.[44] This construction of the home was largely figured on a heteronormative gendered division of labor wherein the wife became the master of home economics. Indeed, consumer goods promised empowerment to white middle-class women by alleviating the labor time of cooking, cleaning, and child-rearing while simultaneously reinforcing the position of the woman as one of mother and caretaker of the family unit and relegating her agency to the privacy of the home.[45] Clearly the blessings of the benevolent corporation were not so evenly distributed and radically egalitarian as advertisers made them out to be.

However, the task of advertisers to reformulate the relationship of the corporation to its publics required the perception of a benevolent personality for the corporation capable of caring for and serving an idealized vision of its public flock. Additionally, advertisers were able to use mass-media technologies and strategies to craft an image of Christ for the modern era. In this way, personalizing the bureaucratic corporation and personifying the seeming ineffable nature of God became a way for those in the business community to meet the criticisms of Progressive reformers in argumentative clash and to rhetorically suture the corporation to evangelical Protestantism. These tasks of personalization, then, were mutually reinforcing. The shift to consumer society, with its emphasis on service, individual choice, and thrift, provided the necessary rhetorical tools for industry leaders to wed capitalism and Christianity and articulate an evangelical capitalist discourse.

Chief among these leaders were Henry Parsons Crowell, president and CEO of Quaker Oats and president of the Moody Bible Institute (MBI), and Bruce Barton, cofounder and president of the advertising giant Batton, Barton, Durstine, and Osborne (BBDO). I argue that though each articulated their particular brands of evangelical capitalism differently, contingent upon their unique theological, political, and industrial commitments, taken together we can gain a more complete picture of the ways in which advertisers were able to meet the criticisms of Progressive reformers against the material excesses and spiritual deficits of corporate capitalism by crafting a corporate soul capable of solving social problems and redeeming society's excesses.

For Crowell the corporation was a steward of society, and for Barton the corporation personified Christ's commitment to serve others. Though each of these rhetorics of corporate responsibility were indeed notable improvements from the earlier Gilded Age, as the power dynamics of the pastoral relationship demonstrate, these rhetorics authorized a hierarchical relationship between corporation and public that dovetailed with technocratic notions of managerialism and benevolent paternalism. Additionally, the vision of society offered by modernity's missionaries reinforced the gendered and racial myopia of the predominantly white Progressive movement, erasing important political and ideological cleavages within the U.S. public. Finally, rather than envisioning a critical, deliberative public that could enact a collective agency capable of checking corporate power, the evangelical capitalist discourse articulated by Crowell and Barton was premised upon a kind of public faith in the saving capacities of the large corporation.

A Man Fully Consecrated: Henry Parsons Crowell and the Rhetoric of Stewardship

Born January 27, 1855, in Cleveland, Ohio, Henry Parsons Crowell was the son of Henry Luther and Anna Eliza Crowell. Luther, a devout Presbyterian and shoe merchant, sought to move his family westward from Hartford, Connecticut, in 1853 in order to explore frontier land and start a business. Luther had his eyes set on either Madison, Wisconsin, or Cleveland, Ohio. Luther ultimately decided on Cleveland, known as a growing metropolis and a "land of silk and money," and the city became the home of Luther's budding shoe warehouse formed with his business partner, John Seymour.[46]

Though Henry Parsons Crowell's father Henry Luther would die of tuberculosis while Henry was only nine years old, there were two crucial lessons Luther imparted to his son. These were the importance of being a good steward and the ability to adapt to the new technologies and methods of the developing business culture. The values of stewardship came from the fact that the Crowell home was devoutly religious. It has been noted that as members of the First Presbyterian Church of Cleveland, the "Crowell home [had] a notable Presbyterian flavor," and that Luther would read a passage from the family Bible before every meal to "offer simple comments of application" to the everyday life of the family.[47] Notable were conversations regarding money. The shoe business had been good to the young Luther Crowell, but he was acutely aware of the trouble money could bring to the follower of Christ.

As Henry Parsons Crowell's biographer Richard Ellsworth Day notes, Luther "had observed, first in his Connecticut hometown, and now in Cleveland, that money kept for two or three generations, will either poison its possessors, or, impart a fine mellowness."[48] Great wealth possessed by a man or family could in other words lead to a loss of Christian virtues. Sloth and greed could corrode one's character. For Luther, and later for his son and business giant Henry Parsons Crowell, one must recognize that not only the tithe but all of one's wealth belongs to the Lord. If one was not cognizant of this fact and instead treated money as an end in itself, they were living not for God but for themselves. One must realize that one's wealth is a gift from God to be prudently managed as a duty of stewardship for the work of the Lord.

70 | Chapter Three

These values of prudence, stewardship, and self-denial were not unique to the Crowell family. Indeed, as Max Weber has shown, these values were a product of the Reformation and the worldly asceticism of Calvinist theology.[49] Arising alongside the development of bourgeois capitalism, Calvinist ethics helped provide a rational, utilitarian value system that rendered labor rather than wealth as the ethical purpose of a Christian life. Sanctified in the notion of the calling, labor became the way in which an individual was able to become anointed as a divine instrument of God's will. The Calvinist life was thus to be lived as one fully dedicated and consecrated to the work of the Lord, in which the individual enacts an ethic of self-control that promises material comfort in this world and salvation in the next.[50]

Stewardship manifested as a "gratitude for the generosity of all God's graces," and demanded thrift and restraint in the face of material excess.[51] While the linkage between Calvinism and stewardship was nothing new, what is unique to Crowell is the way in which he utilized these values to articulate an evangelical capitalist discourse that justified the shift from entrepreneurial to corporate consumer capitalism. As biographer Joe Musser claims, it was this ability to "mediate the conflicts between those who wanted to keep the traditions of the old century and those who pushed for the ways of the future" that distinguishes Crowell's unique vision of an evangelical capitalism from earlier Protestant ethics.[52]

This vision would come to fruition, and Henry's life would be forever changed, as he attended a shoe clerk meeting held at the Second Presbyterian Church of Cleveland in 1873 in which a young Dwight L. Moody had been invited to speak. The young Crowell felt as if Mr. Moody's words were meant expressly for him. Preaching that "the world has yet to see what God can do with and for and through and in a man who is fully consecrated to Him," Moody's words so deeply affected Henry Crowell that he broke into tears.[53] Crowell vowed to be that man, a man fully consecrated to the Lord, stating that though he "would never preach like Moody," he could "make money and help support the labors of men like Moody." Praying, Crowell exclaimed, "Oh God, if you will allow me to make money to be used in Your service I will keep my name out of it so You will have the glory."[54]

After engaging in brief, yet very successful business ventures in North and South Dakota running horse farms, Crowell would return to Ohio wealthier and more business savvy. Selling his farms, he used this money to purchase a mill that came up for sale in nearby Ravenna, Ohio. Though the mill was in financial trouble when Crowell purchased it, the mill also held several promising assets: a new, modernized milling machine using rollers and cutting blades to standardize production, a specialization in milling oats, and the more symbolic asset of holding the name Quaker. Taken together, these assets provided a sound product, a means for producing and distributing this product at a scale and speed required for a mass market, and a name that Crowell hoped would instill ideas of "strength, integrity, trust, and quality" in the minds of consumers.[55] What was needed was the ability to stand out and survive in a crowded milling market.

The methods used by Crowell to market and advertise his goods were nothing short of pioneering. In fact, historian of the Quaker Oats company Arthur F. Marquette has written that the history of Quaker Oats is "the story of modern merchandising."[56] Quaker was the first U.S. company to develop a comprehensive vision of modern consumer advertising, and the first to use consumer packaging as a marketing technique rather than a mere vessel of processed goods.[57] At a time when oats and grains were primarily sold by merchants in barrels or sacks, brands were largely irrelevant to millers. The task of the miller was not to shape public preference but rather to communicate with jobbers and merchants themselves, negotiating solely on the basis of price.[58]

With the rise of manufacturing and the ability to package goods, the benefits of packaging quickly became apparent to dealers, consumers, and ultimately manufacturers like Crowell. For dealers, packaged grains and oats were easier to shelve, handle, and protect from unwanted pests such as mice. For consumers these goods were easier to carry and preserve and provided a sense of overall cleanliness. Finally, for manufacturers, packages allowed for easier direct communication with consumers, allowing them to bypass jobbers and merchants in the distribution process. Taken together, branding, packaging, and consumer advertising worked to shape consumer awareness, preferences, and habits.[59]

Crowell was quick to realize this common purpose and utilized all three to generate consumer demand by experimenting with new advertising techniques and dedicating a large budget for advertising purposes. Yet, these efforts to shape consumer demand and brand awareness did not come without resistance. One of his business partners, Ferdinand Schumacher, was

72 | Chapter Three

adamantly opposed to what he viewed as wasteful spending on consumer marketing. This dispute, representative of industry-wide rifts between the old guard of producer economics and the burgeoning consumer economy, eventually led to a mutiny of sorts in which Crowell and another partner, Robert Stuart, ousted Mr. Schumacher with the approval of stockholders in the then American Cereal Company. After eliminating Schumacher, the company focused its attention almost entirely on the Quaker brand, and in 1901 the Quaker Oats Company was chartered as a holding company for other company assets.[60]

With Schumacher out of the way and with the concurrent rise of the Quaker Oats Company, Crowell was free to continue to innovate in the way of advertising, as his was among the first modern, quasi-public corporations to approach advertising with a consistent philosophy. Developing a theory of constant exposure, Crowell sought to make the Quaker name and logo ubiquitous through the deployment of billboards, news columns, metal signage, free sample displays, attractions at local and national fairs, postcards, scientific endorsements, box-top giveaways, and more.[61] Indeed, though many of these techniques became commonplace and are mundane to us now, Crowell was a trailblazer with regard to many such appeals. Employing these techniques before the rise of the modern ad agency, Crowell and Quaker Oats built a brand from the inside out in an industry in which brands were nearly unheard of.

Displaying a quiet strength, industrious attitude, and moral vision, in many ways the Quaker logo was an extension of Crowell himself. As H. J. Thornton has observed, "gentle of speech, serene of heart, keen of mind, and vigorous in action, he [Crowell] is, indeed, the personification of the alert and genial 'Quaker' whose name and spirit have given life and substance to the organization."[62] This should come as no surprise. Seeking to build success in the business world was never a goal Crowell undertook for himself. He sought to imbue his business with a Christian ethos, building a business empire not for self-satisfaction but for God. The Quaker logo was thus not only a representation of the characteristics needed to succeed in industry, but also a moral avatar for Crowell's vision of a Christian industrialism and an evangelical capitalism.

Becoming an immensely successful Christian businessman was no doubt fulfilling for Crowell, making good on his promise to himself and to God.

Yet, this was not enough. It was only after moving to Chicago when the corporate headquarters of Quaker were relocated that Crowell came into contact with William Newell, a young pastor and Bible teacher at the Moody Bible Institute near the Gold Coast neighborhood of Chicago's downtown. The two became dear friends and conducted Bible studies in the Crowells' Rush Street home. As a result of these classes Crowell felt a burning desire to do more for the Kingdom of God, undergoing a crucial transformation from a mere Christian businessman to a Christian statesman.[63] This shift was symbolic of Crowell's larger commitment to evangelical capitalist ideals, marking a deeper commitment to and development of a rhetoric of stewardship.

Doubtless in a spiritual homecoming of sorts, Crowell, shortly after meeting Newell, joined the MBI staff. The institute at the time was struggling financially and was having difficulties keeping afloat. Placed on the board of the Moody Bible Institute on April 24, 1901, and made president three years later, Crowell was largely brought on board to save the sinking ship with his financial acuity and business acumen. Building the institute "on a business basis," Crowell utilized industrial logics to corporatize the organization, engineering it for growth, expansion, and stability.[64] Using much of his own money to help get the institute back on track, Crowell saw the MBI as a worthy cause of his devotion. Additionally, Crowell saw the institute as the locus from which to fight what he perceived as the creeping modernism within the Presbyterian Church. Seeking to build a "Pure Religion" capable of overcoming the threat of modernism while projecting a kind of "nondenominational 'orthodoxy,'" Crowell and the MBI produced a series of essays entitled *The Fundamentals*. Designed to be a "religious equivalent of muckraking journalism," the essays were penned by theologians and marketed by Crowell.[65] Utilizing mailing lists, Crowell and MBI sought to create demand from below from religious consumers, so to speak, helping create a unified front opposed to biblical modernism.

However, equally as important is the fact that the so-called "orthodoxy" created through *The Fundamentals* was one inherently amenable to the larger corporate evangelical outlook of Crowell and the MBI, bolstering the credibility of the institute and a larger vision of the symbiotic relationship between religion and capitalism.[66] Indeed, the marketing techniques Crowell first developed at the Quaker Company became essential for the

Chapter Three

creation, distribution, and marketing of a religion fit for consumption in the religious marketplace, much as was the case with the Quaker's oats. In a modern, corporate culture, religion too had to adapt to the realities of the market. As with product marketing, religion demanded a theory of constant exposure, keeping the message before the eyes of consumers, using new communications technologies to spread the good news far and wide, much like the sower of the Gospels. These technologies included radio, as Crowell invested large amounts of time and money in the development of WMBI, the Moody Institute's own superpower radio station dedicated to the transmission of the Gospel and MBI's pure religion.[67]

Through his investment of both his time and money at Quaker and MBI, we can begin to see the outlines of a rhetoric of stewardship that undergirded Crowell's Christian statesmanship. Recognizing his "entire personal fortune as a stewardship from God," Crowell sought to create religious institutions and a moralized society through concerted effort.[68] Stewardship, for Crowell, was thus a means of social change and of social control premised on managerial means. Crowell's understanding of stewardship was threefold: a Christian statesman ought to be a good steward of money, time, and action. Derived from Puritan notions of frugality, self-denial, and thrift, these values nevertheless had to be retailored to fit the realities of a burgeoning consumer culture. As the traditional Protestant ethic appeared to discourage consumption, leisure, and enjoyment, the value system of old had to be reimagined in a culture seemingly predicated on the worship of mammon. Aligning the often-contradictory ideologies of mass consumption and thrift, Crowell was able to articulate a rhetoric of stewardship that preserved a rational, utilitarian, Christian ethos in the creation of an evangelical capitalist vision of business and society.

For Crowell, stewardship consisted of faith, perseverance, thrift, prudence, and ultimately a sanctification of one's time, money, and deeds. Faith for Crowell was a faith in works—a faith premised upon social action. Crowell's rhetoric of stewardship thus had a performative aspect, whereby Crowell practiced what he preached, becoming what Day has called a "business priest" who used his social position as his personal "altar where he serves the king." With social action as a central component of Crowell's Christian statesmanship, time and money became the primary means through which to affect social change. As explained by Day, "Mr. Crowell's rule of thumb for social action was adequate legislation, in harmony with Christian ideals, and backed up by courageous citizens." For Crowell, this rule of thumb played out in his involvement in the Chicago Committee of Fifteen. Consisting of leading industrial and political members of the Chicago community, the group put together their monetary resources and dedicated themselves to overturning vice and organized crime in Chicago. The group helped pass legislation such as the Mann Act, a state law against pandering, and the Injunction and Abatement law, and ultimately helped to shut down the red-light district.[69] Taking on the perceived problems of the city with a reformer's zeal, Crowell used his resources and business connections to help create a moralized downtown Chicago.

In addition to his involvement in the Committee of Fifteen, Crowell also used his fortune as a means of sanctification. Righting the finances of MBI with his own money, donating to over one hundred Christian businesses in his lifetime, providing financial assistance to ministers, missionaries, and friends, and giving regularly to the church, Crowell saw charity as a means to continually recognize that his wealth was a "sacred trust" with the Lord.[70] Wealth for Crowell was not simply an end in itself, nor was labor. Rather, each was a means from which to give glory to the Kingdom of God. This sentiment is embodied in Crowell's president's message at the dedication ceremony for MBI's administration building, which included the Tower Studios of WMBI in 1939, in which he claimed that though "improved equipment frequently brings new temptations—perhaps the temptation to glory in material things rather than in the Lord," the MBI's new facilities made possible by material wealth were not an exercise in self-glorification but rather were to be "set apart for His glory." The new facilities represented, then, "not endowment of money, but enduement [sic] of power" for the Kingdom of God.[71]

Yet, if Crowell can be seen as a business priest and a key figure in the development of an evangelical capitalism, it is important to note his articulation of this discourse was only partial. Though crafting a pure religion fit for consumption by the masses, Crowell's theological outlook remained traditional and fundamentalist. Crowell's particular brand of evangelical capitalism thus married Christianity and the corporation in order to utilize advertising and marketing strategies to more effectively spread the word of

God and not the other way around. In other words, while he gained notoriety as a business priest for using business techniques to spread the Word, he was unwilling to use the Word to sell big business.

Such an act would be for Crowell a sacrilegious debasement of Christ's work. Crowell's staunch theological commitments demanded the maintenance of a hierarchical separation between the spiritual and the material realms that kept him from embracing modern and rational accounts of the Christian faith. Indeed, for Crowell the spiritual could not fully be reduced to the material realm as wealth, success, and power were merely means toward more spiritual ends. Taking the Bible as true and authentic history, the liberal theology espoused by ministers across the country and throughout Crowell's Presbyterian Church was a sign of secularism's assault on the institution of the church through evolutionary science.[72] Success in this world, Crowell held, amounted to nothing if not fully committed to the development and expansion of the kingdom of God.

The economy of abundance was merely a sign of God's blessings, for which businessmen and the corporate community must act as benevolent stewards. The corporation itself, as synecdoche for industrial power and progress, must be a steward of God's blessings to the U.S. public. By providing an abundance of consumer goods for an affordable price, the large corporation was able to share God's blessings and distribute a higher quality of living than politics. The Quaker logo provided a constant reminder of the benevolence of the corporation, providing a face and animating personality that acted as a spiritual intermediary between management, owners, and the mass consumer public now separated from individual personalities of business by an economy of scale. The Quaker, much like God, provided assurance, safety, and stability from afar through a kind of benevolent paternalism.[73] The corporation, in an evangelical capitalism, would look out for its public flock of consumers as it recognized its moral duty to consumers as a holy trust with the Lord. Great wealth necessitated great responsibility.

However, one did not need an abundance of time or money to take action. Rather, what was required was the thrifty, economic usage of each to produce effective, efficient change. With the rise of a managerial, corporate economy, Calvinism's moral utilitarianism underwent a shift to a kind of "worldly utilitarianism," and ideals of thrift and frugality were actively being resignified and imagined to comport with managerial logics of efficiency, therapeutic adjustment, and self-actualization.[74] While being a steward of one's time was always central to the rationalized Calvinist ethos of capitalism described by Weber, temporal thrift took on a new significance in a corporate economy. Thrift became intertwined with the Progressive faith in progress and efficiency, seeing a doctrine of "personal efficiency" replacing older notions of self-control.[75] Resonating with neoclassical economics, time itself became a commodity, making efficiency in labor as well as consumption and action essential to personal success.

This shift, as James Davison Hunter notes, was premised on a "subtle redefinition of thrift from saving to 'wise spending' and 'proper use,' and from personal restraint . . . to prudent and efficient release."[76] The linchpin binding Victorian and Progressive managerial notions of thrift became the "recoil from waste" that both saw as detrimental to moral and social thriving.[77] In this sense, a good steward need not replicate the methods of Crowell. Indeed, efficient consumption and prudential spending became emblematic of faithful stewardship. Cast in this light, consumerism was not a shallow exercise in self-gratification or wastefulness, but instead became a moral duty in itself. In an economy of abundance, the traditional doctrine of stewardship became inverted. In other words, spending rather than saving was necessary for national growth and prosperity.[78]

Seeking to meet the task of resignifying traditional Protestant values to comport with the realities of modernization, advertising professionals such as Crowell thus underwent a steady process of rhetorical craftwork. The shift from traditional Calvinist Protestantism to a secularized form of Christianity's utilitarian ethos was not an overnight phenomenon. Nor did it arise solely ex nihilo from the minds of the captains of industry. As Jennifer Scanlon argues, "what marks the change from religiosity to secularism, and from thrift to consumption, is not overthrow but accommodation." Individuals such as Crowell were responding to larger cultural and economic shifts that were altering the face of public life and morality. These responses crafted a new vision of industry that sought to legitimize consumerism and the large corporation through a religious rhetoric of benevolent stewardship and service. However, it is equally as important to note that men such as Crowell were not solely producing change but were themselves products of large-scale change.[79] The larger discursive shifts of the age actively shaped the available sources of rhetorical invention as Crowell and others were

78 | Chapter Three

actively participating in the refashioning of industrial, rhetorical culture, both paving the way for future rhetorical actors.

Continuing to devote his time, money, and person to God until his passing in October 1944, Crowell will no doubt be remembered for his faithful stewardship. In several obituaries published across the nation and in many posthumous writings on his life, writers continually point to his service and charity as his lasting legacy. The *Chicago Tribune* published an obituary on October 10, 1944, recalling his endowment to his Wyoming Hereford Ranch.[80] On the same day, the *Daily News* cited his active participation in the Committee of Fifteen as a "militant opponent of prostitution" in Chicago.[81] Nearly a month later the *Tribune* announced that Crowell's $3,100,000 fortune was largely dedicated to "Christian works and educational projects," after his passing.[82] An essay in *Church Builders* recalled that Dr. Will H. Houghton, then president of MBI, called Crowell "the most Christ-like man I have ever met."[83] Joe Musser proclaims that despite his great success, it is Crowell's "stewardship of his time and money that holds such interest and value for today's readers."[84] No doubt, Crowell's impact is lasting, though his name is rarely invoked. Surely, this is precisely the way he would have wanted it.[85]

Meeting the challenge of comporting Protestantism with modern industrial realities, Crowell is an important figure in the salvation of the corporation. Though welcoming industrial progress, Crowell nevertheless fought the creeping tide of modernism within the Protestant church. However, while Crowell was able to portray the corporation as a spiritual bedrock in the shift to modernity, advertising professional and public relations advocate Bruce Barton would more fully develop a modernized, evangelical capitalist framework. Building upon Crowell's groundwork, Barton was able to personify the corporation and Christ as modern persons that promised well-being through a rhetoric of service.

The Forger of Institutional Souls: Bruce Barton and the Rhetoric of Service

The son of a traveling preacher, Bruce Barton was born in Robbins, Tennessee, August 5, 1886. By the time he was a young boy, his father William had moved the family to Ohio, Boston, and Oak Park, Illinois. Becoming pastor at the First Congregational Church of Oak Park, William became known for his powerful sermons. Graduating from Ohio's Oberlin Theological Seminary in 1890, William held a liberal theology, eschewing religious dogma and Puritanism. Faced with the task of reconciling "the earlier Calvinist, producer-oriented, republican moral strictures of the nineteenth century with the corporate, consumption-driven, bureaucratic world that supplanted it," William Barton, unlike his contemporary Crowell, held that Christ ought to be reimagined to fit the complexities of the modern era.[86] This line of thought had a profound impact on the young Bruce, who looked up to his father greatly.

Indeed, it may be safe to say that the tensions between traditionalism and modernism proved formational for Bruce Barton. Barton's adolescent home of Oak Park was indicative of the larger cultural shifts of the age, placing him at the crux of modernity's transformative power. As Barton's biographer Richard Fried notes, Oak Park was "a way station not only between the metropolis and the great agricultural hinterland" of Illinois, but also "between an older, small-town, individualistic, church-led, producer-oriented ethos and a metropolitan, consumption driven, corporate society."[87] The dialectic between these two different eras played out before Barton's eyes and encompassed the social geography of his upbringing.

As an adolescent, Barton proved to be a promising student and energetic young man. Managing the glee club, editing the student newspaper, and debating during his high school years in suburban Illinois, he ultimately attended Amherst after spending a year at his father's alma mater, Berea College.[88] A voracious reader, skilled debater and orator, and a gifted writer, Barton emerged as a star pupil during his time at Amherst, being voted most likely to succeed by his graduating class. However, the young Barton experienced a "crisis of faith" while away at school, turning away from his longtime plans of entering the ministry after graduation. During a visit home, William sensed this drift in his son. After talking with his father, Bruce ultimately remained committed to a liberal theology, adopting a "syllogistic approach" to faith that saw religion as a "simple, rational, reasonable and pleasant part of life."[89]

Though remaining committed to his Protestant faith, Barton no longer wished to follow in his father's footsteps as a preacher. After graduation

80 | Chapter Three

Barton remained unsure of what profession he would devote himself to. When he graduated in 1907, the market panic made many options difficult. Turning down a fellowship in history at the University of Wisconsin-Madison—an offer made directly to Bruce from Frederick Jackson Turner—he decided upon a career in publishing.[90]

Working at *Home Herald*, a religious monthly in Chicago, Barton solicited advertisements and wrote editorial copy.[91] Quickly recognized as a standout at his job, Barton became managing editor of the magazine as well as two others in the Chicago area. With these publications going bankrupt in the wake of the financial crisis in 1907 and 1908, Barton again was without a job. His work, however, was noticed and brought him job offers in New York. Bouncing from magazine to magazine in New York City, Barton found steady work in 1912 as assistant sales manager of the P. F. Collier & Son publishing house.[92]

Throughout his early, hectic, and eclectic career in publishing, Barton continued to pen articles, editorials, essays, and short stories for several religious publications. A reformer as a youth, Barton embraced the message of the Social Gospel. Importantly, Barton would abandon this line of faith sometime around 1915, likely brought about by the vagaries of the First World War. Even in his youth, however, Barton's Social Gospel was a mild iteration of some of the more radical attempts to use Christianity to bring about structural reform. To borrow Fried's words, "Barton emphasized the spiritual over the socioeconomic service the mission performed," seeing in the Social Gospel a means for individual reform rather than large-scale cultural redemption.[93]

One constant between his earlier religious writings and his later ones was his insistence on a Jesus fit for the modern age. Inviting Christians to "unite and take back our Jesus," he painted an image of Christ as "manly, strong, courageous, sociable, quick-witted, dynamic, charismatic, exuding vigor, teaching that religion was a matter of spirituality, not ritual."[94] Central to this vision of a modern, rugged, masculine Jesus was a sense of service to society. Eschewing his muckraking past, Barton's social Christianity slowly widened its scope to include benevolent businessmen. As Leo Ribuffo points out, by 1914 Barton had "called business the nation's 'greatest force for righteousness,'" seeing a moral capitalism as the most effective means for achieving social reform. These doctrinal shifts can be detected in many of

Barton's published works of this time period, including numerous editorials, his 1914 *A Young Man's Jesus*, a serialized story in *American Magazine* entitled "Finding God in Millersville," and in his only novel, *The Making of George Groton*.[95] The novel, a fictitious look at the ethical dilemmas posed by the shift to a modern society, ultimately praises a benevolent, self-regulating capitalism, offers service as a virtue, and is emblematic of Barton's own changing political beliefs at the onset of the war.[96]

Fundraising for the Salvation Army and managing publicity for the Young Men's Christian Association (YMCA) throughout their wartime efforts, Barton's work during World War One would prepare him for his career as an advertising executive.[97] Seeing advertising and publicity—in his own work, the works of others, and George Creel's Committee on Public Information (CPI)—as an essential means for securing peace through diplomatic means across the globe, Barton increasingly came to see a benevolent capitalism as crucial for social progress.[98] Seeking to bring this view of advertising to fruition, after the war ended, Barton took his industrial and newfound political connections from his publishing career and partnered with Alex F. Osborn and Roy Durstine, both veterans of the United War Work Campaign and advertising professionals, to create Barton, Durstine, and Osborn (BDO). Founded in 1918, the agency would quickly rise among the ranks of Madison Avenue, earning a reputation for offering "a broad array of 'service' to the client."[99] This emphasis on service would become a cornerstone in Barton's evangelical capitalist lexicon, even as the company grew to incorporate George Batten and changed its name to BBDO.

The great clients brought in by BBDO included the National Biscuit Company, General Motors (GM), and General Electric (GE), among others. The services offered to these clients by BBDO and Barton himself included writing copy, doing market research, producing motion pictures, creating names for subsidiary companies, designing packaging, holding cooking demonstrations, designing uniforms for corporate clients, and much more.[100] Advertising not only offered a diverse array of services for clients. Equally as important for Barton were the services provided to consumers by the advertising industry. Advertising, at its best, offered a kind of public education as to the benefits of free enterprise, business bigness, and consumer culture. Indeed, in a brief editorial in the *New York Evening Post* in 1928, Barton called advertising "the voice of business," capable of aligning the

82 | Chapter Three

corporation with "ideals of quality and service" to the public. Advertising, for Barton, thus represented a benevolent force with the "power to keep business striving for high ideals" through public education and standardization of consumer demand.[101] Aligning consumer goods with notions of public service, Barton became adept at creating personalities for large corporate clients capable of conveying sincerity and assurance to consumers.

In his work for GM, Barton was perhaps at his best. As Marchand observes, in his quest to raise public visibility for GM the company came to view him "as its mastermind," utilizing metaphors of the corporate family to create a unified sense of personality for GM's disparate subsidiaries. Deeming him the "forger of institutional souls," Marchand notes Barton's sincerity and commitment to a language of service as essential components to creating corporate personalities.[102] Not alone in this assessment, then president of GM Alfred Sloan's biographer claimed that Barton, "like the great romantic poets, knew how to imbue bloodless entities with great human emotion and spirituality."[103] As with his GE ads, Barton marketed business bigness with its capacity to serve others. In a series of institutional advertisements from 1924 to 1925, Barton imbued not only GM but the automobile itself with notions of service by rhetorically aligning the service of the auto industry with the work of doctors and ministers alike. The 1924 campaign won the Harvard Advertising Award, adding academic legitimacy and authority to BBDO's work.[104]

This growing cultural authority of service in the business community came to fruition in the idea of business statesmanship. With an emphasis on service over personal profit, business statesmanship recognized a broader responsibility to consumer publics in the shift from a producer to consumer culture. While the old guard in the business community saw mass production as the sole justification for bigness, Barton, like Crowell and others before him, crafted an industrial vision premised on values more noble than material wealth. Though Crowell maintained a distinction between the spiritual and material realms, keeping a hierarchical relation of subordination of the material to the spiritual, in Barton's more liberal theology the two were never far apart.[105]

In his June 5, 1923, speech, "And there arose a new King which knew not Joseph," delivered to the National Electric Light Association in New York City, Barton articulated a notion of service that brought together his vision of a socially responsible industry and evangelical Christianity.[106] Drawing business lessons from biblical passages, the speech brought together themes from his earlier writings and presaged the publication a year later of his number one bestseller *The Man Nobody Knows*. Consisting of two parables on the relationship among Christianity, advertising, and public relations, Barton positions the Bible as a text of business history offering valuable lessons to the modern corporate professional. The first of these stories takes a less direct comparison, creating an argument from analogy of the church bell and advertising messaging. Echoing the sentiments of Crowell's theory of constant exposure, the story depicts an advertising man attempting to persuade a local merchant as to the value of advertising. The local proprietor asks, "Why should I advertise? I have been here for twenty years. There isn't a man, woman or child around these parts that does not know where I am and what I sell and how I do business." Responding to this inquiry, the advertising man asks the merchant, "what is that building over there?" Referring to the church across the street, the advertising man continues his interrogation, asking "how long has that been there?" Replying "Oh, I don't know; seventy-five years probably," the advertising man reaches the parable's lesson, claiming, "And yet, they ring the church bell every Sunday morning."[107] In this parable, the constant ringing of the church bell signifies the constant and continual repetition of advertising messages. Regardless of how long a business has operated, how long a product has been created, and how long this product has been in demand, there will always be more out there who have not yet heard the good news. In this sense, the task of the advertising man is akin to that of the evangelist, constant repetition and the large-scale broadcasting of the message to anyone willing to listen.

The lesson of the first parable leads Barton to his second and primary message to his audience as to the merits of public relations. Returning to the Bible to cast a lesson for modern businessmen, Barton recalls the story of Joseph and his "very remarkable business career." Claiming that the story of Joseph offers "one of the most amazing, one of the most staggering lines that has ever been written in a business history," a line so powerful and resonant with Barton that he claims it "ought to be engraved deep on the office wall of every man who has anything to do with public relations," Barton draws direct parallels and lessons from the Bible to corporate, consumer society. The powerful lesson offered by Joseph is encapsulated within the eponymous

84 | Chapter Three

line "And Pharaoh died, and there arose in Egypt a new king which knew not Joseph." Positing this line as "the greatest sermon ever written on the subject of public relations," Barton draws from this sermon the lesson that regardless of what any man, woman, or company has "built up in the way of good-will" in the minds of their consumer publics, this goodwill must eventually pass.

Temporality is thus the perpetual driver of the necessity of publicity. As one generation of consumers leaves this earth and several others are born, the task of consumer education and of crafting consumer desires begins anew. As Barton notes, "Nobody has ever told them that 'Ivory soap floats' or that children cry for Castoria, or what sort of soap you ought to use if you want to have a skin that people would like to touch." Most importantly, "Nobody has ever told them any of the other facts that are so vital in maintaining existence in these complex modern times."[108] Echoing Marchand's arguments about the great parables of advertising, Barton figures public relations as essential to new logics of living in a modern corporate economy.

As missionaries and mediators of the transition to modernity, public relations professionals must be ever vigilant in their constant broadcasting of corporate messaging. In their commitment to the public, sincerity, genuine care, and service are of utmost importance. Business and public relations on any other ground are built upon a shaky foundation. Proper public-relations technique requires not only this commitment to service, but also a strategy that engages the public in a simple and brief language that they can easily comprehend. Not only can simple and brief messages be more easily circulated and recirculated, but they also have a stronger sticking power. Drawing this lesson from Lincoln's Gettysburg Address, Barton argues that the greatness of Lincoln's oratory stemmed from his understanding of these simple facts. The man that spoke before Lincoln spoke for hours, and as Barton reminds us, no one "can remember a single word that he said." The great lesson of Joseph, then, is that public relations is a constant task to be undertaken sincerely, simply, and briefly as an appeal to the king that knows not Joseph.[109]

The powerful message taught by Joseph and Barton's interpretation of the Bible as a text for modern businessmen came full circle a year later in his bestselling *The Man Nobody Knows*. Using his uncanny ability to forge personalities for bloodless persons, Barton created a portrait of Jesus as an innately modern man. Blending his liberal theological orientations with his understanding of the evangelical function of advertising, Barton's book painted a portrait of Christ that "minimized theological controversies, slighted miracles, and stressed Jesus's humanity." Doing so, Barton reimagined Christ for a modern era.[110] Rejecting feminized images of Jesus common in Sunday-school accounts of the Gospels, Barton emphasized Christ's masculinity. Indeed, Barton writes that "Jesus pushed a plane and swung an axe; He was a good carpenter. He slept outdoors and spent His days walking around His favorite lake. His muscles were so strong that when He drove the moneychangers out, nobody dared to oppose Him!"[111] This rugged masculinity was a new interpretation of Christ's personality—one that placed the supposedly feminine emphases on service and speech on sacred and masculine grounds. Yet, this masculinity was only one component of a modernized Jesus.

Alongside his rugged nature, Christ was also depicted by Barton as an indelible executive. Among the qualities that gave Him such a "power over men" was a "personal magnetism which begets loyalty and commands respect," the ability to "recognize hidden capacities in men," and an "unending patience" in training and grooming these capacities in those that are chosen. Through these capacities Jesus was a powerful executive that stood as a model for the modern industrial statesman and advertising professional. For the industrial statesman, Christ's life was emblematic of the importance of a dedication to service. As Barton explains, Jesus said, "There is a success which is greater than wealth or titles," and this success "comes through making your work an instrument of greater service and larger living to your fellow men and women."[112] Seen in this light, the life, teachings, and deeds of Christ made him the first true industrial statesman.

Taking a group of twelve men and creating an organization capable of altering religious preferences in a crowded marketplace, Jesus marshaled his executive powers to create consumer demand and reform the social order. Taking Jesus's message as the origin of the "spirit of modern business," Barton was able to justify an enlightened self-interest and corporate self-regulation through his connection of evangelical Protestantism and corporate capitalism. As Ribuffo argues, "Jesus personified a new spirit of generosity instead of institutional reform," bolstering Barton's belief that "benevolence by regenerate individuals could transform society."[113]

Chapter Three

For the advertising professional, Jesus's methods offered an implicit theory of publicity to be heeded by modern communications officers. Painting Jesus as a prolific strategic communicator and rhetor par excellence, Barton insists that Jesus was able to create consumer demand for a new religion in a market that "was already over-supplied." Beginning like many an entrepreneur with nothing but a "revolutionary idea," Jesus was able to persuade consumers through multiple techniques premised upon His knowledge of the common mind.[114] The genius of Christ's campaign to win over the indifferent and ignorant, Barton claimed, is akin to the modern sales methods pioneered in the fields of psychology and business. Barton's Jesus readily understood that in order to sell another on the benefits of your product, you must first

> Put yourself in the other man's place; try to imagine what he is thinking; let your first remark be sincere and honest but in line with his thoughts; follow it by another such with which you know he will not disagree. Thus, gradually, your two minds reach a point at which small differences are lost in common understanding of a truth.[115]

Through this passage we can see that Barton saw Christ's success as premised upon a process of identification in which common ground leads to a common frame of reference, shared truth, and consubstantiality.[116] Sounding a common note in his writings, Barton also notes the importance of sincerity and genuine care as undergirding a Christian notion of service. Sales need not be simply an exercise in self-interest, but rather by placing oneself in another's frame of mind may allow for the construction of a common public interest. This kind of enlightened self-interest was central to Christ's "higher type of leadership" that offered rewards more noble than self-aggrandizement and mere material wealth. This higher type of leadership, one that promised more obstacles than instant rewards, was what Barton viewed as lacking in the industrial community. As he writes, "Every year in our country there are thousands of conventions—political, charitable, business. Most of them are a waste. They are conducted on the false assumption that overselling and exaggeration are potent forces—that the energies of men respond most powerfully to promises of easy victory and soft rewards."[117] As this passage illustrates, the empty promises of manipulative advertising and blatant overselling were vices to be avoided. What Christ's life and methods illuminated was the primacy of meeting the other on a common ground—the primacy of relating to and understanding one's public as a means to sound executive leadership and effective advertising.

In addition to his understanding of the common mind and emphasis on ethical selling, Jesus also offered the advertising professional lessons on the proper rhetorical packaging of messages to reach consumers. As a man that came to this earth not "to establish a theology but to lead a good life," the ideals of Christ and the church are posited by Barton as the undergirding animus of "all civic enterprises." Indeed, as Barton implores, if Jesus were alive in the modern era, "He would be known only by His service" and "would not neglect the market place." The social space of the circulation of goods and ideas, the marketplace is where the modern Jesus would dwell, peddling his message in the magazines, newspapers, and radio stations of the corporate economy. As Barton explains, these new communication technologies "are now the street in Capernum," replacing the personalized trade of old with the new, impersonal mass market of an economy of scale.[118] Yet even if Jesus's success came in a localized market setting, his parables offer lessons applicable to modern advertising strategists and copywriters alike. These lessons stress the need for effective messaging to be condensed, simple, sincere, and repeated again and again.

Echoing the sentiments expressed in his speech regarding the lessons of Joseph to public relations professionals, in his discussion of Jesus's powerful brevity Barton again references Lincoln's Gettysburg Address. Additionally, Barton notes the power of the introduction of the book of Genesis, capable of putting forward a reformed vision for "the moral structure of the world" in merely six hundred words. Yet not only was Christ economical in his word choice, He was also a master of audience adaptation. Stressing the simplicity of His message, Barton argues that Jesus's words were selected so that even children could easily understand. This is partially a consequence of His selection of illustrations from "the commonest experiences of life," adapting His messages to the *doxa* of His communal culture and eschewing complex ideas in the pursuit of simple turns of phrase and illustrative examples that would resonate with the common man. The simplicity of the message adapted to local audience expectations led naturally to the third lesson of Jesus for advertising men—sincerity. Speaking in the vernacular of one's

Chapter Three

audience creates the appearance of genuineness, care, and respect. As Barton writes, "Persuasion depends on respect for the listeners, and in Jesus great respect was coupled with great love."[119] His sincerity thus followed from an ethic of care for his flock, much as the modern advertising professional, to be successful, must demonstrate genuine care for their consumer public.

In order to guide this public consumer flock to salvation through material well-being and self-actualization, a commitment to an ethic of care emblematic of Christ's commitment to service must undergird the capitalist order. It is in the constant repetition of this message of service that Jesus offers his final lesson. Jesus was cognizant of the fact that the success of his revolutionary idea was contingent upon its constant circulation. Claiming that "reputation is repetition," Barton's Jesus teaches the business community that the reputation of business as a force for social betterment depends on advertising and public relations. This final lesson stands as a testament to the necessity and legitimacy of advertising and public relations as cornerstones of modern corporate culture. Rather than wasteful exercises in public suasion, corporate communications became vital to defending the reputation of free enterprise and saving the corporate soul. Much as in Peters's discussion of the parable of the sower, though indiscriminate scattering may mean that some seeds never reach fertile ground, it is a necessity that the seed be spread as far and wide as possible to continually shape consumer preference and demand.[120]

If, in Barton's formulation, Jesus stood as an exemplar of the ideals of service and care representative of an enlightened self-interest and business statesman, the public figured as the corporate flock in need of care, guidance, and salvation. These ideas are most clearly articulated by Barton in his December 4, 1935, speech "The Public," delivered to the Congress of American Industry at the annual convention of the National Association of Manufacturers (NAM) in New York City. An ardent critic of Franklin Delano Roosevelt and his New Deal policies throughout the 1930s, Barton used this speech as a chance to legitimize public relations as a necessary business function to the NAM and to implore his audience to use new communications techniques to sell free enterprise as morally superior to the perceived statist policies of FDR. Though much more secular in tone than many of his other texts, as I have argued elsewhere, when read through a conceptual hermeneutic of evangelical capitalism the technocratic implications of the address resonate with Barton's moral vision for industry as a shepherd to a lost and adrift public flock.[121]

Arguing that it is the task of public relations to spread a narrative of corporate benevolence and material salvation through consumption, Barton tells his audience:

> We say that Business does not find the people poor and leave them poor. We say the automobile business found the poor man chained to his own poor-yard, with no horizon but the borders of his own little hamlet, and it has made him the monarch of time and distance. We say that the farm implement industry found man only a little higher than the animals—a valet to horses and chickens and cows; and it leaves him riding like a conqueror over his fields doing the work of ten men, and yet not too tired for the radio or movies at night.[122]

In this formulation, the business corporation, through the powers of modern technology, industrial combination, and managerial science, is capable of freeing man from his shackles and providing a kind of worldly salvation through the production and distribution of consumer goods. Additionally, this message positions the corporation as the primary driver of modernity and material progress, processes not to be feared but to be welcomed as redemptive.

Yet if the corporation as agent of modernity is positioned as a saving shepherd, the public is characterized as a flock in need of care, guidance, and salvation. The locus of the benevolent care and service of the corporate shepherd, the public is understood in terms similar to the technocratic public intellectual Walter Lippmann's "public herd."[123] Such a paternalistic picture of the public seemingly belies Barton's discussion of persuasion as premised on listening and the establishment of common ground, seeing instead simplicity in messaging as a dumbing down capable of reaching a largely irrational public mass. Such depictions are not only paternalistic, but also patriarchal. Indeed, the irrationality assigned to the consumer public by advertising professionals was largely attributed to its feminine characterization.[124] As Barton explains in his address,

90 | Chapter Three

> It took only one generation of horses to learn not to be afraid of automobiles, although the threshing machine and the railroad train had frightened them for years. There were more automobiles, and they taught their lesson every minute of the day instead of once in a while.[125]

Abandoning his more religious analogies of the primacy of repetition to business success, Barton compares the constant presence and sounds of the automobile as a pedagogical tool for a frightened and bewildered public in the wake of the complexities of the machine age. The relationship of the public to the corporation, then, is a submissive one in which the behaviors and attitudes of the public are regimented and aligned to the realities of the corporate economy rather than the other way around.[126] This submissive relationship is representative of the pastoral power relationship between shepherd and flock where advertising men acted as what Ewen calls "captains of consciousness," attempting to guide, manipulate, and regiment behavior in the fashioning of the subject position of the "commodity self" capable of purchasing salvation in the marketplace.[127] Unfolding within the submissive nature of the pastoral relationship, corporate communications are to be understood here as primarily a unidirectional exercise rather than a dialogical act of critical reflexivity with regard to the interests of the public, locating public agency not in collective action but in the individual choice of acceptance or rejection of the mass message. Dovetailing with pragmatist technocratic philosophies of governance, Barton's evangelical capitalism can be seen in this reading as a defense against the perceived attacks of FDR's New Deal and a ploy for self-regulation through a rhetoric of service and enlightened self-interest.

Barton's anti-Roosevelt position was further solidified in his continued holy war for advertising throughout the 1920s and 1930s and was reinforced in media coverage of Mr. Barton. In an article in the *New York Journal* on December 4, 1935, entitled "Trade Heads Challenge Raw Deal Policies," the paper claimed that "Barton urges fight" in his outspoken position against "government guardianship."[128] Barton's reputation as an ardent critic of Roosevelt alongside his business and political connections, running publicity for Coolidge throughout the 1920s pro bono, quickly earned him favor within the ranks of the Republican Party. Eventually running for and winning the position of representative in the state of New York's

Seventeenth Congressional District in 1937, Barton positioned himself as a liberal Republican opposed to the New Deal as a misguided platform bent on destroying the advertising industry.[129] Barton's anti–New Deal position later earned him coverage in major newspapers such as the *Herald Tribune* and the *New York Times* in 1939 as he criticized the president's leadership, citing thirty-nine different emergencies since 1933, claiming that this "is at the rate of one new emergency every six weeks for six years—an all-time high in American history." This atmosphere of panic and crisis, Barton asserted, made it impossible for industry to create new jobs, leaving private enterprise and the public at large "exhausted and demanding a change."[130]

Although he ran for a Senate seat a year later, Barton's political career ended in 1940. Fearful of a third Roosevelt term, the looming threat of war, and a perceived creeping statist platform, Barton's campaign expressed these concerns, but not to the tune of the general public.[131] Spending the rest of his political career as a publicity man and occasional adviser for Republican candidates such as Dwight Eisenhower and Barry Goldwater, he was always best remembered for his account of Jesus as the first advertising professional and consummate business statesman in *The Man Nobody Knows*. The book was reprinted multiple times, and the outpouring of letters from thankful readers shows its popular impact. It was the same set of skills that made Barton successful in advertising that ultimately led to the success of the book—his ability to craft humanizing personalities for the largely mysterious and ineffable persons of God and the corporation. Indeed, at a time when the complexities of modernity left citizens desiring a human touch, Barton was quick to meet the demand.

Countless letters from grateful readers recount this fact. Charles Adams, president of the Cleveland Hardware Company, wrote to the Bobbs-Merrill publishing company claiming the book "has given me an entirely different opinion of Jesus and his life, and I visualize him so much idifferent [*sic*] than I ever have before, and I think of him as a man like myself, with the same troubles and the same worries, and the same problems."[132] Another letter from W. Robert Catton, assistant minister and education director at the Plymouth Church in Minneapolis, states that the book captures "His many sided personality," also commenting on the sincerity of Barton's writing, making the book a "magnificent discovery of a vibrant, vital personality which leaps from every page." Others noted the way the text humanized

Chapter Three

Jesus, making Him "a real human being," and someone "by whose side we would be happy to sit at a dinner."[133] Barton's writings struck a chord within the modern man.

All of this is not to say that Barton's interpretations of Jesus and his articulation of evangelical capitalism were met unanimously with open arms. Criticized from both the cultural left and portions of the religious right, many found his reduction of Jesus to a businessman either sacrilegious, a banal reduction of Christ to the language of modernity, or both. While perhaps both viewpoints may be true to some degree, they no doubt both miss the important cultural work of translation Barton performed. The one-time railroad bridge builder was indeed a fine architect. As Fried points out, Barton was "particularly adept at building bridges," but these bridges were ones "between tradition and modernity."[134] Despite the loose theology and at times contradictory ideals Barton espoused, his work resonated with many that desired animating personalities in an economy of scale. In doing so, Barton was able to respond to trends of secularization by corporatizing Christianity and simultaneously Christianizing the free enterprise system itself through an evangelical capitalism premised upon a rhetoric of benevolent service.[135]

Conclusion

As I have demonstrated in this chapter, the rise of corporate communications at the turn of the century adopted a religious function. Many early advocates and practitioners of advertising and public relations saw in the new techniques of mass communication parallels between their work and the work of missionaries and preachers of Jesus's message across the nation. Promising a salvation of this world for consumer publics, equally as important to these men was the salvation of the corporation itself. At a time of crisis for corporate moral legitimacy, Crowell and Barton stood as key figures capable of refashioning the large corporation on an evangelical basis. In the process, these men both defended the corporation and Christianity by reimagining the relationship between the two in a consumer culture. While for Crowell material abundance was to be recognized as a means to spiritual ends, for Barton material abundance was itself a means of salvation through self-actualization. Largely collapsing a distinction between the material and the spiritual, Barton read the Bible as business history and Christ's life as a lesson in the values of industrial statesmanship.

Importantly, however, Crowell and Barton did not stand alone in their efforts to link Protestantism and corporate capitalism, nor was Barton isolated in his endeavors to use evangelical capitalist language to defend industry from the New Deal policies of FDR. As Gloege has demonstrated, the marriage of consumer culture and Protestantism was brought about by the rise of a corporate evangelical network that mutually reinforced the cultural authority of both in U.S. society.[136] Likewise, a committed group of Christian libertarian businessmen would help craft, alongside their traditionalist counterparts, a conservative movement that sought to overthrow the supposed godless statism of FDR's New Deal. Indeed, the nascent conservative movement in the United States would make the relationship between Christianity and capitalism a defining issue during the Cold War. Tracing the development of the conservative movement, the next chapter illustrates the particular economic theology of Cold War capitalism and of a corporate, Christian libertarianism. It is in this political culture that the corporation would be granted a legal voice, knighted as a holy warrior in the crusade for Western Christian civilization.

CHAPTER 4

Voice

The discourse of evangelical capitalism would not disappear after the end of World War Two. Rather, it would undergo a significant revision. The only nation to emerge from the war more prosperous than it had entered, the United States became a global superpower thanks in large part to the wartime production efforts of its leading corporations. In the process, the industrial system itself had changed, seeing the growth of both the state and the corporation. Rather than enemies fighting for the soul of the nation, many came to understand that the two could work in tandem. Indeed, as the nation entered the Cold War, such cooperation was seen to be necessary in order to stave off the specter of Communism on the global stage. Here, the state and the corporation were allies in the struggle for the spiritual and Christian inheritance of the West, embodied by the promise of the United States itself. What emerges in the Cold War era is thus what historian Jonathan Herzog has labeled the spiritual-industrial complex—a marriage of state, corporation, and religion that produced a domestic religious revival and offered an international defense of Western values in the form of a powerful free-market Christian nationalism.[1]

96 | Chapter Four

Crafting such a unified front of state, corporation, and religion was necessary to many in order to combat the avowedly atheistic forces of Soviet Communism and its welfare state variants. Indeed, the Cold War was framed as a struggle not just between liberal capitalism and Communism, but also between the rival theological value systems that undergirded these economic systems. From this perspective, Western civilization itself was under attack, including the Judeo-Christian principles from which ideas of an open society and free market were said to emerge.[2] Christian capitalism was at war with a godless Communist state that sought to (re)make the world in its image.

Though many could agree on the need for a unified front against the spread of Communism, the specifics of how best to defend Western society was a source of great dispute—particularly within the budding conservative movement. Coming into existence with Crowell, Barton, and others in opposition to the New Deal policies of FDR, the conservative movement reached political maturity in the Cold War era. Yet, whereas Bruce Barton was comfortable marrying together Christianity and corporate capitalism to combat the statism of FDR, this was perhaps *the* dividing issue between the traditionalist and libertarian factions of the insurgent movement. In other words, whether or not markets or moral order should be the primary means of defending the West became a clear dividing line among various iterations of U.S. conservatism during the Cold War.

The dispute between the traditionalist and libertarian conservatives in the mid-twentieth century was in some regards a rehashing of the debate ushered in during the age of Jackson: should conservatives return to their European roots, either in Burke or elsewhere, in order to maintain intellectual and philosophical integrity, or should they adapt to the forces of liberalism in order to seek pragmatic political advantage? Should they prioritize liberty or tradition? Markets or social order? These philosophical disputes permeated all the way to the core of epistemological and ontological assumptions of conservatism, with each camp offering a different understanding of the relationships among state, economy, and society on the one hand, and of the person on the other. That is to say, each offered a different vision of politics: one that championed the immanent, profane forces of capital markets, and another that bemoaned the loss of transcendent, sacred values on the altar of modernity.

While hardened zealots on either side of this conservative split would not budge, a larger portion of conservatives would find common ground between these two competing visions of society; that commonality was forged on the rhetorical grounds of the dignity of the person, a deep suspicion of political liberals (distinguished from philosophical liberals) in the Democratic Party, and a commitment to Western values, culminating in a vicious anti-Communism. It is with the rise of such a conservative fusionism that the corporate person would find its voice and become a powerful weapon in the struggle for Western civilization. A crucial actor in the fusionist movement who would craft the corporate voice was Lewis F. Powell Jr. What would happen, however, is that while still employing a rhetoric of individual freedom and the value of the human person, this particular brand of conservatism would empower the corporate person at the expense of the individual.

A House Divided: Conservative Libertarianism, Traditionalism, and Anti-Communism

The end of the war and its tide of prosperity were cause for celebration for many. Yet, for a smaller cadre of individuals it was the harbinger of imminent doom—the decline of the West. As George Nash has noted, the allied victory had left the United States as "a domestic superstate, [with] a partially controlled economy, millions of conscripts under arms, and widespread fears of reversion to depression once demobilization set in."[3] Coupled with the rise to power of the Soviet Union, the nation "faced a theologically alien enemy," deeming Communism "a powerful religion of materialism, complete with its own scripture, prophets, and eschatology."[4] These twin facts demonstrated, to hardened classical liberals, that the very principles of democracy were being sacrificed domestically and abroad, and that in defeating the totalitarianism of Hitler we were willingly marching along a similar path at home. To the traditionalists it represented a sacralization of the state itself, ushering in a repudiation of the Judeo-Christian heritage of the West and a broader faith in transcendent order. The time was ripe for a conservative backlash.

98 | Chapter Four

The libertarian position was common in the United States yet was given its most triumphant defense by an Austrian-born professor at the London School of Economics (LSE), Friedrich Hayek. Hayek's 1944 *The Road to Serfdom* was an indefatigable defense of liberalism in the face of what he identified as a creeping state socialism in the West. Arguing that all forms of collectivism and state planning, however well-intentioned, create conditions favorable to totalitarianism, Hayek maintained that too much democracy undermines the goals of freedom and order that lie at the heart of liberal political theory. Opposing liberalism and democracy in this way, Hayek championed the former over the latter as democracy could—and if unchecked, naturally would—erode the privacy of the market.[5]

As Quinn Slobodian argues about Hayek and other so-called Geneva School neoliberals, the tension between politics and markets, democracy and liberalism that lie at the core of neoliberalism was first described by the famed Nazi legal theorist Carl Schmitt. Proposing that the world was bifurcated in terms of political and economic rule—indeed, prefiguring the economic theological problem of sovereign reign and market governance—Schmitt argued that global politics was split between *imperium* (the sovereign rule of peoples and territories) and *dominium* (the immanent government of goods). While Schmitt bemoaned this doubled order as it threatened the unified powers of an absolute sovereign, the Geneva School ordoliberals found in this split an order worth preserving and meticulously defending through the positive force of law.[6]

These ideas, among others, would find a receptive audience in the Walter Lippmann Colloquium and later in the Mont Pelerin Society as a committed group of intellectuals sought to remake liberalism to comport with shifting geopolitical realities. The error of classical liberalism, as Pierre Dardot and Christian Laval argue, was that it had been gradually "transformed into a narrow conservatism, opposed to any advance by societies, in the name of absolute respect for the natural order." The naturalism of classical liberalism was to be discarded in favor of a liberalism that understood the state as a crucial actor in crafting and maintaining conditions favorable to a market society. Liberalism became "not a jungle of egotisms but a rule-governed game of self-realization" through the competitive structures and functions of the market.[7] For the libertarians and early neoliberals, it is in the market that the individual becomes a fully realized person as they engage their competitive and rational faculties.

The early roots of this neoliberal vision can be traced to differing intellectual and practical manifestations in France, Germany, and the United States.[8] Yet, in the United States they are cast in a straightforward manner by Milton Friedman, who advocated a strong juridical state capable of making and enforcing the rules of this game of self-realization. As Friedman argues in his *Capitalism and Freedom*, the state must act as rule-maker and umpire, providing a way to modify the rules of the game when necessary and to enforce compliance with these rules when they are violated. Freedom, then, is the absence of governmental coercion during game play; it necessitates the protection of a private sphere of economic liberty and self-realization that is to be untouched by the state. For Friedman, however, this freedom was under assault externally by Communist forces and internally by those of good will who "wish to reform us" through the expansion of the welfare state.[9] In this way, Communists and progressive reformers were allies, even if accidentally—both sought to destroy liberalism through radical democracy.

For traditionalists such as Richard Weaver, Russell Kirk, and Eric Voegelin, politics rests on a metaphysical bedrock of absolute truth. Yet, unlike the libertarians—Christian or otherwise—the traditionalists were no friends of the market. The rise of modern society, for these men, was marked by a drift away from first principles and a loss of truth itself. As Michael Lee argues, following Isaiah Berlin, traditionalism was marked by a rhetorical style of the hedgehog argument. That is, its arguments offer "an assertion of one core truth that explained the scope of history and a tragic narrative about the collapse of that truth in the modern world." For Weaver, for instance, the target was nominalism—a philosophical view that came to prominence through the medieval scholar William of Ockam that rendered language a pragmatic tool as opposed to a transcendent mode of truth. For Voegelin, however, it was Gnosticism—the ancient heretical Christian doctrine—that proclaimed that man was perfectible.[10]

Each of these enemies amounted to an attack on what Kirk called the permanent things as they set the groundwork for and shared intellectual affinities with modern liberalism.[11] For these writers, liberalism and Communism were next of kin as each threatened to "immanentize the eschaton,"

100 | Chapter Four

or more plainly put, each attempted to create God's kingdom on earth through state administration.[12] The problem of modern society was thus the loss of transcendence and its descent into an abyss of pure immanence and bureaucratic managerialism. Materialism had triumphed over idealism. Substance had bested form. Freedom toppled virtue and order. Society was no longer an organic whole but had become a machine. In the process, the human person had been stripped of its dignity before the total state and displaced by a concern for the masses. For the traditionalists, unlike the libertarians, the market was not an answer to these maladies but part of the problem.

This was particularly the case for Weaver, a committed southern agrarian in his later years. Studying under the tutelage of John Ransome Crowe and Donald Davidson at Vanderbilt University, he argued that it was industrialism as much as it was the concentration of state power that had eroded the feudal fabric of southern culture. The proper remedies to the spiritual ailments of the time, for Weaver, were threefold: a resuscitation and protection of private property—the last metaphysical right of Western culture; a rehabilitation of the poetic and divine nature of language; and the adoption of a pietistic outlook towards the self and towards the earth. When read together, this amounts to a (re)sacralization of modern life, beginning with the human person.[13]

Indeed, the argument that property is the last metaphysical right is by no means a defense of the market but of the person. As Weaver argues, "property in this [the industrial] sense becomes a fiction useful for exploitation and makes impossible the sanctification of work. The property which we defend as an anchorage keeps its identity with the individual." This is perhaps most evident in the aforementioned split of ownership from management in the modern corporation—a split that fueled the rise of finance capital and joint-stock ownership. Stock ownership is emblematic of this artificial property that Weaver rails against. In owning stock, the individual holds no real property but rather a fictitious piece of the corporation that he capitalizes upon without investing any labor or effort. True property ownership, for Weaver, is not impersonal but "provides a range of volition through which one can be a *complete person*, and it is the abridgment of this volition for which monopoly capitalism must be condemned along with Communism."[14] Much like Communism, monopoly capital threatens the dignity of the person—Under Communism this threat comes in the form of the total state, and under liberalism this threat comes in the form of the large, quasi-public corporation.

The critical task for Weaver was to cultivate the individual personality instead of a mass society. The mass is faceless, impersonal, and has no soul. The individual personality, however, is "that little private area of selfhood in which the person is at once conscious of his relationship to the transcendental and the living community." To do so, Weaver suggests, requires the restoration of traditional Western values and civilization by requiring training in literature and rhetoric on the one hand, and logic and dialectic on the other. Such training would rehabilitate the transcendental aspects of language and human experience and would lead to an attitude of piety toward the world—an attitude that "admits the right to exist of things larger than the ego, of things different than the ego."[15] The cult of self-interest and the reduction of the human to a pragmatic utility maximizer offered by liberal economics was, for Weaver, as much of a debasement of the person as was Communism.

As should be apparent, there was a seemingly inseparable chasm between the competing conservative camps. One side emphasized liberty, markets, and a rehabilitation of classical liberalism as a means of preserving the promise of individualism in the face of an ever-expansive state apparatus. The other praised the virtues of order, transcendent truth, and organic community as a way to resacralize society and the human person. One saw liberalism as the means of fighting Communism; the other saw liberalism and Communism as siblings born of the same parents: the Gnostic-inspired Protestant Reformation and the equalitarian atheism of the French Revolution. Where could there be common ground between two parties so seemingly diametrically opposed to one another?

In 1952 there seemed to be an answer to this question with the publication of Whittaker Chambers's *Witness*. Chambers, a once loyal Communist turned conservative, became a household name as a writer-editor for *Time* and later for testifying before the House Un-American Activities Committee (HUAC) against Alger Hiss and other supposed Communists in the state department. Chambers himself had been a member of the Soviet Underground during his time as a member of the Communist Party and was enlisted as a spy within the U.S. government—much of which came to light during the

102 | Chapter Four

trials.[16] When *Witness* was published, however, the nation received a wake-up call and the conservative movement gained an icon.

The book, penned as a conversion narrative, told the story of Chambers's departure from Communism as a form of spiritual revelation. Likewise, he portrayed the ascendancy of Communism as a story of a good versus evil. Yet, as Lee argues, it was "Tolkien in reverse: the forces of darkness prevailed over the forces of light."[17] This tragic framing established a political and spiritual urgency in the Cold War and cast it in something of a millennial framework: the battle between capitalism and Communism was a battle for the very soul of Western civilization. The United States must fight, or usher in its own demise.

Winning widespread acclaim, the book was touted by political and religious leaders alike. Likewise, *Witness* reached bestseller status, seeing a serialized reprinting of key excerpts in the *Saturday Evening Post* and even having portions of its foreword read aloud on national radio and television. According to Herzog, it was largely "Thanks to Chambers" that "many Americans in the 1940s and 1950s considered Communism not only a philosophy but also a religious system," in many ways leading the charge to understand the Cold War in spiritual terms. In many ways resonating with the arguments of Hayek and Weaver, he struck a cultural chord when he bemoaned the eclipse of Western culture and values. Much like Arnold Toynbee before him and James Burnham after him, he argued that unbridled material wealth led a nation to decadence and decline. Indeed, Chambers "bemoaned the secularization of twentieth century America, and called on his countrymen to recognize that religion and politics were symbiotic."[18] Spiritual vitality without material prosperity made a nation holy but weak on the world stage. Material prosperity without spiritual vitality made a nation powerful, but likely to crumble. Here, it seemed, was a marriage of libertarian and traditionalist conservatism. Faith and freedom required one another.

Chambers was neither the first nor the last to attempt to reconcile these competing camps, but his was a powerful public testimony to the secular faith of Communism. Others, notably Frank Meyer, would preach the gospel of conservative fusion, helping to create a conservatism fit for larger audiences.[19] Yet, while conservative intellectuals were busy debating the merits and demerits of liberalism, other political actors and organizations were actively undertaking a campaign for a religious revival in America. Led by an amalgam of crusading businessmen and conservative religious leaders, their rhetorical might, combined with the politics of the Cold War itself, would lead President Harry S. Truman to frame the Cold War in a spiritual mold. This would ultimately be extended in the Eisenhower administration as the "spiritual-industrial complex" came of age. Whether libertarians or traditionalists liked it or not, a mainstream conservative fusion was being crafted for the masses.

Conservative Fusionism Goes Mainstream: Truman, Eisenhower, and the Molding of a Public Faith

Historian Kevin Kruse notes that while the number of Americans who claimed to hold a faith and belong to a house of worship stayed relatively constant between 1910 and 1940, hovering around 40 percent, that number skyrocketed to 69 percent by the end of the 1950s.[20] How to account for such a meteoric rise? Perhaps the latent religiosity of public discourse surrounding the early Cold War accounts for part of this rise. Perhaps the related fear of nuclear disaster accounts for part of this equation. But as Kruse deftly argues, the primary factor here is a concerted campaign by industry and religious leaders who successfully lobbied the government to wed faith and free enterprise in the creation of an American creed.

The campaign, which began in the 1930s as a reaction to Roosevelt's New Deal, targeted its buildup of state power and its liberal, secularizing Social Gospel theology. The New Deal, they argued, was merely Communism in disguise. It promised freedom and equality under an all-powerful state, using its bureaucratic arms to create heaven on earth. Making a false idol of the state, the New Deal was thus a rebuke of God, the one true sovereign. Salvation could be found by denying the god of the state and finding God's promise of freedom within the market.

Led by James Fifield Jr., these men argued that the welfare state and its Social Gospel variants were a perversion of God's word. Offering a rebuke of the liberal Social Gospel theology, Kruse details, "they argued that the central tenet of Christianity remained the salvation of the individual." To help lead this crusade, Fifield cofounded—with Carleton College president

104 | Chapter Four

Donald J. Cowling and Harvard philosopher William Hocking—Spiritual Mobilization, an organization committed to the marriage of capitalism and Christianity. Quickly gaining notoriety among business leaders, Fifield would deliver a rousing speech in 1944 at a meeting arranged by Senator Albert Hawkes at the Waldorf-Astoria that would garner the support of other industrial giants, including J. Howard Pew of Sun Oil and Harvey Firestone of the eponymous tire company.[21]

To help matters more, Spiritual Mobilization gained the support of Leonard Read, founder of the Foundation for Economic Education (FEE). Read, the former head of the Los Angeles Chamber of Commerce, founded FEE as an organization committed to spreading the word of libertarian acolytes, including Hayek, Von Mises, Bastiat, and others. According to the great conservative historian George Nash, Read was heavily influenced by anarcho-libertarian Albert Jay Nock and his notion of the "Remnant"—the idea that each generation bequeathed a small intellectual elite who would preach the folly of the nation—and his FEE became something of a "secular monastery" devoted to the virtues of capitalism.[22]

Also drawn from the ranks of the FEE and an ardent follower of Nock, Edmund A. Opitz was a conservative congregationalist who proselytized for Christian libertarianism. For Opitz, both Christianity and the market recognize the inherent limits and imperfect nature of the human such that each asks that the individual place faith in a transcendent order that is beyond rational calculation.[23] All attempts to rationalize and subsume the providential workings of God and the market are thus heretical. Arguing against those state planners and Social Gospel advocates, he argues, "Communism has been called a Christian heresy. The point is not well taken. If one must talk in these terms he is on safer ground if he affirms that liberalism is a Christian heresy and Communism is a liberal heresy." The Enlightenment vision of the human as a purely rational, sovereign individual spawned both modern welfare liberalism and its logical extension—Communism. Further, liberalism and Communism shared a commonality for Opitz as "All movements that enhance the powers of the state correspondingly diminish the stature of the individual person. Big government means little people."[24] The dignity of the person was thus the common target of both liberalism and Communism. Each must be staved off by the conservative. Opitz's answer was thus to craft Christianity and the market as complementary pieces of the puzzle—each required the other. Economics was primarily concerned with immanent means, Christianity with transcendent ends.

A means of rallying the troops and bringing together like-minded individuals, the partnership of Spiritual Mobilization, the FEE, and other organizations would prove more ineffective in terms of pressuring elected officials to adopt their positions. They were, however, placing their finger on the pulse of something significant. It would be Billy Graham, however, who would prove himself capable of entering the halls of power and preaching the virtues of Christian capitalism—first in his attempts to influence President Truman and later in his successful ploy to craft Eisenhower as a spiritual leader of the nation.

Though Truman would shoo away Graham's advances, the spiritual nature of the Cold War was not lost on Truman. Indeed, as T. Jeremy Gunn argues, it is largely Truman who is responsible for inaugurating an "American national religion," suited for the Cold War. This national religion was composed of three primary elements: governmental theism, military supremacy, and capitalism as freedom. The turning point for Gunn is 1947, the year that the term Cold War was first used—by New York financier Bernard Baruch—and in which the Truman Doctrine was announced to Congress.[25] Truman's Doctrine was significant as it pitted freedom versus slavery as the dominant motif of the Cold War, and it announced a policy of containment to combat the Communist threat. This vision would be codified in the now infamous policy document National Security Council (NSC) 68, described by Herzog as a kind of moral treatise that justified state and military expansion as the United States began its holy war against Communism.[26] Indeed, as Ned O'Gorman argues, "the overarching policy point of NSC 68 was that the crises of the Cold War called for a new wartime economy and society in the United States."[27] Thus, even though Truman pronounced a religious and ideological war with Communism, ramped up military forces, would authorize loyalty oaths and sign into law an annual National Day of Prayer, he would catch the ire of conservatives. By some he was denounced as being too lenient on Communism, while others felt he was willing to wage war without congressional approval. By the time he left office in 1952 the nation was ready for political change.[28]

Facing off against his Democratic opponent Adlai Stevenson, Republican Dwight D. Eisenhower, at the urging of Graham, infused his campaign

106 | Chapter Four

with a vague spiritualism and religiosity that would prove successful at rallying the Republican Party and a vast majority of voters. As Herzog argues, "Eisenhower would not abandon Truman's holy war; he would intensify it."[29] Eisenhower (named Dwight after the evangelist Dwight R. Moody) understood that defeating Communism would require a revival in public faith. Indeed, it would be under Eisenhower's watch that the nation would add the phrase "under God" to the Pledge of Allegiance and would offer "In God We Trust" as the country's first official motto—one that would be added to U.S. currency to remind the citizenry of the divine nature of the free market during its battle against Communism.[30]

Importantly, Eisenhower's American religion was a vague one. As a sophisticated leader, Kruse avers, he understood that "religion could serve a public role only if it was reduced to its lowest common denominator—or perhaps, its lowest common denomination."[31] A loosely defined public religion would prove capable of uniting Americans and would enable a coalitional, interfaith movement united against Communism and its denial of the dignity of the person. Echoing Chambers and others, Eisenhower thus maintained "that American democracy depended on religion, that Communism was at its heart a dangerous religious creed, and that successful nations balanced material and spiritual strength."[32] Even as embattled conservative intellectuals were trying to forge a middle ground between their more radical libertarian and traditionalist counterparts, Eisenhower offered a fusion of faith and markets for the mainstream.

However, much to the ire of the insurgent conservatives, this particular brand of politics used religion not to dethrone the state but to sacralize it. Christian faith and free enterprise were thus married to state military power, furthering rather than eroding the superstate status of the United States after the Second World War. The spiritual-industrial complex was able to cement itself in part through the very efforts of those radical conservatives who would come to abhor it. Their arguments provided the rhetorical resources to create a marriage of state power, free markets, and a vague Christian faith that helped mold a middle-of-the-road political consensus—one that proved powerful in drawing boundaries around an acceptable form of conservatism. As Lee argues, "The accepted performance of conservatism halted where libertarians became hostile to religion, where antistatism became antimilitarism, where libertarianism and libertinism were indistinguishable."[33] The insurgent force of conservatism was blunted, at least for now.

The Crumbling of Consensus: New Left v. New Right

What was once a united interfaith front against Communism's assault on the dignity of the person became a sectarian battleground in the 1960s. Eisenhower's vague American religion proved capable of proving everything and nothing as it refused to offer a firm theological stance for those in the religious right and failed to challenge state authority for those more libertarian extremists. It seemed even Eisenhower himself came to trumpet these concerns as he left office, warning of the creeping military-industrial complex he helped create. In 1964 the conservative movement would get a shot in the arm in the form of Arizona senator and Phoenix native Barry Goldwater.

Goldwater's fiery brand of libertarianism took aim at the mechanistic welfare state that emerged under Truman and Eisenhower.[34] Capturing the growth of a technocratic form of government dependent upon the close relationship between state and corporation, the automatic society was the product of the so-called liberal consensus and another form of the specter of a creeping totalitarianism under the guise of a planned economy. According to Jason Stahl, this new liberal consensus in the Cold War era entailed a value system that believed that American capitalism was now fundamentally different from its historical antecedents in its ability to act responsibly and meet the demands of social change. Accompanied by a capacity of the state to "sustain unending economic growth," manage consumer demand, and diminish the need for labor unions, the United States saw in the new capitalism a means of achieving social equality and harmony.[35] Through the implementation of a scientific approach to social problems, economic planning, and governance, this form of liberalism held that technocratic and professional decision-making was capable of providing for all at home and of defending this uniquely American way of life abroad.

This smacked of Communism to the Phoenix firebrand Goldwater. For him, Eisenhower's brand of politics was a form of socialism that paid lip service to the market while subjecting it to the imperatives of state planning.

108 | Chapter Four

It was not concerned with the individual but with public welfare—and as such was merely an extension of Keynesian doctrine. Challenging the automatism of this vision of society, Goldwater championed a conservative notion of freedom that saw in the large state the demise of individual liberty. His particular brand of politics struck fear not only in political leaders but within the business community, which feared his staunch libertarianism would undermine corporate-governmental relations. Coupled with his defense of the family, the church, and the Christian faith, Goldwater was one of those conservatives who proved capable of uniting traditionalists and libertarians, albeit tenuously. Yet, unlike those who came before him, he was capable of mobilizing this sentiment into a mass, insurgent movement against the political establishment of the time.

As traditionalist conservative intellectual Paul Gottfried argues, "If postwar conservatism had been a series of movements rather than the orderly unfolding of a single force, the Goldwater campaign is the most crucial turning point in its history," and one that for Gottfried proved ultimately damning. Representing the triumph of libertarian conservatism over the traditionalist vision, while Goldwater's campaign demonstrated the political power of conservatism—a power that had been cultivated for decades now—it ultimately equated "its social philosophy almost entirely with free enterprise," and made the movement "more concerned with electoral victories than unifying principles."[36] Pragmatism and profits triumphed over piety and principles. It seemed the traditionalists were unable to stop the descent of the Judeo-Christian West in the face of economizing liberalism.

Now effectively pushed into the background, these conservatives no longer had to be concerned with the metaphysical diatribes of traditionalism. They could now spend their efforts mobilizing the youth, electioneering, and getting conservatives elected into office. Fecklessly praising Goldwater, popularizing the writings of the divisive William F. Buckley and his *National Review*, and utilizing new media technologies, this group became what Richard Viguerie and historians of conservatism have called the New Right.[37] As David Ricci writes, the New Right "argued that its predecessors were weak on strategic thinking, that they mainly reacted to liberal pressures rather than initiating their own projects, and that they had not fashioned the organizations which . . . would enable conservatives to combine their efforts in order to line up public opinion behind conservative causes."[38] Traditionalists, content to diagnose the failures of liberalism and whine about the loss of Western culture, did not have what it took to mold a winning brand of conservatism. Focused on taking back Washington and Hollywood from liberal elites, individuals such as Phyllis Schlafly, Paul Weyrich, and Buckley were central to creating an institutional network for conservatives that developed and sustained American conservatism in the mid-twentieth century.

This new brand of conservatism was central in the emerging culture war between the New Right and the nascent New Left. Inaugurated by the development of the Students for a Democratic Society (SDS) movement on campuses across the country and the codification of their ideology in 1962 with the drafting of *The Port Huron Statement*, the New Left railed against the "failure of corporate liberalism, the bankruptcy of the Old Left and the New Deal, the inadequacy of the welfare state, and the destructiveness and obsolescence of the Cold War," while championing civil rights causes.[39] Framing themselves as an insurgent and confrontational group of political agitators, the New Left utilized the language of the "establishment" and "counterculture" to describe the political and economic structures that stunted the radical equality and democracy that the movement so ardently championed.[40]

Ironically, then, just as Daniel Bell would famously proclaim the end of ideology, new radicalisms of the left and right had emerged to challenge the liberal consensus.[41] While those on the left challenged the establishment of corporate power, the burgeoning military-industrial complex, and state violence, those on the right portrayed a reality wherein the welfare state and the rising counterculture represented minoritarian rule and a creeping totalitarianism of the left.

Indeed, for many in the New Right, the increasing demands of peoples of color, women, and those within the LGBTQ community amounted to an attack that threatened the sacred sphere of privacy by constant political and state intrusions.[42] The market could not be free if the domestic sphere that supported it was to be tampered with.

Of course, conservatives—libertarian and traditionalist alike—had no qualms about using the state to enforce a stratified social order, contrary to

110 | Chapter Four

their claims of a minimal state. The tactic was to make the case that it was in fact white southern men and the business community who were being pushed out of the public sphere by the entrance of these "radical" voices. With these movements representing a supposed loss of power by white men at the hands of a tyrannical, minoritarian state, many of those in the conservative movement more broadly and the New Right specifically made the argument that the present political order marginalized not the voices of peoples of color, but those of white conservatives in the United States.

This opinion was held by many, including William Baroody, former campaign manager for Goldwater, New Right activist, and head of the American Enterprise Institute (AEI). Originally known as the American Enterprise Association (AEA), the organization was founded in 1938 and incorporated in 1943. Created to combat FDR's New Deal, the AEA nonetheless had to navigate its partisan ideals within the political culture of the "apolitical politics" of the liberal consensus. This would remain the case when Baroody was brought on board in the 1950s to revive the struggling think tank. Attracting funding from conservative industrialists and large corporations who demanded more aggressively conservative messaging, Baroody and company nonetheless "needed to walk a fine line in the early 1960s between garnering support from conservatives who were considered outside the mainstream of the liberal consensus and maintaining a relevancy within the institutions of that same liberal consensus."[43] This rhetorical double bind would eventually lead Baroody and others within the conservative movement to discover a new means of engaging the political debate.

The power of the liberal consensus to, in a manner, police the rhetoric of the conservative right led Baroody to deploy arguments regarding the existence of a liberal establishment that shut off conservative dissent and a truly open debate. Indeed, as Baroody saw it, there was no debate to be had. The free market "had no defenders in Washington" and thus lacked any kind of access, representation, or voice in U.S. politics.[44] This viewpoint was given further intellectual credence in the writings of neoconservative Irving Kristol, who extolled the rise of a liberal "New Class" of technical experts that ran the Washington establishment.[45] These sentiments resonated with many in the business community. Here, Kim Phillips-Fein is worth quoting in detail on the growing perception of marginalization within the business community:

The student demonstrations at Columbia University, the University of Chicago, and Kent State, the bombs at the Bank of America, the accusations of Ralph Nader, the new government regulations, the sudden new working-class militancy, the activists invading corporate offices—all of it seemed a single continuum, one discordant challenge rising against American businessmen.[46]

In light of such realities, it was becoming clearer to conservatives of all stripes that business could no longer keep its mouth shut or be content to remain on the political sidelines. None other than Russell Kirk, the father of conservative traditionalism in the United States, would argue that businessmen must concern themselves with the political fortunes of the nation. Couching his call for business political action within his notion of an imaginative conservatism, Kirk argued that "We hear a lot about the political power of U.S. business, but the country suffers far more from the political indifference of the businessman than from his alleged political influence." Sounding something like Bruce Barton, Kirk demanded that businessmen be mindful of the health of the larger industrial system that individual businesses operated in. Unlike Barton, however, Kirk argued that this necessitated a class of politically educated and active businessmen committed to the preservation of Western civilization. To his point, Kirk averred, "If businessmen don't assume some political leadership, leaders of a disagreeable and violent sort will make themselves felt in the field." As the "accidental leaders" of American politics, it was up to the business community to lead the political charge against Communism and the radicalisms of various domestic movements for social justice.[47]

Of course, Kirk was not alone in making this call for a more politically active business community. Lewis F. Powell Jr. would make a similar demand just over a decade later in his infamous memorandum "Attack on American Free Enterprise System"—now colloquially referred to simply as the Powell Memo. Yet, Powell's memo was the crystallization of a much longer effort to mobilize lawyers, businessmen, politicians, and education leaders in common purpose against the growing radicalism of the political left during the Cold War. In typical accounts of the role of Powell's memo in the conservative movement and the rise of neoliberalism, Powell appears as a kind of libertarian market apologist who commanded his vast network

112 | Chapter Four

of influence to marshal the corporate world in defense of laissez faire.[48] However, this only tells part of the story.

Indeed, by the time Powell was appointed to the Supreme Court, he had held membership on various corporate boards and became known as a defender of the large corporation. Appointed to the U.S. Supreme Court by then President Nixon in 1972, Powell, as John Nichols and Robert McChesney write, "was a jurist who aggressively promoted not just the legal fantasy of corporate personhood but also the remarkable political infrastructure that would come to assert corporate political power" in the United States.[49] But Powell was also a native Virginian who was raised and educated in a segregated culture during the heyday of Jim Crow. Powell would continue to identify with the Southern culture that nourished him, bequeathing a complex legacy on integration, civil rights, and diversity that developed alongside his defense of markets and corporate persons.

In other words, I argue that a more holistic look at Powell's social, political, and legal philosophy more properly situates him not as a libertarian darling but rather as a conservative fusionist who delicately balanced concerns for localism, tradition, and moral order with those of competition, liberty, and individualism. These competing visions would, perhaps ironically, find common ground in his understanding of diversity—a through line that connects his opinions on (de)segregation, affirmative action, anti-Communism, and corporate speech. In this light, Powell represented what the conservative traditionalist Kirk demanded: a learned lawyer and businessman committed to preserving the humane values of Western Christian civilization against Communism and zealous reformers who sought to topple the rule of law.

Lewis F. Powell Jr.: Southern Virtue, Free Markets, and Diversity

Described by legal historian Earl Maltz as a "pillar of the white establishment in Richmond, Virginia," Lewis Powell was a model of southern gentility and virtue.[50] Born September 19, 1907, in Suffolk, Virginia, Lewis Powell Jr. was a bright child, excelling in English and history.[51] Going on to attend the segregated, all-male Washington and Lee University to study law, Powell became president of his fraternity and student body president before graduating magna cum laude in 1929.[52] Graduating with a LL.B just two years later from Washington and Lee, Powell then moved on to Harvard Law School, where he received his LL.M in 1932. As Powell's biographer John Jeffries Jr. notes, Powell's legal education strengthened two attitudes that were central to his career and jurisprudence: one was a respect for authority and the rule of law, and the other was a practical understanding of the law as an institution that shaped society. Though at times these attitudes conflicted, Powell offered a kind of "sociological jurisprudence" that mitigated the "tension between respect for authority and the need for change."[53] So, too, did his political philosophy balance between individual liberty and cultural pluralism. Writing on this balance, Anders Walker notes that "This link between localism and liberty was central to his political philosophy, something that he shared with the Agrarians," including Donald Davidson, Robert Penn Warren, and Richard Weaver.[54]

This balancing of conservative concerns for order and liberal adaptation to change embodied New Right and conservative fusionist ideals. For Powell, liberty was the ultimate promise of liberal democracy and the rule of law, but liberty was best fostered by protecting local custom and cultural pluralism from the homogenizing force of federal power. A distinctly southern political philosophy with roots in Confederate resentment over Reconstruction, such an emphasis on cultural pluralism was here wed to economic liberty. Indeed, for Powell, economic liberty and cultural pluralism went hand-in-glove, as one would be impossible without the other. The individual and the community found common sources of freedom from the threat of socialism and state power in the privacy of the marketplace, protected from the masses by the force of law. Here, we can certainly find rumblings of the Hayekian move to encase the market, separating the *imperium* of political rule from the *dominium* of the market, but must also note that such an understanding of markets was tethered to cultural concerns regarding southern tradition, custom, and regional identity.[55] The common affinity that Powell finds in both individual liberty and cultural pluralism, I argue, is to be found in his notion of diversity—an idea that he would develop over his long and storied legal career.

Eventually serving as president of the Richmond Bar Association, joining the Richmond school board, and becoming partner of Hunton,

114 | Chapter Four

Williams, Gay, Moore & Powell, Lewis Powell Jr. occupied several positions of power and authority.[56] Representing several large corporations, Powell became a "legal darling" of the tobacco industry among others, later serving on the board of eleven major corporations.[57] Becoming president of the American Bar Association in 1964, the position represented for Powell "a bully pulpit" where he could shape the agenda of the association and speak on matters of the importance of the rule of law and decry the tactics of civil disobedience used by many in the Civil Rights Movement.[58] Indeed, questions of integration, racial parity, and civil rights were central to Powell's pragmatic conservatism and his commitment to law and order. As chair of the Richmond city school board, immediately after the decision of *Brown v. Board of Education*, Powell was critical of federally mandated integration and defended an image of southern virtue and noble local tradition.

As a pillar of the white establishment—as a lawyer and school board official—Powell occupied a crucial position in the debates about integration in Richmond. Sitting between those who backed the *Brown* decision and those like James Jackson Kilpatrick—the author and journalist who backed a campaign for massive resistance to *Brown*—Powell instead argued for compliance with the spirit of the law while using local powers and pressure campaigns to maintain a more-or-less pre-*Brown* racial composition in the schools of Richmond.[59] While Kilpatrick at first vociferously opposed such a pragmatic move, the two ultimately aligned on Powell's strategy and quickly realized that part of such a strategy necessitated mobilizing their professional networks and local communities to counter federal power, collectivism, and ultimately the Civil Rights Movement itself, as each posed significant challenges to the segregated order of the South.[60]

To combat these tendencies, Powell maintained that a vigorous education on the nature and principles of Communism—and their destruction of liberty under law—was necessary at every level of education across the United States. In a speech delivered to the Connecticut State Bar Association in 1962, for instance, Powell argued that the ultimate concern was not simply for education, but that such education mattered because "The real issue is the survival of freedom—and perhaps of survival itself." Drawing from his time on the Richmond school board, Powell cited studies conducted in Virginia and across the country to indicate that educational programs on the nature of Communism met no real standards of academic rigor and failed to educate the majority of the population as to the existential stakes of the Cold War clash between capitalism and Communism. Urging the organized Bar Association to take the lead in educating teachers and mobilizing their resources at the local level to improve educational standards, Powell's ultimate plea was that "The affirmative teaching of the values of our American system, and its rich legal and cultural heritage from Western civilization, must of course be the foundation of our social science education."[61] Upon such a foundation, the purpose of the educational system would be to enshrine liberty under law as the cornerstone of American liberal democracy lest such collectivist ideals take root in America, too.

The concerns about the fate of Western civilization would be voiced more directly years later in his speech—figured as a "lay sermon"—to the 1972 prayer breakfast of the American Bar Association in San Francisco. Raised himself as a Presbyterian, Powell seemed to retain a meaningful sense of personal faith; yet his faith rarely seeped into his legal and political affairs—this is perhaps the reason for his self-professed unease at leading the prayer breakfast. His training, after all, was in law not theology. The tenor of his speech struck a different tone, then, emphasizing the humane values of Western civilization embodied by the church.

Rebuking the "unanchored individualism" of the counterculture, Powell argues that our connections to the "humanizing authority" of intermediary institutions such as the "home, church, school, and community" have been severed. These institutions anchored individualism and the pursuit of happiness within a larger, transcendent framework. The immanent, profane pleasures of the self were thus always tethered to something that pointed beyond the self—values of honor, duty, loyalty, work ethic, self-discipline, and patriotism. For Powell, redeeming these lofty values, as well as the promise of liberty under law, means recognizing that institutions that train the individual for the ethical life, such as the home and church, are indispensable. Indeed, he closes his speech by stating that "I affirm my belief in the worthiness of religion, and its indispensable role in the development of the human spirit."[62] A return to religion was a vital part of the triumph of liberal capitalism and the rule of law.

Over time, Powell would come to understand Martin Luther King and the Civil Rights Movement as perhaps the biggest domestic threat to liberty under law, and would use his position as president of the American Bar

116 | Chapter Four

Association to levy critiques of King and his doctrine of civil disobedience. For instance, in his 1966 essay "A Lawyer Looks at Civil Disobedience," published in the *Washington and Lee Law Review*, Powell refers to civil disobedience as a "heresy" that places "the old wine of revolution into the new wineskin of constitutional government."[63] Figuring civil disobedience as a kind of spirit that, if imbibed, would get the masses drunk on promises of freedom and revolution, Powell saw the ultimate *telos* of civil disobedience as lawless anarchy in which all men and women followed not the law of the land, but the natural law of their own moral conscience. The theology of King was not compatible with that of Western civilization, Powell seemed to argue, despite King's clear attempts to build this connection in his "Letter from a Birmingham Jail."

Significantly, Powell's larger fear, however, was that the doctrine and tactics of King's civil disobedience were not confined to the Civil Rights Movement, to the problems of the South, or to unjust laws, but were instead spreading like wildfire across the diffuse New Left. Taking the examples of the 1965 demonstrations in Berkeley and Chicago, Powell argued that civil disobedience was being brandished as a kind of political weapon by those who found the normal avenues of democratic and legal redress too cumbersome. The radical and participatory democracy espoused by groups such as the Student Nonviolent Coordinating Committee (SNCC) of Stokely Carmichael and Students for a Democratic Society (SDS) evidenced the creep toward socialism and away from the rule of law for Powell, as these groups used civil disobedience—among other, more aggressive and sometimes violent tactics—to attack the bases of U.S. liberalism.

The danger in such a politics, for Powell, was that the legitimacy of the rule of law itself was destroyed in the process. As Powell writes, "The logical and inescapable end of civil disobedience is the destruction of public order, and in the anarchy which follows, all liberty would be lost."[64] In this sense, Powell drew on a familiar conservative argument—that democracy is a means not an end, and that too much democracy threatens the promise of freedom and liberty it was meant to provide. Forced to choose, Powell would take liberalism over democracy, using the rule of law to encase the realm of privacy and individual freedom.

Powell's commitment to law and order was recognized and rewarded. President Johnson would task him with leading a commission on crime, and he was approached by Richard Nixon, upon his election in 1969, to join the Supreme Court. As Anders Walker argues, that Powell would be approached by Nixon was not entirely surprising, as Nixon was actively searching for a southerner who could shore up votes and could extend the reach of the Republican Party well into the South with growing political power.[65] Powell's position as a respected southerner who rebuked outright racism and its strategies of massive resistance yet maintained a defense of southern culture, as well as being the president of the American Bar Association, made him a perfect candidate. Though he would turn down the appointment in 1969, Powell would be appointed in 1970 to Nixon's Blue Ribbon Defense Panel, where, in a confidential paper entitled "Political Warfare," Powell outlined the struggles of the war as inherently ideological, claiming that the United States had failed to recognize itself as in the middle of a "critical war of words and ideas." Indeed, Powell maintained that the nation "must put aside the self-deception that the techniques of political warfare are unethical or immoral," and engage in the vagaries of ideological struggle.[66]

Such commitments would strengthen over the coming year, and when Nixon again approached Powell for a spot on the Supreme Court in 1971, Powell would accept the nomination. It was also at this time that Powell would pen a memo to his friend, colleague, and chairman of the Education Committee of the U. S. Chamber of Commerce, Eugene Sydnor Jr., "Attack on American Free Enterprise System." I will return to this memo in a moment, but for now I want to note the continued development of Powell's understanding of diversity and its relationship to matters of race and corporate speech.

The most infamous case in which Powell would espouse his understanding of diversity was that of *Regents v. Bakke* in 1978—the same year in which Powell would hand down the majority opinion regarding protections for corporate speech in *First National Bank of Boston v. Bellotti*. The *Bakke* case concerned a man by the name of Allan Bakke, who was denied entrance into a graduate program in the Medical School at the University of California-Davis. Bakke blamed his rejection on the program's quota system, which guaranteed sixteen of the possible one hundred positions to members of historically underrepresented minority groups. Arguing that the school's affirmative action program had discriminated against him, a white man, on the basis of race because he was not able to compete evenly

118 | Chapter Four

for all one hundred positions, the case made its way to the U.S. Supreme Court, where it would be narrowly decided by Justice Powell.

As M. Kelly Carr argues, Powell's opinion in *Bakke* was a central moment in the rhetorical invention of diversity, one that "privileged the commitment to diversity, broadly defined, over the commitment to social justice" by invoking classical liberal values to wed diversity to "the principle of individualism."[67] In other words, multiculturalism was a laudable goal insofar as it enhanced individual freedom rather than being used as a rhetorical ploy to create state-sanctioned egalitarianism. Walker reaches a similar conclusion, writing that in *Bakke*, diversity emerges as "a standalone principle, a guarantor of liberty rather than a 'ruse' for equality." For Walker, however, this prioritization is not merely the legacy of *Bakke* but is Powell's constitutional legacy more broadly—one that continues to have very real effects in our political culture.[68]

The groundwork for Powell's opinion was laid before *Bakke*, however, in cases such as *San Antonio v. Rodriguez*, *Keyes v. School District No. 1*, and *Milliken v. Bradley*, where Powell challenged the distinction between de jure and de facto segregation, pushed against northern claims to superiority on racial matters, and enshrined local rights of communities over their school districts. Through these cases Powell was able to make the case for southern America against northern and western embraces of federal power. As Walker argues, "His rulings successfully protected unequal funding between districts in *Rodriguez*, absolved the South of moral guilt in *Keyes*, and now helped provide the rationale for holding school districts constitutionally insurmountable in *Milliken*."[69] These decisions, read along with that of *Bakke*, illustrate a commitment to diversity and cultural pluralism—one that valorized localism against a perceived imperialism and authoritarianism of state power. The privacy of the market and sovereignty of local communities protected traditional values from governmental erasure. In other words, diversity would be enshrined in and through individual rights, cultural pluralism would be preserved in and through the free market, and the rule of law would be restored through local and social custom.

These rhetorical moves were not the product of Powell alone. Indeed, as Carr eloquently argues, his opinion was the product of a much larger rhetorical process of invention that involved appeals to legal precedent, amicus briefs, letters and conversations between Powell and other justices, as well as the larger political culture that the Court found itself within. However, drawing from these rhetorical resources, Powell's understanding of diversity was made possible through a particular narrative regarding race in the United States, an outright denial of the continued existence of structural racism in America, and the placement of issues of racial discrimination within the First Amendment. Each of these rhetorical moves pushed concerns for structural redress of racial disparities downward to the more concrete level of the individual, shifting the "constitutional safeguards against racial discrimination and guaranteeing equality articulated in the Fourteenth Amendment to the individual freedoms asserted by the First Amendment."[70] The central concern was not about eliminating barriers to equal access—for Powell, there were no structural barriers to be found—but rather about allowing a greater diversity of voices and viewpoints within the classroom that might benefit all individuals in the educational process. The concern was less about the quality (or equality) of representation, and more about the quantity of diverse persons and viewpoints in the educational system—an idea represented in Powell's notion of race as a "plus" factor of diversity to be arithmetically tabulated among other attributes and factors for acceptance into a university.

Ultimately, Powell would defend the constitutionality of affirmative action in the United States but would defang the law from its more emancipatory potential. Likewise, his arguments would set the stage for claims to reverse and colorblind racism.[71] More notable for our purposes here, however, is the striking similarity between Powell's notion of diversity in *Bakke* and his arguments about the lack of diversity of viewpoints in public dialogue in the Powell Memo and in *Bellotti*. So, too, are the implicit claims to the marginalization of businessmen and the corporation in political life, shut out of the public sphere by the liberal and leftist monopoly of the market of ideas. The answer for Powell, much as in *Bakke*, was to emphasize the importance of diversity at an aggregate, quantitative level in the speech marketplace. However, unlike *Bakke*, here Powell does not entirely sever diversity from structural concerns about inequality, arguing that the corporate person has been treated unfairly by a left-leaning political establishment. Liberalizing—and literalizing—the metaphor of the marketplace of ideas

120 Chapter Four

became the surest way to ensure diversity and protect economic liberty in the political warfare of the era.[72]

Words as Weapons, Money as Speech: Responsibility and Survival in Lewis Powell's *Attack on American Free Enterprise System* and *First National Bank of Boston v. Bellotti*

In *Attack on American Free Enterprise System*, Powell takes great pains to define the constitutive problems at hand for the business community as well as to locate potential solutions within the possibilities of collective action. A sharp, concise, and well-articulated vision of the standpoint of the businessman, the document follows a problem/solution format that blames not only a burgeoning radicalism of the left but the corporation itself for the woes of free enterprise in the United States. Laying out the dimensions, sources, and tone of the attack, Powell turns to what a largely apathetic and accommodationist business community can do to elevate the corporate voice. Identifying the campus, the courts, and the public sphere as the sites of ideological battle, Powell calls upon corporate executives, young conservatives, and the Chamber of Commerce to utilize their vast material and symbolic resources to defend the free market.

Utilizing a realist rhetorical style, Powell's memo portrays a monopolized public conversation that threatens the very survival of the large corporation and free enterprise. In order to challenge this monopoly, the corporation must take on a new set of social responsibilities and actively engage in the public sphere. Crafting words as weapons, Powell's rhetoric oscillates between a Hobbesian understanding of brutal competition and the state of nature on the one hand and a more humane vision of the balancing and civilizing powers of the market on the other. In this sense, Powell's sometimes militaristic rhetoric is softened by the language of a competitive market in need of correction. Seeing the radical elements of a revolutionary left as eroding the social contract and engaging in ideological warfare, the corporation must meet its adversaries in combat. This combat, however, is seen as a means not to destroy or eradicate the enemy, but rather to restore law and order, economic freedom, and a diversity of opinions in the market of ideas. Indeed, the solution to the problems facing the corporation lies in the civilizing republican virtues of a competitive market wherein conflict is resolved through the providential powers of exchange and consumer demand, not via the violence of state force or ideological assault.

Beginning with a powerful usage of the declarative tone, Powell writes to Sydnor and the Chamber that "No thoughtful person can question that the American economic system is under broad attack." Using such language to place the problem outside the scope of debate, Powell's move at the onset places corporate marginalization in the realm of fact. While those at the Chamber were likely in no need of being persuaded of this belief, such an unequivocal stance helps reinforce Powell's already strong ethos as a defender of the market and a representative of the voiceless corporation. Though Powell is careful to note that criticism of free enterprise is nothing new and is in fact a necessary component of a balanced market of ideas, what the corporation now faces is "quite new in the history of America."[73]

This contrasting of the present circumstances with past iterations of the debate regarding free enterprise and corporate power calls attention to something inherently more insidious, subversive, destructive, revolutionary, and most importantly, anti-democratic. Not simply engaging in civil debate regarding the merits and shortcomings of free enterprise, activists of the New Left engaged in tactics of political warfare, sabotaging the foundations of Western society. The New Left stood as an internal threat comparable to the external threat of Communism, which if left unchecked would topple the rule of law and bring about social anarchy. Under such exceptional circumstances, the corporation has no choice but to defend itself by utilizing its vast political arsenal.

Indeed, not only is the corporation dealing with a more militant left, but the left is also portrayed as "more numerous, better financed, and increasingly . . . more welcomed and encouraged by other elements of society."[74] The present crisis is not just an ideological assault by a radical fringe, then, but is seeping into and saturating the political mainstream in a way that poisons the grounds upon which industrial society rests. Coming from all angles—college campuses, pulpits, the media, journals, elected officials, and the legal system—the free market and Western values of individualism were under attack by radical Communist forces. The anxieties of the Cold War and the lessons offered by conservative intellectuals cannot be overstated

122 | Chapter Four

here. Communism was a problem not only to be contained abroad but to be eliminated at home.

Further, as Friedman argued, Western capitalism was in jeopardy not only from Communist forces but also from those well-meaning reformers who unwittingly were paving the road to totalitarianism through the construction of the welfare state.[75] For those in the conservative movement, and for Powell as well, it was not only the exportation of liberal democracy abroad but the active education and public-relations campaign domestically that were capable of providing economic literacy in the fundamentals of free-market capitalism. Echoing the argument of Leonard Read decades before, more information, a balanced and diverse market of ideas, and equal access to political debate for all were the inherent solutions in this diagnosis, for if only the public could hear the business case, they would recognize the evils of state planning and the inherent benevolence of the market.

Rather than mounting such a campaign, however, Powell indicted the business community itself as part of the problem. Indeed, he writes that "One of the bewildering paradoxes of our time is the extent to which the enterprise system tolerates, if not participates in, its own destruction."[76] With campuses funded by corporate taxes, industry leaders on boards of trustees, and a corporate media industry, the business community either failed to recognize its direct channels of influence, failed to recognize the fundamental assault on free enterprise, or recognized these matters and refused to act. In any scenario, Powell demanded that this complacency and ignorance be overcome. Whether they recognized it or not, he maintained, the business community was being dragged into war.

Led on the frontlines by the likes of consumer activist Ralph Nader, Marxist intellectual Herbert Marcuse, and Harvard environmentalist Charles Reich, the militant left held that the free enterprise system was the source of all social ills. Reducing the intellectual works of these and other leftist writers to "rifle shots which undermine confidence and confuse the public," the New Left was polluting the market of ideas with mere noise that detracted from legitimate debate and sought only to confuse and undermine the very mechanisms that facilitated exchange. Labeled unprepared and ill-equipped "to conduct guerilla warfare with those who propagandize against the system," the business community is portrayed as a bereft, sabotaged, and ambushed victim of an enemy who refuses to operate within the proper rules of engagement. This militaristic language crafts a metaphor of a diffuse yet unified enemy, one well regimented and guided by a strategic imperative to undermine the capitalist system.[77] Simultaneously, the language portrays the large corporation and its various interests as an ill-equipped militia that does not yet recognize the enemy at the gates. The largest problem facing the corporation was thus a lack of strategic vision and efficient organization to meet its enemy head-on.

Taking on this problem, Powell doubtless saw himself as adopting the position of general in the war of ideas, crafting a strategic vision and programmatic solution that utilized the vast material and symbolic resources of the corporate community to marshal the troops to victory. The first step in this strategic mission, however, was persuading his compatriots that the time "is long-overdue for the wisdom, ingenuity, and resources of American business to be marshalled against those who would destroy it."[78] A rallying cry for self-defense and active counterattack, this call was likely a contentious one that sought to unite doctrinaire libertarians opposed to corporate involvement in politics and a more conciliatory group of corporate liberals that did not want to rock the boat in Washington. Part of the rhetorical force of Powell's argument is that if one accepted the severity of the problem and the declaration of war announced against the corporation by the left, then the conclusion was all but certain: even if business wanted to stay away from politics it would be pulled into ideological warfare. All is fair in war, and though philosophical consistency is important, the messiness, pragmatics, and realism of politics demanded a certain flexibility that the academic realm seemed not to provide.

Fundamentally challenging notions of government and business cooperation, Powell heralded a unilateral relationship of influence between the corporation and state. This was, in fact, the first and most important step to be taken. As Powell claims, "The first essential—a prerequisite to any effective action—is for businessmen to confront this problem as a primary responsibility of corporate management."[79] Moving effective and responsible corporate management beyond a mere commitment to maximizing shareholder return and maintaining profitable margins, Powell redefined the primary responsibility of the corporation as political action. To be a

124 | Chapter Four

responsible corporate person was to make one's voice heard in the market of ideas. Moving beyond the militaristic language of ideological war, speech here is not simply a matter of survival and self-defense, but also signals a larger responsibility to the common good through a defense of Western society. Corporate responsibility is not simply to its own survival, but also to the larger survival and preservation of the industrial system and the Judeo-Christian values it is built upon. To engage in the war of words was thus an act of citizenship, one that maintains law, order, and the freedom of the market.

Making this case further, Powell argues that "The day is long past when the chief executive officer of a major corporation discharges his responsibility by maintaining a satisfactory growth of profits, with due regard to the corporation's public and social responsibilities."[80] The imperative that corporations speak and act in the public realm is articulated by Powell not just as something necessary to protect corporate privilege and power, or to maintain a free enterprise system, but also something done for the benefit of the public at large. Corporate speech in this sense benefits all in the deliberative processes of democracy. Portraying the New Left and the state as potentially totalitarian instruments that suppress freedom and destroy an open society, the interests of the corporation can stand in for the interests of all who are concerned about maintaining a truly open market of ideas. Offering corporate speech as a balancing force, one that maintains openness and fairness in democratic conversation, Powell utilizes the rhetoric of civic-republican notions of speech and citizenship to make the case for the corporate voice. By offering its unique perspective and making its preferences known to the larger community, the corporation is portrayed as just as valuable and legitimate a participant in deliberation as any other citizen.

An increased emphasis on offices of governmental affairs, corporate lobbying, and political publicity work offered the most direct means of making sure the corporate voice was represented in the corridors of established politics. Importantly, however, the individual corporation could not gain such access and influence alone in a hostile marketplace. Calling for carefully orchestrated campaigns and collective action, Powell writes that "Strength lies in organization, in careful long-range planning and implementation, in consistency of action over a definite period of years, in the scale of financing available only through joint effort, and in the political power only available through united action and national organizations."[81] As the current liberal monopoly prevented proper competition and threatened to undermine the structures that stabilized and brought order to civil society, opening this market through deregulatory measures and liberal policies, supplemented by careful planning, promised to maintain equilibrium through competition and influence rather than by cooperation and the centralized administration of state socialism.

The primary target of this disruption, for Powell, must be the college campus. Rather than equipping students for the job market or training students in the classical virtues of citizenship and civic-mindedness, the campus is portrayed as a hotbed of leftism that destroys these Western virtues in the name of a radical egalitarianism. Using arguments of the left against itself, Powell called for a public education and political action campaign that championed values of free speech, claimed an unwillingness to listen to a diversity of viewpoints on the left, and portrayed the corporation as a marginalized actor denied inclusion in the public sphere. Here, Powell was able to tap into familiar arguments made by various iterations of conservatism regarding the liberal suppression of speech on campus. Traditionalists such as Russell Kirk and Paul Gottfried, neoconservative and fusionist rhetors such as William F. Buckley, and libertarian intellectuals including Friedman, for instance, all lamented the liberal biases of higher education. A powerful way of uniting a fragmented right, this line of argument was the pillar of Powell's strategic plan, rallying the troops against a common enemy.

Writing about this plan, Powell claims that those in the business community must "aggressively insist" upon equal time, and must, if these requests are denied, attack the left as "publicly refusing a forum to diverse views." Again careful to mitigate the tension between political warfare and a humane, free, and competitive market of ideas, Powell takes great care to make it clear that he is not advocating the suppression of liberal speech. Though there is a tendency toward a liberal bias in university faculty, this mere fact for Powell is "not a criticism *per se*, as the need for liberal thought is essential to a balanced viewpoint. The difficulty is that 'balance' is conspicuous by its absence on many campuses."[82] Seeking to strike a balance between his militaristic language on the one hand and his

126 | Chapter Four

appeal to deliberative inclusion and fairness on the other, Powell posited that balance becomes recognizable in its absence by those whose opinions are left out of debate. On this, for Powell, there is no room for debate—readjusting the market so that balance and diversity may again be achieved cannot be negotiated but rather dictated by the marginalized corporate person. In this vein, corporations must use any and all available means of persuasion and influence to bring about balance in the market.

These tactics include utilizing corporate influence on boards of trustees to ensure pro-business faculty hires, creating a staff of scholars and speakers to lecture on campuses across the country, and evaluating textbooks for liberal bias, among others. There was a startling flex of corporate and governmental muscle to shape campus and classroom environments, especially when considered in light of his later decision in *Bakke*. Calling for support in these matters from the Chamber of Commerce, the vast reach, influence, and infrastructure of the organization proved for Powell indispensable resources in mobilizing and facilitating the coordinated action necessary to challenge the liberal campus monopoly.

Much like conservative think tanks emerging at this same time, the Chamber was to be an intellectual and activist space committed to training young men and women to write and speak on behalf of the corporation and the free enterprise system at large. The networked and managerial structure of the Chamber mirrored in many ways the bureaucratic structures of the corporation itself, offering an efficient means through which to produce, distribute, and promote new ideas in the market. Operating from the centralized national headquarters, local and regional offices of the Chamber carried out national-level tasks and duties with an emphasis on the provincial. Making efficient use of this industrial federalist structure, the daily tasks could be fulfilled by a managerial staff while the primary functions of "control and direction—especially the quality control—should be retained by the National Chamber."[83] Such efficient means of coordination promised to offer sufficient modes of resisting the campus left.

Though the primary target, the campus was not the only area of concern. In the short term, the public itself represented an equally necessary realm of action and target of persuasion. Just as susceptible to a leftist monopoly of ideas, the public sphere, for many conservatives, was controlled and directed by a liberal, cultural elite. One need look no further than Nixon's vice president Spiro Agnew for such a belief. Indeed, in his scathing indictment of television news coverage of the Nixon administration, he refers to an elite "little group of men who not only enjoy a right of instant rebuttal to every presidential address, but, more importantly, wield a free hand in selecting, presenting, and interpreting the great issues in our nation."[84] Echoing this sentiment, Powell claims that "The national television networks should be monitored in the same way that textbooks should be kept under constant surveillance," particularly news programming, "which so often includes the most insidious type of criticism of the enterprise system." Utilizing the Federal Communications Commission (FCC) for corporate ends, effective pressure campaigns and complaints provide a means for correcting and challenging speech deemed "unfair or inaccurate" regarding the system of free enterprise.[85]

Alongside such efforts, Powell makes pleas for conservative representation in "forum-type programs" such as *Meet the Press*, books and pamphlets, and scholarly journals.[86] Calling for a system of what Oscar Gandy terms information subsidization, the Chamber and other conservative political action groups' primary efforts at reaching the public are to be in the publishing and distribution of conservative ideas for cheap and available consumption. Not so much about balance, then, the *telos* of the corporate voice as envisioned by Powell was to flood the marketplace, drowning out other viewpoints with mass-produced and easily accessible corporate viewpoints.

An information subsidy, Gandy writes, "is an attempt to produce influence over the actions of others by controlling their access to and use of information relevant to those actions." Put differently, subsidies are "efforts to increase the use value of information by reducing its cost."[87] By actively checking and surveilling liberal discourse, as well as by utilizing the growing network of conservative activists, think tanks, business associations, and the like, Powell sought to inundate the market with cheap and accessible products that represented the corporate voice in the public sphere. Packaging narratives, data, and statistics for public consumption, the market of ideas was to be brought into balance through subsidized information from rightward-leaning, tax-exempt organizations.[88]

The ultimate measure of the effectiveness of this campaign for the corporate voice was to be found in a revolutionary shift in public attitudes toward the corporation in the long term, and in the short term more

128 | Chapter Four

favorable political representation.[89] Long neglected by corporate actors, political representation and a sustained corporate voice in the public sphere offered the surest path to regained power and legitimacy. Thus, whereas men like Bruce Barton argued that the corporation ought to stay out of political affairs, the system of industrial governance imagined by Powell was one in which the corporation occupied a permanent and integral space in Washington. This move was perceived as necessary in an era of a burgeoning state held hostage by the demands of interest groups, social movements, and political clientelism in which the corporation was said to lack comparable governmental influence.[90]

As Powell notes, "Few elements of society today have as little influence in government as the businessman, the corporation, or even the millions of corporate stockholders. . . . with respect to the course of legislation and government action, the American business executive is truly the 'forgotten man.'"[91] Constructing the corporation as a kind of non-subject, what Phillip Wander deems a third persona in rhetorical discourse, for Powell the corporate person has been negated in language and history from the possibilities of emancipatory action and rhetorical agency in the public sphere by the pretensions of a supposedly open, inclusive, and egalitarian academic left.[92]

Yet, as Robert Asen notes in his critical interrogation of calls for counterpublicity by conservative William Simon, claims to marginality must be mitigated by materiality and textual markers of privilege that may contradict a speaker's assertions.[93] Calling upon the business community to utilize its resources and access to channels of power not available to ordinary citizens thus undermines Powell's claims to marginalization. Hardly the forgotten man, the businessman occupied a position of great power and influence in politics. Underneath claims to suppression and marginality there seemed to be a deeper desire to use corporate power to define its own rights and responsibilities rather than have them dictated by the state and social movements.

Ultimately, Powell's central lesson and call to action that "political power is necessary; [that] such power must be assiduously cultivated; and that when necessary, it must be used aggressively and with determination— without embarrassment and without the reluctance which has been so characteristic of American business" would not fall on deaf ears.[94] A rallying cry of sorts for conservative and corporate free-speech activists, the vision for a pro-corporate campaign offered by Powell would become a blueprint for recrafting the structures of political culture. As Nichols and McChesney note, after the release of the Powell Memo, "The Chamber would triple its budget over the next six years as an infrastructure of pro-corporate think tanks and advocacy groups took shape."[95] Though only in its infancy in the early and mid-1970s, the foundation built in these years would provide the means for what William Simon in his 1978 *Time for Truth* would call a conservative counterintelligentsia and counterrevolution against an establishment left.[96]

As Jean Stefancic and Richard Delgado argue, this emergent corporate speech network and Simon's call for a conservative counterintelligentsia were instrumental in carrying out "a successful war of position" that fundamentally "shifted the grounds of discussion away from liberal solutions to what many Americans believed were real social problems, and toward conservative solutions" to these problems.[97] Published just three years before the election of Ronald Reagan, a shift to monetarism in macroeconomic domestic policy, and austerity politics abroad, Simon's incendiary rebuke of the already crumbling liberal consensus came the very same year in which the corporate voice was granted its largest legal victory.

Appointed to the Supreme Court just one year after the release of the memo, Powell would find himself in a position to act on his own demands regarding an activist-minded Court. In the wake of Watergate and Nixon's impeachment in 1974, public confidence in government and the institutions of the state was waning. To help combat corruption and its appearance in the electoral process, the 1970s saw a flurry of legislation concerning campaign finance. The Federal Election Campaign Act (FECA) of 1971, originally signed into law by Nixon, was amended in 1974 and again in 1976 to limit the size of individual contributions, as well as those made by political action committees (PACs) and other organizational actors.[98] Of central concern was the role of private, corporate spending in influencing and shaping the outcome of public elections.

Challenging these reforms, *Buckley v. Valeo* (1976) rolled back some of the restrictions upon electoral spending. Maintaining restrictions on contributions but holding that limits on spending were unconstitutional,

130 Chapter Four

Buckley held that money was a form of speech and expression protected under the First Amendment.[99] Though crafted as a defense of equality, Smith argues that the loopholes for soft-money spending opened in the *Buckley* decision "created a system that favors the independently wealthy, the major parties, and incumbents" in the electoral process.[100] Further, with the extension of money as speech to corporations in *First National Bank of Boston v. Bellotti* (1978), corporations gained a foothold in the speech marketplace. Deregulating campaign finance law and altering the structures of the marketplace of ideas, *Bellotti* fulfilled Powell's strategic plan, not only giving voice to the corporation but elevating it above others.

A case concerned with the use of corporate treasury funds to create communications seeking to influence a Massachusetts general election ballot measure to implement a graduated income tax in the state, it was held by the appellants that restrictions upon corporate spending flew against the intent of the decision of *Buckley* as well as violated the First and Fourteenth Amendment rights of the corporate person. Delivering the majority opinion of the Court in a narrowly decided 5–4 decision, Justice Powell's rhetoric defends the rights of corporate speech as identical to the rights of natural persons. Absent the militaristic language of his memo, Powell retains his civic-republican framing. However, the true rhetorical brilliance of the decision is the ability of Powell, writing on behalf of the majority, to ignore complicated metaphysical and jurisprudential questions of corporate personality, identity, and voice in the crafting of a simple, pragmatic, and realist account of the value of corporate speech for public debate. Indeed, rather than asking who speaks for the corporation, the Court asks the question: for whom does the corporation speak?—making the decision not about the power and privileges of money, but about the responsibilities and civic duties of the corporate person in maintaining a competitive, diverse marketplace of ideas.

The decision in *Buckley v. Valeo*, while uplifting some restrictions and enforcing others established in FECA, held that corporate political speech is protected when such speech has a "material effect" upon the business holdings, transactions, or property of the corporation. In this sense, the First Amendment rights of corporate political speech extend from the promises of equal protection and due process secured by the corporate person nearly one hundred years before in the *Railroad Tax Cases*. Referencing *Buckley*, Powell writes that "Distinguishing the First Amendment rights of a natural person from the more limited rights of a corporation, the Court concluded that 'whether its rights are designated "liberty" rights or "property" rights, a corporation's property and business interests are entitled to Fourteenth Amendment protection. . . . [A]s an incident of such protection, corporations also possess certain rights of speech and of expression under the First Amendment." Arguing that the statute regarding a graduated income tax did materially affect the business of the First National Bank of Boston, the Court held that corporate political speech was warranted on this issue. However, arguing further, the Court decided that "the 'materially effecting' requirement . . . amounts to an impermissible legislative prohibition of speech based on the identity of the interests that spokesmen may represent in public debate."[101] In this sense, rather than protecting democracy from the occurrence or appearance of corruption through corporate power, the materially effecting requirement draws parameters regarding acceptable viewpoints and opinions in democratic exchange. Under this formulation of the public sphere, those who suffer most from legislative restrictions are in fact consumers of information, not the producers.

This rhetorical move is critical, for as Robert Kerr argues, one of the primary appeals of the corporate free-speech advocates has been to "frame corporate interests as consumer interests."[102] Masking corporate interests under a veil of republicanism, these interests were held as the universal norm by which other individual actors were to judge their own relative positions. If corporate speech was restricted, not only did this hold the possibility that the speech of other social and demographic groups might be silenced in the future, but that the public suffered from a lack of information necessary to make the difficult and important decisions of the democratic project of living together in a community.

The corporate person, understood here as a quasi-citizen, was crafted as having an equal right to express its own opinions, make its interests known, and engage in rhetorical exchange. Stressing the importance of a diversity of viewpoints in the market, particular emphasis is placed upon the transmission and distribution of ideas. Here, more information inherently means better information, and governmental regulation and restriction

132 | Chapter Four

inherently violate the principles of a competitive and open market. That is to say, under this market-based model of speech, "Democratic communication is whatever the market produces" when left to its own devices.[103]

This emphasis on quantity over quality raises important questions regarding the capacity of market logics to shape democratic exchange. Reformulating classical liberal notions of rights, democracy, and speech, the understanding of democratic speech offered under the market of ideas reduces democracy to an empty proceduralism premised on norms of balance, competition, self-interest, and free exchange. So long as the procedural mechanism of the speech market is left to function on its own, the outcome is a democratic one. Here we might understand the procedural mechanism much as a production line. Democratic communication is a linear process of production where the workers are interchangeable parts of a complex whole. The particular identities and histories of each individual worker are stripped away as they become parts of a larger system that generates democracy in their productive and efficient interplay. Each individual, of course, must play by the rules of the game and maintain the norms of balance, competition, and freedom through the expression of self-interest. So long as these rules are adhered to, however, the system is working just fine.

What this model of democratic speech overlooks, however, is the way in which democratic communication is inherently imbricated within and constitutive of broader contexts and cultures within which speech occurs. Narrowing the public realm in this way, politics is rendered an individual endeavor, severing the communal ties that ground individuals within particular cultures and severely limiting any sense of responsibility to anyone other than the self. Much as in the case of *Bakke*, then, diversity in the market of ideas is lauded as a standalone principle and as a guarantor of individual liberty as opposed to larger issues of social justice.

Ironically, as the free and individual self is figured as the locus of all political action, missing from this account of democratic speech is the role of power, history, and identity in shaping the structural elements that construct the self, as well as the limitations to voice and representation. In their removal of the market from the realm of political discourse, market rhetorics deny the rhetorical fashioning of subjects and economic discourses in an adaptation of what Seyla Benhabib refers to as "liberalist dialogic neutrality" that assumes democratic equality under the law, while not considering the broader material circumstances in which speech occurs.[104]

What is most significant about the argument of the Court, however, is that rhetorics of power, identity, and representation, while eschewed or unnoticed in the effects of the ruling on citizen actors, are appropriated in service of corporations within the market of ideas. Employing these rhetorics to argue that the central "question in this case, simply put, is whether the corporate identity of the speaker deprives this proposed speech of what otherwise would be its clear entitlement to protection," Powell and the majority concretize the image of a suppressed and historically marginalized corporate voice akin to the account offered in Powell's memo to the Chamber, without the openly partisan and ideological valence of rhetorical warfare. Indeed, the restriction on corporate speech is said to give "one side of a debatable public question an advantage in expressing its views to the people" through the suppression of other voices and viewpoints.[105] In other words, the corporation was in need of affirmative action so as to have its voice heard.

Harkening to arguments regarding a liberal monopoly over the current market of ideas, governmental regulation of corporate speech contributes to the subversion of the assembly line of democratic communication and thus the free and open distribution of ideas. Powell and the majority hold that, best regulated instead by consumer behavior and demand, "the people in our democracy are entrusted with the responsibility for judging and evaluating the relative merits of conflicting arguments," not a paternalistic state apparatus. While the dissenting opinion of Justices White, Brennan, and Marshall holds that the primary purview of corporate speech is increasing profit and is thus subversive of the "development of ideas, of mental exploration, and of the affirmation of self" that undergirds the First Amendment, Powell maintains that corporate speech buttresses democracy "in affording the public access to discussion, debate, and the dissemination of information and ideas." Indeed, though corporate communication and "advocacy may persuade the electorate," this fact alone "is hardly a reason to suppress it."[106] Persuasion is the primary objective of any advocacy work, and thus this is not a sufficient basis in the eyes of the majority to restrict corporate speech. To do so would not only limit the diversity of viewpoints in the market but

134 | Chapter Four

would also restrict public access to the market as corporate communications also help structure the very market in which they participate.

What this line of argument represents is the complexities and metaphysics of identity, voice, and speech that were intentionally circumvented in the opinion of the majority. Where does the line between corporation as speaker and corporation as facilitator of speech get drawn? Where do the obligations of the corporation to make its voice heard in democratic exchange end, and the threat of corporate power to subvert democratic processes begin? To claim that these questions did not matter to the case at hand, as Powell did, is to elide the central tensions and relationships among personhood, voice, and representation that provided the rhetorical grounds for claims to corporate marginalization. To adapt such a realist style of discourse, as Aune claims, separates power from textuality and assumes that such higher-order questions are of little importance to the realities of corporate speech and political action.[107]

This was, of course, the argument of the traditionalists all along. It was none other than Richard Weaver who had argued that industrial capitalism and the large corporation as much as the state devalued human personality in the mass production of artificial property. Severing humanity from the land in this way led the agrarian theorist to return to and champion feudal metaphysics as opposed to liberal notions of possessive individualism. Of course, we need not adopt such a reactionary view to agree with Weaver that the corporation can often be a dehumanizing force. Indeed, today this seems more a platitude of the left than a clarion call of the right. Regardless, by casting the question of corporate speech not as one of who speaks for the corporation but for whom the corporation speaks and enables to speak, these complex and important questions were cast aside, elevating the corporate person and corporate voice over all others in the process.

Conclusion

Powell's conservative fusion of markets and moral order proved a powerful way of mobilizing those in the business community to the defense of the corporation and of a diverse market of ideas. However, his particular brand of conservatism, even as it drew from the agrarian tradition, came dressed in a suit and tie rather than a pair of overalls and a straw hat. Powell's fusion thus comported southern tradition to the modernizing forces of liberal capitalism and not the other way around. This was a southern-inspired capitalism fit for the halls of power and mainstream Washingtonian politics. However, during the same time period, another version of southern capitalism was being crafted—not in Washington, DC, or prominent eastern think tanks, but in the Ozarks of middle America.

Indeed, the New Right was mobilizing grassroots campaigns across the South and the West in order to defend a particular vision of Christian capitalism. As Bethany Moreton chronicles, the shifts in U.S. politics and global markets during the 1960s and 1970s brought about a powerful Sun Belt service economy that articulated a vision of Christian capitalism amenable to the populist yeoman mythology of the region.[108] What emerges is a kind of populism in which corporate capitalism becomes the primary defender of white patriarchal family structure, rural traditions, and Christian fundamentalism. While Moreton focuses primarily on the role of Wal-Mart in the crafting of this corporate populism—and for good reason—they are not alone in articulating this brand of Christian capitalism.

Significantly, however, what the legacies of Powell and later of Wal-Mart demonstrate is that neoliberalism—at least in the United States—has long been connected with a concern for social custom and moral order against the homogenizing forces of state power. Likewise, both have continued impact today. Indeed, if we may think of Powell's ideas as a precursor to the 2010 decision of *Citizens United*, the rise of corporate populism and the so-called Wal-Mart voter were precursors to the rise of the Tea Party movement and the 2014 decision of *Hobby Lobby*.

In either case, the Cold War crafting of a muscular Christian capitalism and the creation of the corporate voice planted the seeds for continued deregulatory measures and liberal policy reforms, which would come to prominence during the presidency of Ronald Reagan. Likewise, arguments offered by Powell and others on the New Right that corporations and white Christian men were marginalized in the public sphere would become cornerstones of conservative discourse even as they continued to gain legal and political victories. In this way, and certainly others, the New Right helped set the stage for what was to come.

CHAPTER 5

Conscience

The idea that the corporation was a marginalized political actor and that white Christian men were the great silent—and persecuted—majority offered by the New Right in the 1970s would continue to be an organizing point for various stripes of conservatives in the decades to come. Indeed, these ideas were at the heart of Ronald Reagan's political platform and were the backbone of Jerry Falwell's Moral Majority that led to his victory. They would also be cornerstones in the successful 2016 campaign of Donald J. Trump, placing a corporate person in the White House. Somewhere between these two presidencies, however, two rather significant court cases regarding corporate personhood breathed new life into these ideas and represent the tendentious relationship between neoliberal and evangelical strands of conservatism—*Citizens United v. Federal Election Commission* (2010) and *Burwell v. Hobby Lobby* (2014).

Though the two cases may seem disparate to some degree—*Citizens United* concerns the ability of corporations to use nearly unlimited private funds during electoral campaigns as constitutionally protected forms of speech, and *Hobby Lobby* concerns the ability of privately held corporations to be exempt from federal contraception mandates for reasons of religious freedom—each stems from crucial questions of First Amendment

137

jurisprudence. Likewise, in both cases, we see the corporate person and white evangelical Christians portrayed as victims of a powerful state that seeks to control freedom of speech and religious liberty and thus deny the bulk of our nation's freedoms to the majority of its people.

The nexus of these two cases also continues to illustrate the centrality of corporate personhood and conservatism to what William Connolly has called the "evangelical-capitalist resonance machine" in the United States. This resonance machine is sustained by and channeled through the connections among evangelicalism, neoliberal capitalism, an expansive right-wing media ecology, and elements of the Republican Party itself.[1] Corporate personhood becomes imperative to the continued power of this resonance machine as decisions such as *Citizens United* enable corporations to spend excess sums of money to influence the electoral process, while the *Hobby Lobby* decision effectively grants corporate actors and those in the evangelical community the right of exit when they find that federal law violates their rights to conscience. In other words, each case buttresses and expands corporate sovereignty, one by expanding the purview of corporate participation in civil society and the other by allowing evangelicals and their organizations to withdraw from the difficult responsibilities *of* and *to* difference required by democratic life.

In doing so, as Robin West argues, such exit rights function to "exempt their holders from legal obligations which are themselves constitutive of some significant part of civil society," due to claims of conscience, and in the process further harm those already marginalized in society by denying them available legal protections.[2] Here, the significance of the relationship between evangelical Christianity and neoliberal capitalism is laid bare. Indeed, as Connolly suggests, "The right leg of the evangelical movement today is joined at the hip to the left leg of the capitalist juggernaut. Neither leg could hop far unless it was joined to the other."[3] This intricate relationship was made possible, in part, by the advances of the conservative movement as well as significant shifts within conservatism during the years of Reagan and beyond—many of which I will explore in this chapter through an investigation of Trumpism.

Forgoing a nuanced theoretical exposition of the concept of neoliberalism—a task that has been performed by many—I instead want to trace the contours of Reagan's evangelical-neoliberal vision while demonstrating the theological tenets of the neoliberal creed as it emerged in its muscular form throughout the 1980s.[4] After illustrating the significance of Reagan's particular marriage of evangelicalism and capitalism during the Cold War, I will then discuss the paleoconservative backlash to the Washington consensus in the 1990s and early 2000s. Including figures such as Patrick Buchanan, Paul Gottfried, Peter Brimelow, and others, paleoconservatives demand a return to core traditionalist conservative principles and offer a rebuke of what they view as the three-headed monster of a global welfare-state system, multiculturalism, and political correctness. In place of this system, they argue for a conservative, middle-American populism of those white men and women seemingly left behind by establishment politics. In other words, paleoconservatives openly espouse a nationalist politics of white identity premised upon closed borders, free markets, and vindictive Christian moral codes, yet not entirely hostile to corporate capital. These ideas would become significant in the continued rise of populist conservative movements such as the Tea Party, yet would come to the White House in the figure of Donald J. Trump.

Upon first glance this might seem a bizarre proposition—Trump was an East Coast elite, a playboy billionaire businessman who depended upon global free trade for his riches and is nominally Christian by upbringing only. Yet, as early as 2012, Trump wed himself to the insurgent Tea Party movement, championing the racist birther conspiracy regarding then President Barack Obama. This seemingly odd pairing would continue to build over the next four years as Donald continued to imbibe baseless conspiracy theories and rode them to a place in the 2016 Republican primaries and ultimately into the White House. Further, he would do so winning the highest percentage of the white evangelical vote in the history of this country and overwhelming support from other significant portions of the Republican base.

What was it about Trump that brought these factions together? Was there a new fusion of libertarian and traditionalist conservatism being created in this moment? The answers to these questions are complex, but I will argue here that Trump was able to rally conservatives of all stripes together around the key issue of *conscience*—that is, freedom from a godless and all-powerful state apparatus that polices language through a soft totalitarian discourse of political correctness on the one hand, and

140 | Chapter Five

mandates that companies abandon their religious convictions in the name of state-sanctioned multiculturalism on the other. It is here that libertarian and evangelical conservatives have again found common footing and have found their champion in Donald Trump. If, as Corey Robin suggests, conservatism represents a defense of the private life of power, this was a perceived defense of privacy pushed to the inner core of personhood: the right to speak and think freely.[5]

From this vantage, white male and corporate persons are under attack as the Judeo-Christian and free-market foundations of Western society crumble at the behest of a global elite committed to eroding national sovereignty and policing language and thought—*Citizens United* and *Hobby Lobby* meet at a nearly global scale. This is to say that, I suggest, the turn to Trumpism by many on the political right—and some on the left—represents an anxiety about the stability of received orthodoxy about evangelical-capitalist conceptions of personhood and its attendant freedom of conscience in a world in which traditional value systems are challenged and overturned by drastic climactic and geopolitical change.

As I have argued thus far, Christian and market understandings of the person share affinities with one another, insofar as both envision personhood in largely rational and economic terms.[6] Though they certainly differ in significant ways that allow for contestation within and outside of conservative camps and various forms of Christian theology, as Connolly suggests, "Across these modest differentiations, the two parties are bound by similar orientations to the future. One party discounts its responsibilities to the future of the earth to vindicate extreme economic entitlement now, while the other does so to prepare for the day of judgment against nonbelievers."[7] In other words, evangelical-capitalist visions of the person converge in an understanding that man (and specifically man) is the rational individual who presides over the Earth that is here for his present usage.

What unites them is thus a kind of existential resentment and abdication of worldly responsibility in the here and now—an ethos of *ressentiment* built upon "demands of entitlement and revenge," particularly in a political culture that has left them behind economically and a world that has abandoned God's inerrant word.[8] No longer content to simply stand athwart history yelling "stop," as William F. Buckley had previously portrayed the conservative persuasion, conservatives have now created a vision for recrafting politics through a populist (re)assertion of white male Christian and corporate personhood. Donald Trump represents the embodiment of this evangelical-corporate person in its economic entitlement and righteous vengefulness and stands as a Christ-like figure sent to redeem the people who have been crafted in his image.

Offering a new fusion of Christian morality and corporate capitalism, Trumpism is simultaneously a perversion and debasement of both. To quote Phillip Gorski, Trump and many of his followers have thus failed to realize that "too close an association between worldly and spiritual power will ultimately diminish both."[9] The debasement of Christianity on the one hand and democracy on the other fuses them together in a way that transforms each into its opposite: democracy is transformed into a vulgar populism and Christianity is equated with a militant nationalism.[10] Reducing identity, nationhood, and politics to a corporate system, Trump the individual becomes the personification of this new corporate society as well as its redeemer—a model of corporate personhood for his followers to aspire to.[11]

In order to make this argument, I will turn to a rhetorical analysis of the writings of prominent Trump supporter and Christian media mogul Stephen E. Strang. Strang is a charismatic Pentecostal Christian and founder and CEO of *Charisma Magazine*, a leading Christian digital magazine and media company. Gaining notoriety after his publishing house, Strang Communications, published the *New York Times* Best Seller *The Faith of George W. Bush* in 2003, *Time* magazine named him one of the twenty-five most influential evangelicals in America in 2005.[12] He has become even more influential with his efforts to support Donald Trump's candidacy in 2016, his term in office, and his failed reelection bid in 2020.

Strang published four books on Trump and Trumpism in this time—*God and Donald Trump* (2017), *Trump Aftershock* (2018), *God, Trump, and the 2020 Election* (2020), and *God, Trump, and COVID-19* (2020). I examine these texts in particular to outline the rhetorical workings of Trumpism. Broaching several right-wing conspiracies regarding a new world order, demographic replacement, and QAnon-like claims regarding a cosmic battle for the soul of the nation, Strang's works craft Trump as a biblically preordained and anointed redeemer of the nation. In this world, Trump emerges

142 | Chapter Five

as the corporate savior of society from the evils of the state, a Christ-like martyr for the American way of life, the moral conscience of the American folk, and the second coming of the nation's glory.

The Reagan Revolution: Markets, Morality, and the Economic Theology of Neoliberalism

The subtitle above is perhaps a bit of a misnomer. Indeed, I think it is more appropriate to view Ronald Reagan as the culmination of a longer history of competing conservative visions than as a revolutionary figure that single-handedly transformed the face of conservatism in the United States. That is, we must understand Reagan in relationship to the fractions and fissures in conservatism among traditionalist, libertarian, and anti-Communist dialects of conservative discourse and their ultimate fusion in the New Right. Seen in this light, conservatism as a rhetorical discourse authored Reagan as much as Reagan rewrote and reimagined conservative discourse. Reagan the man is not possible without the larger discourses he sought to marry together—namely, Christianity, anti-Communism, and free-market capitalism—nor is modern conservatism possible without Reagan as a node of its articulation. Reagan was not the first to marry Christian faith and the free market, nor would he be the last. He was, however, perhaps the most influential and powerful proponent of their rhetorical imbrication. In this attenuated sense, Reagan was in fact quite revolutionary.[13]

The revolutionary force of Reagan's particular evangelical-neoliberal rhetoric was, I contend, contained within what Craig Smith calls the "master dialectic" of Reagan's rhetoric: that of up/down.[14] Though this dialectic certainly confines itself to no one authoritative reading, one powerful way of interpreting its rhetorical force is by understanding it in terms of the tensions between the transcendent and the immanent in political life. In other words, this dialectic heralded the truth of Western civilization and of the power of the free-market system as resting upon the transcendental truth of God's wisdom and providential design. This reading of the dialectic also helps demonstrate how Reagan's rhetoric, as Meg Kunde has demonstrated, drew upon a longer historical Puritanical discourse of covenantal theology.[15] So long as the United States remained committed to its Judeo-Christian heritage, it would continue to be a beacon for democracy around the world—a Shining City on a Hill, as he often explained.[16]

Such a covenantal system of thought gave way to a covenantal rhetorical form, one that allowed Reagan to "reframe free-market policies as an intricate moral arrangement rather than a form of social Darwinism." The primary concern of "Reaganomics," then, was not material prosperity, but rather the spiritual and humane values of individual freedom from state power. Such freedom was articulated as a means of enabling individuals to participate in God's divinely orchestrated economic system and to maintain their side of the economic covenant between God and man. As Kunde argues, "Reagan carved out a rhetorical space to frame his own economic actions and policies as respectful of God's divine plan in the covenant of grace and as the route by which the people of the United States could embrace their God-given freedom to do the same."[17]

Such a covenantal form also provided the tools for a tactical rhetorical fusion between conservative traditionalists and libertarians. In other words, a covenantal economic rhetoric enabled Reagan to balance traditionalist concerns for order, faith, and communalism with libertarian virtues of freedom, entrepreneurialism, and individualism. Striking such a delicate balance between morals and the market, Reagan "framed his policies as freeing people to serve God through their special gifts, using his policies *not to impose arbitrary order* but *to allow divine order to be carried out*."[18] Put differently, for Reagan, state power and regulation ought to *only* be used to ensure the providential workings of the market, not to impose artificial fetters on it. In this way, we can see in Reaganomics a mature vision of neoliberalism in which government is utilized to create and preserve a space of economic and moral freedom in the market.

Indeed, the economic-cum-Christian actor par excellence for Reagan was the entrepreneur, who was positioned by Reagan "as fulfilling his or her commitment to self through taking risks, to God by having faith in God's grace and plan, and to the community through economic production from which others could benefit."[19] In this way, the entrepreneur walked a proverbial tightrope between freedom and order, faith and work, individualism and communalism. Further, entrepreneurs seek to become an enterprise in and of themselves, standing as a corporeal rendition of corporate models of personhood to which all should nominally aspire.

144 | Chapter Five

Reagan, much as Hayek before him, thus understands the entrepreneur as the backbone and outcome of the unfolding of the market's internal, self-manifesting order. Yet, Reagan makes visible, indeed centers, the theological core hidden and smuggled into Hayek's understanding of market catallactics. As Timothy Christiaens argues, Hayek "completes the movement toward the death of God hidden in providential theology and replaces God's harmonious creation with the price system as an immanent technique for mutually harmonizing individual preferences." Yet, even with Hayekian neoliberalism, the individual subject is secondary and subservient to the imperatives of the market. That is to say that "the success of providential catallaxy depends on the willingness of subject[s] to self-identify as second causes in the spontaneous market order" and its logic of the price mechanism.[20] We might rightfully ask, however, why we should submit to a system that governs via logical abstractions and incentives that are erratically produced as the market continually shifts, evolves, and adapts. Absent a sovereign guarantee that the ills the market produces work in the long term toward the greatest good and ensure the best of all possible worlds, a different rationality is needed.[21] For Reagan, however, the theodicy smuggled into neoliberalism is perhaps its primary justification—the market is the immanent unfolding of God's providential vision for the world.

This moral vision of the market was made possible by those that had come before him—Whittaker Chambers, Ludwig von Mises, William F. Buckley, and Edmund Opitz—many of whom Reagan ardently studied and even befriended, as well as the larger organizational networks of committed Christian libertarians forged in the wake of the New Deal. Indeed, it was in 1979 that committed New Right architect Paul Weyrich would join forces with the famed evangelical preacher Jerry Falwell to create the Moral Majority, an organization that was the backbone of Reagan's presidential ticket. The organization effectively gave voice to White conservative Christians of all stripes committed to defending Judeo-Christian values and Western free-market capitalism.[22]

Regardless of one's view of Reagan—that he was a cowboy actor who merely played the part of president, that he was a flexible and pragmatic statesman-orator, or that he was a heroic figure who single-handedly brought down the specter of global Communism—it was largely Reagan's rhetorical prowess that was responsible for the mainstreaming of conservatism in the takeover of the Republican Party.[23] Yet, conservatism would become a victim of its own successes. For as Michael Lee argues, conservatism has long defined itself negatively, that is oppositionally, in the face of a common enemy. Effective for mobilizing a base, it offers little in the way of a coherent governing strategy.[24] Though Reagan sought to smooth over these issues, once conservatism became part of the political establishment it had betrayed its founding principles. It's tough to stand athwart history yelling stop when you're the one in the driver's seat.

These tensions would become evident after the fall of the Berlin Wall, the waning of the Cold War, and the end of eight years of a Ronald Reagan White House. As Robert Rowland and John Jones have eloquently argued, the early 1990s created a crisis for the performative tradition of conservatism as "the very successes of conservatism had created a symbolic bind." Indeed, this bind played out before the nation's eyes at the 1992 Republican National Convention in Houston, Texas, where the speeches of Pat Buchanan and Ronald Reagan painted two different trajectories of conservative rhetoric and governance in the years to come. The bind facing conservatives and their Republican Party was twofold: first, national defense became less and less a central issue of concern after the fall of the Soviet Union and the end of the Cold War, and second, after railing against liberals and big government for eroding individual freedom and creating massive deficits in the federal budget, having now held the White House for over a decade, conservatives could no longer simply blame the left for the nation's woes. In other words, "The end of the Cold War and the decline of traditional liberalism eliminated two primary 'evils' that conservatives had fought against for decades and, at the same time, eliminated the two primary factors that had unified conservatives."[25] Who or what would be capable of unifying the warring conservative factions in this moment of crisis? What would conservatism look like moving forward?

While Buchanan and Reagan certainly disagreed on these questions—a tension that we will return to later—they both offered an endorsement of George H. W. Bush as the new de facto leader of the conservative Republican Party. He was capable of speaking to both evangelicals and cowboy capitalists and seemed capable, temporarily at least, of keeping the warring factions of conservatism at bay. Yet, it would become abundantly clear to many that Bush was no Reagan, and that "Without Reagan's unifying

Chapter Five

persona and his reformist message . . . the gap between these two branches of conservatism became quite visible."[26] Indeed, the war of words between Buchanan and Reagan in Houston would continue to bubble under the surface of Republican conservatism for the coming decades in the eventual resurgence of conservative traditionalism, now rebranded under the moniker of paleoconservatism.

The Paleoconservative Backlash: Conservative Inc. and Mid-American Radicals

George H. W. Bush would take the Republican ticket and win the presidency, yet many in the conservative movement became frustrated with his governance. Further, after his son, George W. Bush, became president it became quickly apparent that with the Bush family conservatism had become part and parcel of the very establishment the insurgent movement had meant to take down. Indeed, it became clear to many that Bush Sr. was a run-of-the-mill Washington bureaucrat, and his son's brand of so-called compassionate conservatism was nothing but a rebranded neoconservatism that paid lip service to traditionalist conservative principles but continued the growth of state power. Further, as Luke Winslow suggests, after the terrorist attacks of September 11, 2001, "the Bush administration fulfilled the most cynical caricature of institutional incompetence, beginning with the global war on terror and ending with the collapse of the global economy."[27] For many who were committed to the cause of the New Right and Reagan-era conservatism—such as one of its primary architects, Richard Viguerie—Republicans had betrayed the movement. A return to principles was needed.[28]

Given this political recipe, "In the ashes of the Bush presidency, an audience was united by anger, cynicism, and frustration toward any institution's ability to redress the challenges of their own lives." Republicans had sold out middle Americans and had abandoned conservative principles. Add to that the appointment of Mitt Romney as the Republican nominee—a Mormon elitist and moderate Republican who had once proposed the equivalent of Obamacare in his home state of Massachusetts—and eight years of a Black

Democrat in the White House and you have a perfect storm for a reactionary conservative populism. As Winslow has argued, Romney's message could not resonate with the more (white) evangelical and populist base of the party, particularly the burgeoning Tea Party movement, as he couldn't promise to take the country back, for "*It was already his country.*" The rhetorical effect of this chasm was that "space was carved out for the constitution of an older, whiter, rural, and nominally religious audience fed up with tone-deaf party politics."[29] The generation and audiences that largely had their news fed to them from far-right talk radio and websites such as Breitbart.com emerged after the fall of the fairness doctrine, and thus became a more vocal and less fringe component of conservatism. It was their turn to have a go at the Republican Party.

Indeed, according to these individuals, conservatism had lost its principles, its bite, and its insurgent nature as it had become, after taking over the Republican Party, part of the political establishment. Faint echoes of this line of argument can be heard in 1992 from Buchanan's speech at the RNC in Houston. Buchanan's calls for a cultural holy war for the soul of America and the evil, totalitarian nature of liberal Democrats in the United States would be carried forward throughout the 1990s and early 2000s on many fronts but were given their most precise articulation by fellow paleoconservatives Paul Gottfried and Samuel Francis.

According to Paul Scotchie, the term paleoconservative came about in the 1980s, in part as a response to the prominence and influence of neo-conservatism on the Republican establishment, but also as a call to return to pre–Cold War, "Old Right" principles.[30] The origins of this movement were fostered in part by the Mises Institute, yet it primarily was incubated at the Rockford Institute, a traditionalist conservative think tank founded in 1976 by former Rockford College president John A. Howard.[31] This is a complex political position, and paleoconservatives do not all adhere to the same ideology. Indeed, according to Murray Rothbard, paleoconservative Old-Righters were reactionaries that should be viewed as a coalition of ideologies that ranged from "libertarian decentralization to Hamiltonian reliance on strong government within rigid limits to various wings of monarchists."[32] However, there are some unifying threads within the movement—namely, that a return to conservatism's roots and a return to American tradition was

148 | Chapter Five

the only way to revitalize the sovereignty of the nation state, to preserve cultural pluralism, and to defend regional ways of life from the onslaught of multiculturalism and global capital.[33]

Paleoconservatives, much like Weaver, Kirk, and others before them, were thus right-wing critics of capitalism. Yet, in a post–Cold War climate, they were right-wing critics of neoliberalism and offered an alternative economic theology to that of Reagan, Bush, and the conservative establishment. Such an alternative economic theology was, in some regards, a rethinking and retooling of mercantilism—a protectionist nationalism that subordinates economics to culture and nation.[34] More specifically, and unique to the cultural moment, paleoconservatives refashioned the political divide as no longer left versus right, capitalism versus Communism, or even up versus down (to use Reagan's preferred dialectic), but rather nationalists versus globalists. If, as Slobodian argues, those influenced by the Geneva School of neoliberalism thought in terms of global order, paleoconservatives sought to revitalize the nation. Like Schmitt before them, they decried the doubled nature of global politics and longed for a world of walled sovereign states.[35]

Echoing the cries of Irving Kristol and others, paleoconservatives saw the United States as under the spell of a political New Class of managerial bureaucrats, dead set on selling out American principles, virtues, identity, and labor to the highest global bidder. This is what Buchanan would call the Great Betrayal of late neoliberal capitalism and the political establishment. Stating that "Free trade ideology is [thus] a product of a shift in perspective, from a God-centered universe to a man-centered one," Buchanan argues that under multicultural capitalism the sovereignty of the nation is eroded, and the promise of American civilization is threatened.[36]

According to Buchanan, "In the Global Economy, money no longer follows the flag," for "money has no flag." Similarly, "the transnational corporation does not naturally invest 'at home.' It has no home." Augmenting Hayek's warning of the long road to serfdom, Buchanan's ultimate warning is that "Once a nation has put its foot onto the slippery slope of global free trade, the process is inexorable, the end is inevitable: death of the nation-state."[37] Figuring money—or at least the single-minded pursuit and love of money—as unpatriotic and even subversive of loftier, transcendent virtues of national sovereignty and a Christian American moral character, Buchanan's assault on neoliberalism and conservative libertarianism is a scathing one. Likewise, his figuring of the corporate person not as a maligned citizen-orator, as was the case for Powell, but instead as a kind of foreign alien or global parasite on distinct national cultures and sovereign powers recalls Hobbesian and to some regard Jacksonian anxieties about the proliferation and metastasization of corporate bodies.[38] The answer for Buchanan and his ilk was a phrase that has resurfaced in contemporary U.S. politics: to put America first. The enemy was no longer to be understood as primarily one that was coming from abroad—though indeed they were for many paleocons—but rather the primary enemy was the state itself for authorizing the demise of its now ethnically defined national identity.

This point would become clearer in the writings of Peter Brimelow—former *Forbes* editor, anti-immigration advocate, and founder of the white nationalist website VDare.com.[39] In his 1995 diatribe against U.S. immigration policy, *Alien Nation*, Brimelow argues that continued immigration threatens to alienate the nation from itself and its ethnic heritage. Significantly, for Brimelow, it is the state itself that is to blame, for beginning in 1965 with not only the passage of the Civil Rights Act but also the 1965 Immigration Act, the state authored a supposed "ethnic revolution" in which White Americans were destined to become a minority in (supposedly) their own country.[40] The real threat of liberals and establishment conservatives—often referred to as Conservative, Inc.—is thus not only the sacrificing of American sovereignty to the false god of global capital but also the authorization of a white genocide under the rhetorical auspices of multiculturalism and political correctness.[41]

For Gottfried, this new vision of liberalism has birthed a totalitarian left premised upon a politics of atonement and guilt. This new totalitarianism of the left is fashioned as a logical progression of liberal Protestant theology—a kind of secular religiosity in which sensitivity and political correctness feminizes Christianity through the "fusion of a victim-centered feminism with the Protestant framework of sin and redemption." The end product for Gottfried is thus a "reformulated Protestantism that incorporates politically correct martyrologies" and proselytizes "a theology of victimization."[42] According to Gottfried, this theology stems from the progressive refashioning of democracy throughout the twentieth century under the guise of pluralism. Further, this particular form of democracy possesses a therapeutic ethos that enforces the doctrine of multiculturalism and diagnoses unsavory ideas

150 | Chapter Five

and opinions as a social pathology in need of remedy through "a process of sensitization"—a process that leads inexorably to the decline of Western civilization and values.[43] In other words, multiculturalism is enforced by a policing of language as politically correct or incorrect and shames subjects into submission through discourses of white guilt and atonement.

Taking this argument further, Gottfried proclaims that this "therapeutic tyranny" is the logical culmination of the continued growth of the welfare state premised upon "mass democracy featuring entitlements and an expanding list of 'human rights' to a regime that sets out to reeducate world opinion." For Gottfried and many on the far right, those on the left preaching the gospel of universal tolerance, respect, and care for others use this gospel to mask their malicious intent: a totalitarian yearning to control individual thought and public opinion and to redistribute wealth from deserving members of society to a class of state-sanctioned victims, and utilizing tactics of shame to keep dissenters at bay. As Gottfried succinctly puts it, "This updated state masks the exercise of power as a form of caring, while moving toward the abolition of 'private social relations' in order to sanitize group consciousness."[44] Whether they knew it or not, the conservative establishment—in its support of the welfare-state apparatus—was as much a part of the problem as those on the left. The Republican Party was in need of a reckoning. Conservatism needed to regain its insurgent force and founding principles. This was the promise of Buchanan's cultural conservatism and populist nationalism, utilizing the electoral base of "ethnic Catholics and southern white conservatives" to sacralize political culture and economy on the basis of ethnic and religious identity.[45]

If Gottfried provided the philosophical defense of a far-right populist and postmodern identitarian right in the United States, Samuel Francis was its political architect. Describing and constituting a new base for a radical—indeed, revolutionary—conservatism, Francis rhetorically crafts what he labels Middle American Radicals (MARs). A disaffected swath of voters in the Midwest and rust-belt states, MARs represent a voting bloc that spans traditional left-right divides on economic issues while maintaining a staunch conservative attitude toward social and moral ones. As Francis argues, "The political conflict of the future is likely not on the horizontal plane between left and right but along a vertical axis: between a Middle American substratum, wedded to the integrity of a distinct national and cultural identity, on the one hand, and, on the other, an unassimilated underclass in alliance with an alienated and increasingly cosmopolitan elite."[46] Squeezed from above and from below, MARs are committed to a cultural redefinition of America along a supposedly traditional white Christian national identity committed to strong moral and conservative values and a defense of the sovereign borders of the nation-state.

These cultural anxieties first found their political voice in the form of Wal-Mart voters and the later rise of the Tea Party movement. A group of middle-American, largely white male laborers, those in the Tea Party felt they had been left behind by a global economy, feared their jobs were being taken by continued Mexican immigration and that they were being discriminated against in the workforce through affirmative action policies, lamented that America had lost its Judeo-Christian values, viewed Hollywood as a liberal cesspool, argued that politicians had been bought by unpatriotic global corporate interests, and felt they were being marginalized and demographically replaced. These anxieties were on display in the Tea Party's Obama birther conspiracy, in which it was suggested that Obama was a Kenyan, Muslim socialist committed to usurping American sovereignty. Yet while Darrell Enck-Wanzer avers that this kind of "born again racism" lies at the heart of racial neoliberalism—and this is certainly in part true—to label the Tea Party as *simply* a form of neoliberalism is to miss the ways in which it fashions itself as a radical traditionalist response to the very neoliberal policies of the Washington elites they feel have left them behind.[47]

This kind of radical populist conservatism looks backward in order to look forward. Not simply a reactionary force or a return to market orthodoxy, radical forms of conservatism seek to actively create, through concerted will, a future wherein the structures, cultures, and norms of politics maintain a social hierarchy of white, masculine, patriarchal control, and a geopolitical order of tribalism and ethnic conflict. Reducing the political to a state of nature, it is "kill or be killed"; and under a global welfare regime, it is said that Western culture and white civilization are slowly dying under the pressures of free trade, open borders, and cosmopolitanism.[48] In this context, the radical right finds in the co-optation of identity politics a powerful rhetorical tool to reassert this supposedly natural political order that sets white men atop the social hierarchy. This is the temporality and social vision inherent in Trump's slogan "Make America Great Again."

152 | Chapter Five

Trumpism and Evangelicalism: Fundamentalist Discourse and the Rhetorical Homology

After Trump's victory in the 2016 election, one thing was clear: his ability to rally the evangelical vote was a decisive factor in his campaign's strategic success.[49] The larger question, however, was why evangelicals flocked to—and still defend—a man who has been married three times, has engaged in numerous extramarital affairs, is a notorious playboy, has little grasp of Christian doctrine or theology, and who has bragged of sexual assault behind closed doors. Writing for *Newsweek* in September 2016, Kurt Eichenwald averred that the evangelical community was being duped by a wolf in sheep's clothing. As Eichenwald writes, "By pretending to be a Christian, Trump has fooled those who *want* to believe he is like them. They are being conned, into giving up not only their money but their vote."[50] The end result of this electoral fleecing was not only a Trump presidency but a debasement of Christianity and an evangelical community that cares more about political influence than the Word of God.

In an interview with Renée Montagne on NPR's *Morning Edition* in March 2016, the head of the Faith and Freedom Coalition, Ralph Reed, suggested not that evangelicals were conned but rather that like most voters, "they're driven by issues. And on the social and moral issues—marriage, abortion, religious liberty, support for Israel—Trump not only checks all those boxes . . . but if you go to one of his rallies . . . it's surprising how much of his stump speech speaks to those issues."[51] In this account, Trump won the evangelical vote because he spoke their language. His message simply resonated with them.

This was doubtless true. According to Alex Morris from *Rolling Stone*, Donald Trump met with several conservative Christian leaders in 2016 to discuss messaging and strategy on central issues regarding "religious liberty" in the United States. Present at this meeting were Dallas, Texas, megachurch pastor Robert Jeffress, conservative Christian author and radio host Eric Metaxas, and senior Heritage Foundation fellow Ryan Anderson, among others. Over the course of their conversation these men stressed the significance of the Affordable Care Act's contraception mandate, prayer in school, funding for private Christian schools, transgender bathroom rights, and pro-Israeli foreign policy. As Morris suggests, throughout this meeting these leaders of the Christian right realized they had found a champion in Donald Trump—not because he fashioned himself "a true believer," but rather "as a strongman, the likes of which the religious right had never seen." Trump was no theologian, then, but a warrior who would engage in combat for the evangelical right.[52]

It is this explanation, and others like it, that are more interesting and perhaps closer to the truth than the idea that evangelicals were too ignorant to see Trump for who he really was. Indeed, the fact of the matter appears to be just the opposite. Something about Trump's radical conservative rhetoric resonated with core values and key concerns of many white evangelical Christians in the United States. Part of this resonance is perhaps explained by Trump's vague adherence to the teachings of the so-called prosperity gospel—a rhetorical admixture of Christian theology with self-help and positive-thinking psychology that preaches that God materially and financially blesses those who live in His truth.

Though perhaps the most infamous preacher of the prosperity gospel is the notorious televangelist Joel Osteen, one of the pioneers of this train of thought is Dr. Norman Vincent Peale—a man who also happened to be the officiant of Trump's first wedding, to Ivana. Peale was a foundational figure in the history of the prosperity gospel movement, but also of the insurgent conservative movement against FDR. Writing on Peale's history for the *Daily Beast*, Christopher Lane, professor of English at Northwestern University, explains that Peale would often use his pulpit to politick about pressing contemporary issues. Further, Lane states that "Anticommunism was to Peale and his allies a pro-Christian stance, even if the religious component was not strictly necessary for the critique to hold."[53] Anti-Communism, for Peale, was the spark that would set the nation on fire for the message of Christ—to start a new religious revival premised upon a personal religion of positive thinking and self-help. This kind of vague spiritualism and personal religion (faith in faith, as Lane puts it) is central to Trump's worldview and sense of entitlement.

This fact may help explain, to some degree, the like-mindedness of Trump and the evangelical right. However, it misses more than it reveals. Something deeper is at work here than paying lip service to issues and principles of religious freedom on the one hand and a vague commitment to a personal religion of positive thinking on the other. Indeed, Winslow's

154 | Chapter Five

argument regarding the homological relationships among fundamentalist, anti-environmentalist, pro-gun, and pro-Trump rhetoric is perhaps the most compelling argument to date regarding evangelical support for Trump.

Defining a homology as a set of "symbolic points of formal correspondence operating across disparate texts, media, and experiences," Winslow states that "homologies order experiences; they offer an explanation for how formal parallels appearing across texts may equip an audience with motives appropriate for their social situations; and they instruct audience members in how to respond to the larger social dimensions of their day-to-day existence."[54] The homology that unites disparate audiences, texts, and media regarding Christian fundamentalist and Trumpist (as well as anti-environmentalist and pro-gun) rhetorics is one of catastrophe: a shared sense that destruction and chaos are the surest way to restore social order to a world out of sorts. More specifically, this catastrophic homology consists of five formal points of rhetorical correspondence for members of these disparate communities: a perceived sense of marginalization, a perversion of the prophetic style of rhetorical discourse (what Winslow calls a hermeneutic of systematicity), a militant form of individualism, and a telic temporality that understands moments of crisis and disorder as necessary steps on the path toward redemption.[55]

A form of conservative Protestantism that emerged in the early twentieth century in response to the modernizing forces of industrialism, scientific progress, and urbanization, fundamentalism was birthed in part by Henry P. Crowell's efforts at the helm of the MBI. It was a form of Christianity that adhered to a biblical literalism that maintained that the Bible was the true and clear Word of God. Garnering a significant following, the fundamentalist and literalist position toward scripture became less tenable as U.S. Protestantism gradually embraced a liberal theological stance. As Winslow argues, if fundamentalism was content with staying on the theological margins this would not have been a problem, but a desire to confront modernist thought and engage in the public sphere required a shift from literalism to biblical inerrancy as a theological and hermeneutical strategy. A strain of theology that "synthesiz[es] versions of Catholic exegesis with a particular strand of Puritan Calvinism," inerrancy provided a more rhetorically flexible and politically robust means of responding to the forces of modernism.[56]

This rhetorical flexibility came from an appropriation of scientific vocabularies, methods, and standards of reason, and an incorporation of such secular reason into a seemingly coherent and rational worldview—a systematic hermeneutic for interpreting the world. This hermeneutic maintains that God's truth is accessible to all who care to observe it, rendering each individual a potential prophet of or witness to God's telic design for all human affairs. Capable of transforming a perceived marginalization into the proof of their righteousness, inerrancy provided spaces for rhetorical invention not previously available to the evangelical community. Acceptance of this truth was, as Winslow avers, "the primary constitutive demand, the price of admission into the community"—a demand that insists on maintaining a dogmatic adherence to its precepts even in the face of evidence to the contrary.[57] Such a demand often comes with steep political costs and consequences.

In terms of the political stance of fundamentalism, the adherence to the hermeneutic of inerrancy also entails a belief in a telic temporality. This temporal orientation understands chaos, crisis, and disorder as necessary and even preordained events that are required for the eventual salvation of God's faithful remnant of believers. As Winslow suggests, "Rather than prevent or mediate chaos," fundamentalists often "hasten the progression of history" by bringing about the necessary violence that precedes God's resplendent return. This is to say that "fundamentalism encourages the most pernicious type of political activity: the anticipation of perpetual chaos."[58] The militant individualism, the perversion of prophetic witnessing, the telic understanding of history and temporality, and the perceived marginalization offered by fundamentalist inerrancy find formal resonance in the rhetoric of Donald Trump, suggesting a deeper logical symmetry, a homological structure, that connects Trumpism and fundamentalism. It is here, I argue, that we witness the unique construction of a new economic theology in the rhetorical workings of Trumpism.

Trumpian Anxieties: *Ressentiment*, Personhood, and Economic Theology

The homologous relationship of Trumpism and fundamentalism is eye-opening insofar as it both explains evangelical support for Trump and points to

156 | Chapter Five

the theological nature of Trumpism and its rhetorical inner workings. Yet, I want to suggest that the relationship is not simply one of homological, formal correspondence, but that for many fundamentalists Trumpism is itself infused with their theological worldview. Indeed, I suggest that we should view Trumpism not simply as having points of formal, logical correspondence with fundamentalist theology, but that Trumpism itself stands as *its own fundamentalist theology*—one that offers a heretical fusion of neoliberal and Christian discourses.

To borrow from Adam Kotsko, heresy here implies neither apostasy nor rebellion, but rather signifies a means to "reclaim and purify" a particular faith, often in a conspiratorial manner that decries the "illegitimate authorities that have hijacked and corrupted the gospel."[59] In this way, Trumpism is both a move away from and an extension of neoliberalism, intensifying and purifying its commitment to corporate power and the reconstitution of the state, yet simultaneously wedding the corporation to a virulent xenophobic nationalism while preaching democracy in the service of oligarchic rule.[60] The corporation does not so much supplant the state and bend it to its will, but rather, in this heretical variant, the corporation destroys the state and offers salvation through its destruction. Significantly, while Trump of course did not, could not, and never actually planned on the destruction of the state that was so necessary to his power, his refusal to play by the rules, his promise to drain the swamp, his reckless attitude toward governance, and the hollowing out of several federal departments represented this apocalyptic vision for his followers.

Heretical narratives thus often take on apocalyptic forms regarding destruction, catastrophe, and redemption. Though such logics have always been present to a degree in neoliberalism (we may think here of the Schumpeterian notion of capitalism's creative destruction), here they are intensified to their most extreme.[61] For instance, themes of the threat of Communist atheism and the evils of state bureaucracy proffered during the Cold War are now pushed to their conspiratorial extreme, seeing the state itself—in nearly any form—as the wellspring of all evil at a cosmic scale. This is indicated in many far-right conspiracies regarding malicious Deep State operatives, state-authorized white genocide, and a cabal of global and political elites bent on ushering in a new world order (organized in part, no less, through a child sex-trafficking operation run out of the basement of a pizza parlor). This is neoliberalism pushed to a point of indistinction with paleoconservative traditionalism, a point in which market ideology and pro-corporate sentiment merge with transcendental claims regarding the evils of pluralism and the totalitarian desires of the hedonistic, progressive left. Such a rhetorical move requires a refashioning of the distinction between immanence and transcendence—markets and theology—that simultaneously debases both.

When seen in this light, Trump and his supporters' embrace of conspiracy theories and their blatant disregard for reality are thus part of a broader problem of political and economic theology. Namely, as Kotsko argues, conspiratorial rhetorics are exemplars of "last-ditch efforts to save an order of legitimacy and meaning that is breaking down—a state of affairs that the conspiratorial narrative both denies and unconsciously acknowledges."[62] Evangelical and neoliberal assumptions of a world that is either subject to rational mastery or was created for human enjoyment are rapidly being challenged by the ever-looming possibility of environmental catastrophe and degradation on the one hand and the perceived erasure of white men on the other.[63] Far from a rational self-possessed individual, the person under such conditions becomes marked by an inherent, embodied vulnerability that challenges fundamentalist Christian and neoliberal understandings of the person alike.

When confronted with such an era of existential crisis, apocalyptic narratives about the crumbling of the social order or the decline of the West offer respite and reassurance for those who are incapable of or unwilling to dwell on the uncertainty of life. While perhaps correctly identifying and feeling the inherent precarity of human life—a precarity that white men in particular have not had to grapple with as many women and peoples of color have historically been forced to confront—the explanation offered is not that these insecurities are the logical outcome of an always incomplete and misguided understanding of personhood and markets, but rather that they are the outcome of short-sighted or even evil attempts by the state to curtail white male freedom and autonomy. Indeed, the hardened heretic argues for the inevitability of the present system and will try, or say, or do anything to prove their point—even if it means denying the very reality before them. For instance, I initially wrote this passage just one day following the unprecedented storming of the nation's Capitol building by thousands

158 | Chapter Five

of pro-Trump rioters insistent that the election was fraudulently stolen from him as part of a larger globalist conspiracy. In this way, such concerted efforts belie their self-proclaimed certitude in their very act.

This heretical form mirrors what Joshua Gunn has labeled the perverse rhetorical style. The perverse style, Gunn avers, is premised upon a simultaneous disavowal and demand that is captured in the rhetorical device of *occultatio*, colloquially expressed as: "I am not going to speak about the reality I affirm by denying it, or I know what I am doing is bad, but I am going to do it anyway."[64] The pattern of simultaneous disavowal and demand in the case of Trumpism's heretical neoliberalism is represented in its apocalyptic narrative and its conspiratorial visions, which work in tandem to both affirm the reality of neoliberalism's waning legitimacy and to deny this reality in preaching the inevitability of its purification and rebirth in the hands of Trump the redeemer.

Yet, as Gunn claims, "one denies a reality they affirm because they insist on something," the demand that comes with the disavowal. Typically, this demand is for "at the very least the adoption of a particular point of view, but more grandiloquently for the restoration of a social order that never existed."[65] In the case of Trumpism it seems clear that the demand couched within its disavowal of reality is not that we avoid apocalypse or catastrophe, but that we welcome and even accelerate it so as to return to our former glory and restore a supposedly natural social order that, indeed, never existed.[66] The often-latent function of such a rhetorical style is thus an attempt to (re)gain social control and mastery by defensively imposing their will upon others and reasserting a sovereignty that was assumed to be under siege or lost.[67]

That the discourse of Trumpism would traffic in such a rhetorical style should not be surprising, as many of Trump's followers—including the large majority of fundamentalists and evangelicals—suffer from a perceived sense of marginalization and shame under the auspices of a secular, multicultural society and its insistence on political correctness. As Donovan Schaefer argues, "Trump responded to a situation in which the fever of white shame was boiling over and was able to exploit that for political power through rhetorical techniques that converted shame into a felt sense of dignity."[68] That is to say, that Trump enabled white folks to feel not shame or guilt in their whiteness but rather pride, dignity, and glory in the accomplishments of Western civilization and the racial exclusions upon which it was built.[69]

As Casey Kelly suggests, such a rhetorical style points to a particular "emotional-moral framework in which victimization, resentment, and revenge" are not simply tolerated but rather refashioned as "civic virtues" in and of themselves.[70] Theorizing this emotional-moral framework as one of *ressentiment*—à la Nietzsche and Scheler—Kelly argues that *ressentiment* is a particular form of melancholia, a perpetual longing for an object thought to be lost yet that one never had to begin with. Thus, in the case of Trumpism, the loss of a supposedly natural white, Christian, patriarchal social order in which America had realized its greatness.

However, for Kelly, *ressentiment* is not merely an emotional-moral framework, but also appears representative of the general cultural condition of our age. William Connolly reaches a similar conclusion, yet comes to define *ressentiment* differently, in a manner supplemental rather than oppositional to that of Kelly. Indeed, for Connolly, *ressentiment* is theorized as *existential resentment*, which is to say that it is "resentment of the most fundamental terms of human existence."[71] Following Nietzsche, for Connolly it is Christianity and neoliberal capitalism that represent the great storehouses or wellsprings of such existential resentment as they deny the sensuous irrationality of being and as they proclaim a sense of universal certainty or rationality about the course of history.

Yet, as Wendy Brown notes, *ressentiment* here is the adverse of Nietzsche's accounting, for whereas he argues that Christianity and its secular variants espouse equality and meekness as virtues in order to take down the powerful they wrongly blame for their subordinate position, under our reactionary neoliberal moment *ressentiment* is espoused in reverse: empowered white Christian men and corporate persons claim marginalization and blame others for their dethronement. This is on full display in the claims of federal infringements upon religious freedom in cases such as the aforementioned *Hobby Lobby* or in the *Masterpiece Cakeshop v. Colorado Civil Rights Commission* that supposedly marginalize those in the business and evangelical communities.[72]

This is, in fact, one of the similarities between Christian and (neo) liberal ontologies of the person, and one that finds particular strength in

160 | Chapter Five

the evangelical-capitalist assemblage of the United States. This is because both evangelical Christianity and neoliberal capitalism demand "that the cosmos be treated 'as if' it were for us in the last instance."[73] That is to say, both evangelical Christianity and neoliberal capitalism contain a sense of existential entitlement and revenge, insofar as they seek to transcend the limits of corporeal existence and the finitude of time—one through the promise of everlasting life and the other through the promise of an infinite investment in and perpetual creation of the future.[74] Trumpism, then, is merely an extension and refiguration of this assemblage, one that intensifies its affective culture of *ressentiment* and pushes a thin notion of democracy into outright fascism.

This is perhaps not so surprising, for as Connolly suggests, *ressentiment* is "activated when people who have imbibed traditional monotheisms and/or secular humanist notions of human uniqueness encounter living evidence on behalf of a bumpy, multitiered world of becoming."[75] The anxieties provoked regarding the general hospitableness of the earth by, for instance, the waning of a system of political-economic legitimacy in the face of massive income inequality, rising levels of racial violence, the threat of the eclipsing of the United States as the dominant global superpower, the supposed loss of white masculinity, a looming climate crisis, and a global pandemic thus push people ever more strongly into the clutches of their received orthodoxies rather than seeking other possible answers to the world's problems. Those who challenge the current order of things, then, are demonized, cast as heretics, and are scapegoated as the "others" responsible for the problems in the first place. The rhetoric of Trump the man and of the discourse of Trumpism are representative of this phenomenon.

To be sure, Trump the individual is significant for the larger rhetorical functions of Trumpism, even as it continues without him, for as Kelly notes "in adopting the role of suffering martyr, Trump becomes a transcendent figure whose sacrifice offers his audience an illusory sense of redemption and wholeness."[76] This is to say that the politics of white male victimhood offers Trump as a Christ-like martyr who suffers for the salvation of his base, for the nation, and by proxy evangelical-capitalist visions of the person that he embodies. Through Trump, his followers find wholeness and the promise that evangelical-capitalist understandings of personhood are not only still plausible, but are universal, timeless truths.

Such a secularized martyrology appropriates identity politics and notions of embodied vulnerability in the service of white nationalism and of Trump's own financial self-interest. In the process, Trumpism also appropriates Christianity, hollowing out its theological precepts and abusing its claims of moral authority. Rebuking social norms and the niceties of civic culture, Trumpism's perverse style simultaneously acknowledges and disavows—indeed, disavows in its acknowledgment—the social customs and norms that have traditionally governed political discourse for self-advancement. Further I suggest that in Trumpism's destruction of social norms and the political establishment, such a politics points toward a particular kind of eschatology: one that offers redemption of evangelical-capitalist visions of personhood through the apocalyptic destruction of politics-as-usual and constructing in its place a neofascist corporatocracy.[77]

Whether or not Christians were duped by Trump's hollow commitment to Christianity is beside the point here, as Trump becomes an anointed vehicle of God's divine plan for redeeming the United States from its collective (or rather, collectivist) sins. Clayton Crockett is worth quoting at length on this idea, for as he argues,

> Evangelical Christians know very well that Trump is not a Christian, but many support him nonetheless, because they claim that God put him into power for a reason, and Christians should follow Paul's admonition to the Romans to obey the current political rulers. God is using Trump to accomplish God's ends, which is to return America to its white Christian identity and to repudiate the idolatry of multiculturalism. Here kingship is not about a literal king but about seeing Trump as God's flawed but anointed vehicle for saving the USA from moral relativism and secular humanism. Sovereignty here is not a thing or a person but rather the *essential link* between corporate capitalism, American nationalism, and white southern Christianity in cultural terms.[78]

Trump as sovereign, then, is the rhetorical and material glue that binds together corporation, nation, and white Christian personhood. The person of the corporation, nation, and individual are one and the same, and are to be found in Donald J. Trump. A triune figure, the secular Christology of Trumpism refashions the transcendent/immanent dialectic, seemingly

162 | Chapter Five

collapsing the transcendent into the immanent while simultaneously performing this rhetorical work through overt appeals to Christian morality. In other words, the culture of *ressentiment* both enabled Trump to become president of the United States and also points to the continued significance of Trumpism as a loosely coherent discourse after he leaves office—one that seeks to reclaim and redeem evangelical-capitalist notions of personhood while simultaneously draining Christianity and neoliberal capitalism of their very legitimacy. To illustrate these claims, I turn to the resonance machine itself and observe the writings of Stephen E. Strang. Indeed, Strang and his Charisma publishing house are representative of the rhetorical intersections of far-right conspiracy theories, white Christian nationalism, and anti-statism that herald Donald Trump as a corporate Christ-like figure, chosen by God, to redeem the nation.

Inside the Resonance Machine: Stephen Strang and Trump the Redeemer

Stephen Strang is a seasoned Christian journalist and founder of Charisma Media. Created in 1975, the magazine is now one of the top Christian magazines in terms of influence and circulation. Since its creation, Strang has turned *Charisma* into a media empire, with its website hosting a series of podcasts, publishing short-form essays and opinion pieces, and operating a publishing house through its auspices. Strang's success in the Christian media world found him rated as one of the twenty-five most influential evangelicals in America by *Time* magazine in 2005, and his influence has continued to grow as he has authored several books and hosts his Strang Report podcast.

A leading figure of Pentecostal evangelicalism and charismatic Christianity, Strang rubs shoulders with prominent conservatives, including Dennis Prager, and the forewords to his books are written by a veritable who's who of the evangelical right, including Mike Huckabee, Jerry Falwell Jr., Erica Metaxas, and Lorri Bakker. Strang even conducted a one-on-one interview with Trump for *Charisma* magazine. Proclaiming Trump to be God's chosen instrument to restore America to its (white) Christian past, to expose and dismantle the liberal Deep State apparatus, and to summon a new religious awakening in the United States, Strang's rhetoric exemplifies the economic theology of Trumpism.

In doing so, Strang espouses conspiratorial arguments regarding the coming of a new world order and a one world government. Like Pat Robertson and others before him, Strang thus melds political economy and a zealous white Christian nationalism into conspiratorial musings regarding a struggle for the soul of the nation. In the process, Strang has emerged as a supporter of QAnon and arguments regarding demographic replacement. What emerges is an account of political economy at the level of a cosmic Manicheanism in which the state is pure evil and the market is pure goodness. Indeed, Trump's saving grace is his status as a corporate outsider to the political establishment. He is in the (political) world but not of it, and to be a good American is to follow in his footsteps.

The narrative structure of Strang's evangelical-capitalist accounting of Trumpism crafts Trump as prophetically preordained as he has been anointed by God, like King Cyrus, to restore God's will on Earth. Further, Strang portrays the Democratic Party as a group of demonically possessed socialists, funded by a vast network of billionaire radicals led by George Soros, bent upon eroding national sovereignty, destroying the Judeo-Christian value systems of Western society, stealing the country from its white Christian ethnic core, and implementing a new world order of global bureaucratic rule. In this formula Trump is a redeemer, sent by God, to disrupt this nefarious plan and redeem Western culture. Trump's garish masculinity and rebuke of established norms of diplomacy become his strengths, allowing him to speak out against the totalitarian impulses of political correctness and its restrictions on religious freedoms. Indeed, Strang proclaims that the secular new world order will persecute Christians and destroy the church, replacing God with the worship of state power. Liberalism here is rendered nothing other than a secular religion that culminates in Communist state-sanctioned atheism.

We can observe the catastrophic homology at play in Strang's narrative, employing a perversion of prophetic witnessing, a commitment to a telic temporality, claims to a sense of victimization and felt marginalization in a secular world, and a sense of militant individualism and rabid anti-statism that are bent on fighting off a Chinese Communist threat. Taken holistically, each of these elements supports a systematic hermeneutic for understanding

164 | Chapter Five

contemporary politics—one rooted in a supposed "master blueprint" laid out for God's followers in the pages of the Old Testament. As I undertake my rhetorical criticism of Strang's texts, then, I will use and extend the catastrophic homology as a framework to guide my interpretation and argument about its discursive functions as an economic theology.

Beginning with the presumption of a systematic hermeneutical framework derived from Old Testament teachings, Strang cites the work of his friend and messianic Christian pastor Jonathan Cahn. Cahn's books *The Harbinger, The Paradigm,* and *The Oracle*—published by Strang's Charisma Media—turn to the stories of King Ahab and his wife Jezebel to explain the preordained nature of contemporary affairs. According to scripture, King Ahab and Jezebel were a powerful political couple bent upon destroying God's kingdom and implementing a secular government, building in the city of Jerusalem a shrine to the pagan god Baal. Cahn finds in Ahab and Jezebel a forewarning of Bill and Hillary Clinton, and in Donald Trump a modern Jehu who commands an uprising against the House of Ahab.

Writing on this supposed biblical foreshadowing, Strang states that "just as King Ahab rose to power during a time of deep national apostasy and stood at the front of a culture war that championed anti-biblical values, so did Bill Clinton, who became the first US president to champion abortion and homosexuality and led the nation at a time when the term culture war was just entering public discourse." Further, as Ahab ruled in tandem with his wife Jezebel, a woman who was power hungry and a more staunch opponent of biblical morals than her husband, Strang argues that this dynamic is paralleled in Hillary Clinton. Ultimately, the House of Ahab was overthrown by Jehu, a commander in Ahab's army and an insurrectionary leader who was used by God to fulfill prophecy and return Israel to His teachings. Here, Strang states, "Similarly, Trump is a fighter who promised to reform Washington and 'drain the swamp' as president."[79] The parallels of biblical and modern politics point to an irrefutable truth for Strang, that Trump is a preordained and anointed vehicle—a "divine wrecking ball" as he calls him—sent by God to redeem history and ensure the rule of God's kingdom on Earth.

As further support for this divine reading of political history, Strang turns to modern-day prophetic faith leaders, including Frank Amedia, religious adviser to Trump, and Mark Taylor and Mary Colbert, authors of the book *The Trump Prophecies*, among others. The strategic function of such a rhetorical move is that it simultaneously distances expertise and authority from traditional institutions, supposedly dispersing and democratizing access to knowledge and even to God's divine will, while re-consolidating power and authority in a top-down manner. Take, for instance, Frank Amedia, a supposed marginalized outsider to Washingtonian politics, yet a man who was also a spiritual advisor to Trump and the founder of a global religious ministry network. What such a perversion of authority and expertise accomplishes, Winslow avers, is that it "allows catastrophic rhetors to define the terms of debate," as they concentrate power and seek to reify their marginalized identities vis-à-vis established orders of power by "leverag[ing] the betrayal of sacred documents and founding texts" to make their case.[80] Whether it is the inerrant word of the Bible or the original intent of the Founding Fathers as written into the Constitution, Strang and others in the resonance machine are quick to define the debate as one of a war of religious freedoms; to label their opposition traitors, Communists, and the like; and to portray themselves as righteous-patriotic outsiders in a country that has turned its back on its Judeo-Christian history.

Defining the terms of the debate in this way allows them to make claim to a felt sense of victimization at the behest of modernizing global secular forces. Again, this is where we see the evangelical-capitalist resonance machine proffering (and profiteering from) the culture of *ressentiment* in which nihilism and neoliberalism intermingle. Forced to reckon with the inherent vulnerability of the human estate after forty years of neoliberal liquidation of political and social life, white men blame political correctness, globalism, and so-called cultural Marxism for their political losses.[81] It could not be the case that white Christian capitalism could have been at the root cause of such displacements, so naturally they look elsewhere and find demonic forces at work.

For Strang and many others within the resonance machine, quite literally, the devil is in the details, pulling the strings of a masterfully orchestrated global conspiracy run by a cabal of globalist bogeymen intent on creating a new world order. This cabal is run by a cadre of radical socialist billionaires, including Warren Buffett, Bill Gates, and Jeff Bezos, and orchestrated by George Soros and his Open Society Foundations. Leaving aside the laughable notion that any of these men is a radical socialist (if

166 | Chapter Five

the war cry of socialists is to "eat the rich" then Bezos must be committed to the practice of auto-cannibalism), such conspiratorial musings offer a narrative in which Christian identity, national sovereignty, and free markets are under assault by a shadow party of well-connected elites with tentacles in every corner of public life. Indeed, for Strang globalism is not merely about geography, but rather is "a spiritual issue that is demonic at its core. It means the dismantling of American sovereignty, opening our borders to the world, and abandoning our great heritage of freedom and independence based on the Christian worldview of the Founding Fathers."[82] The battle between nationalists and globalists that seems to mark our contemporary moment is thus not simply one between reactionaries and progressives but is coded in biblical terms as "spiritual warfare"—a battle between God's divine kingdom on one side and "principalities and powers and evil in high places" on the other.[83]

For Strang, the telos of globalism is "to eliminate nation states as we know them, along with their individual laws, customs, currencies, and traditions, in order to empower a global cadre of educated and progressive elites to rule all the people." This is the goal of Soros, the Clintons, Obama, the Deep State apparatus, the liberal court system, the so-called fake news establishment, and their ground troops in Black Bloc Antifa and the Black Lives Matter movement. Supported by a soft-totalitarian discourse of political correctness in which "freedom of speech is virtually impossible, religious freedom is threatened, and everyday conversations can be risky and sometimes even lethal," the enemy seems limitless in its power.[84] This is the Goliath that fundamentalists have created for themselves as evidence of their persecution and that only a muscular white Christian nationalism could defeat.

This muscular white Christian nationalism was given its champion in God's chosen vehicle (a bulldozer no less) of Donald Trump. While the demonic forces of the Democratic left had everything in place to complete their globalist anti-Christian task, with Obama laying the groundwork for a Clinton presidency to complete, God delivered President Trump at the eleventh hour. The seeming impossibility of Trump's 2016 victory is thus fashioned as a way for Christians to "once again stand for righteousness and push back against the demonic agenda we were under so we could change the trajectory in which this nation was headed."[85] And yet it was not simply that God's hand was on Trump and guiding history, but that there was something about Trump himself that was so essential to his abilities to disrupt established orders.

That Trump's redeeming power is somehow inherent to his personhood is clear to Strang, for as he argues, Trump "may be the *only person* I can think of who could have taken such a daily beating and yet continue to win, pushing back against the nefarious agenda and those who seek to destroy him and our country. This is most likely why God chose him to lead us through this very significant time in history as we battle for the very future of our country."[86] Strang's musings on Trump's masculine prowess and the image of Trump as a Christ-like martyr should give us pause. As Kelly notes, it is this marriage of rhetorical tropes of "toughness and vulnerability" that undergirds Trumpist discourse. Such a unification of an inherent or ontological vulnerability with a performance of a powerful masculinity is what Kelly dubs an abject masculinity that "is valorized for its capacity to suffer."[87] Suffering for his supporters much as Christ did on the cross, Trump's masculinity arises from his virtue and nobility, and his virtue and nobility arise from his masculinity. Unlike the effete and emasculated left, Trump is a holy figure willing to stand up to secularizing forces and suffer the harangues of the feminizing and politically correct social justice warriors for the future of the United States.

Claims to Trump's virtue and nobility ought to give us further pause, for while Strang and many of those within the resonance machine claim Trump as a champion of conscience, he seems to lack any form of moral compass whatsoever. This is a claim that Strang takes pains to confront throughout his books. From arguing that the garish and offensive Trump we see on television and Twitter are strategic performances that do match his demeanor behind closed doors, to arguing that Trump is a committed father to his children, that he was the lesser of two evils when compared to Hillary Clinton, to arguing that his agenda is the most pro-Christian in history, Strang offers a clear apologia for Trump's past indiscretions. Yet, the most common defense of Trump—and perhaps most rhetorically powerful for his audience—is through his comparison to Cyrus the Great and the doctrine of common grace.

Quoting theologian and friend R. T. Kendall, Strang describes common grace as a kind of grace given by God to all human beings, not simply

168 | Chapter Five

born-again Christians. Common grace is thus common "not because it is ordinary but because it is given commonly to all people of all ages in all places in the whole world. It is a creation gift not a salvation gift."[88] This notion of common grace explains how God was able to use even the unlikeliest of people to accomplish his divine will. For instance, the great Persian King Cyrus was "a pagan used by God to allow the Jews to return to Jerusalem from the Babylonian captivity." This comparison became particularly salient as Trump officially recognized Jerusalem as Israel's capital, reclaiming the Promised Land, with the comparison of Trump and Cyrus even being made by Netanyahu himself.[89]

Yet all of these defenses amount to nothing more than rhetorical gymnastics that avoid the ultimate question of moral dubiousness in Trump's proclaimed renewed Christian creed. For the ultimate question of morality fades into the background as political expediency in this world becomes the most important task at hand. Faith without works means little, yet works without adherence to one's self-proclaimed tenets of faith drains Christian theology of its very core.

This inherent contradiction is reconciled for Strang and his followers as this nihilistic form of Christian capitalism, as Wendy Brown suggests, renders morals merely contractual. As she writes, "Trump's evangelical base does not care who he is or what he does so long as he delivers on Jerusalem, abortion, the trans ban in the military, prayer in school, and the rights of Christian business and individuals to discriminate." The "most pro-Christian agenda" ever becomes the only matter of concern, as Trump promised to repeal the Johnson Amendment, uphold conscience protections, set aside a $130 billion dollar budget for school choice, promote conservative originalist justices to the U.S. Supreme Court, and end Christian persecution in the Middle East. What is truly at stake is thus the political fate of white male conservative Christians in the public sphere who understand themselves as displaced. As Brown suggests, "Trump's boorishness and rule breaking, far from being at odds with traditional values, consecrates the white male supremacism at their heart, whose waning is a crucial spur to his support."[90] His rebuke of political correctness and verbal displays of white male privilege and supremacy are thus part and parcel of the entitlement and ethos of revenge at the heart of the resonance machine.

The ruthless individualism and anti-statism of Trumpism and fundamentalist rhetoric is laid bare here in its crusade for a return to Christian values against a global state system that seeks to install a Communist world government and supplant Judeo-Christian moral values. For Strang, this, too, marked the significance of Trump's 2020 reelection campaign. In their defeat in 2016, the internal rifts between establishment and progressive members of the Democratic Party saw significant gains in the 2018 midterms and the election of Alexandria Ocasio-Cortez, Ilhan Omar, Ayanna Pressley, and Rashida Tlaib to the U.S. House of Representatives. These "radical leftist" women of color, along with Tulsi Gabbard, now Vice President–Kamala Harris, Julian Castro, Cory Booker, and other politicians of color represent the Democratic establishment and Deep State's goal to remake America in its image. That is to say, the state is at war with its own heritage and seeks to create a future in which white conservative Christian men are minorities in a country they have claimed as their own.[91] This fear of a "New American Majority" and the related conspiratorial musings of demographic replacement are at the crux of the globalist agenda and its erosion of sovereign borders. To stand for Judeo-Christian and Western heritage is thus to denounce collectivism and the state.

Yet, not only is state-sanctioned demographic replacement emblematic of these problems, but so too is the moral cesspool of Hollywood and the growing influence of China in the global economy. Here again, Trump's garishness is a virtue for Strang, as his reckless approach to diplomacy in North Korea, his withdrawal of the United States from the Paris Agreement, and the aforementioned recognition of Jerusalem as Israel's capital, all become much-needed rebukes of moral relativism, political accommodationism, and globalist environmental policy that encumber America's national exceptionalism. So too do Trump's Twitter feuds with Meryl Streep, Rosie O'Donnell, and other Hollywood celebrities signify to his followers his masculine prowess as a dealmaker and doer. As Jerry Falwell Jr. writes in his foreword to Strang's *Trump Aftershock*, his motivation for supporting Trump was The Donald's business acumen. Though Trump certainly was no theologian, his status as "a pragmatic businessman with common sense" was enough for Falwell to know that he "would come down on the right side of issues."[92] Likewise, his self-styled brand as the consummate dealmaker

170 | Chapter Five

would ensure that he could get things done and make good on his promises. Coupled with his pro-Christian agenda, Trump becomes a metaphorical and literal godsend for the fundamentalist conservative Christian community.

Despite all of Strang's professed faith in his modern-day prophets and the inerrancy of God's master plan for a second Trump term in 2020, there was, as with all matters of faith, some professed doubt. In his *God, Trump, and the 2020 Election*, Strang lists several possible reasons that Trump could lose the election, including overconfidence, social media censorship, voter fraud, evangelical Never Trumpers, and economic collapse, among others.[93] Of course, Trump supporters would cite nearly all of these reasons to explain Trump's loss in 2020—chiefly voter fraud, social media censorship, and economic collapse at the behest of a global pandemic. The crises of economic collapse and global health brought on by the COVID-19 pandemic, however, do not break Strang's faith in the providential, telic unfolding of God's will. Rather, fitting with Winslow's keen insight, "telic messaging encourages an orientation toward time that aligns the painful stages of crises with catastrophe's ultimate renewal and restoration."[94] Even if Trump were to lose, as he did, this too could not disprove the idea that God had chosen Trump to redeem the church, the nation, and the world, but rather would be proof that we had collectively turned our backs on God and accepted the alluring appeals of Satan's demonic forces. Redemption will ultimately still come, but through God's righteous vengeance rather than Trump's.

Indeed, something as catastrophic at a global level as the COVID-19 pandemic is seen by Strang as part of God's providential plan for a national reckoning and spiritual awakening with Trump at the helm. For God's church, the pandemic is thus a kind of blessing in disguise—through our suffering comes redemption. Turning again to his prophetic colleagues, Strang crafts the pandemic as a "modern-day Passover" that provides a real opportunity for a spiritual rebirth of the nation.[95] Despite the promise of renewal, the pandemic is accompanied by the pitfalls of further spiritual decline as the state refuses to recognize religious services as essential services during the pandemic, while abortion clinics such as Planned Parenthood were able to remain open. That Planned Parenthood and other centers offer a panoply of other important healthcare services to already vulnerable groups of women, or that abortion itself may be medically necessary to protect the life of the mother are apparently irrelevant here. So, too, is the fact that the right's agenda to defund Planned Parenthood has been, to this point, largely successful, negating claims to marginalization by a radical feminist agenda. Further still, the idea that one's conscience is not violated by stating that you should not gather to worship in ways that threaten public safety is entirely lost. Instead, what becomes clear is that Strang's key concern is less with religious liberty as such and more so with the mobilization of "religious liberty and free speech to permit the (re)Christianization of the public sphere."[96] Such rhetoric turns the democratizing potential of the First Amendment against itself in the buttressing of white male Christian superiority.

Yet, as such, the pandemic and the election of 2020 are thus crafted as a divine mandate "to once again stand for righteousness and push back against the demonic agenda we were under so we could change the trajectory in which this nation was headed" toward that of an anti-God "death culture" that sacrificed the unborn to the whims of radical feminism. The stakes of the 2020 election during the midst of the pandemic could not be higher. The choice could not be simpler. You either vote for God, Trump, and spiritual and economic renewal, or you vote for Joe Biden's radical Democratic machine, the demonic forces of a global new world order, and the ultimate realization of the "beast system" they were preparing for the world. To fail to do so would be to fail God's plan for the United States, the outcome of which would be a world in which individual rights suffer and in which "Christians will be target number one."[97] Either way, however, the telic orientation is confirmed as both paths fulfill "the desire to advance history forward toward a definitive end."[98] Regardless of which way we choose, we stand at the end of days. We may receive collective redemption either through Trump's mighty vengeance or through God's ultimate sovereign rule.

The anti-democratic and existentially dangerous implications of such an apocalyptic worldview should be clear. These implications are given voice by Ed Black in his observation of the rhetoric of the John Birch Society, when he argues that it evinces a suicidal fatalism that aligns with an eschatological view of history.[99] Winslow, too, points to the fatalism of such a politics, stating that for audiences and rhetors enmeshed within a catastrophic worldview and its telic understanding of history, any effort to address economic, religious, environmental, or political crises "smacks of futility and weakness."[100] Better to let the world burn and accelerate its

Chapter Five

demise, for only on its ashes can true order be restored. A better slogan for the existential resentment of our political culture can hardly be crafted.

Conclusion

In this chapter I have observed the rhetorical intersections of conservatism, corporate personhood, and economic theology in the discourse of Trumpism. Central to its rhetorical and persuasive work is a felt sense of marginalization and a culture of *ressentiment* as white masculine notions of personhood are being eclipsed and displaced. Cases such as *Hobby Lobby v. Burwell* and *Masterpiece Cakeshop v. Colorado Civil Rights Commission* illustrate this anti-Christian agenda, which is said to have a chilling effect on evangelical and corporate speech. The two targets of the secular state and the subjects of political marginalization in our late neoliberal moment are thus not women, peoples of color, or members of the LGBTQ community, but rather "businesses and moral-religious traditionalists" who are being forced to act against their conscience.[101]

Arguments for business and religious persecution on the right, of course, are not new. Nor is there anything new about arguments regarding liberalism as a secular religion, a left-leaning bias in the mainstream press, university campuses as hotspots of radicalization, the Judeo-Christian exceptionalism of the West, or the inherent evils of statism. These arguments were incubated in the days of the New Right, came of age in Paul Weyrich and Jerry Falwell's Moral Majority, and have only now reached full maturation. This maturation process occurred throughout the years of Reagan, the traditionalist and paleoconservative refashioning of the right in the United States, and the white backlash to the nation's first Black president, all of which were abetted by the rise of what Connolly calls the evangelical-capitalist resonance machine. Trump was the apotheosis of these crucial shifts, and he paints a picture of the world—and offers an alternative to it—that resonates with white evangelical men and women across the heartland of the nation. This is a "world of 'fake news' all the way down, one where conservative Christianity, property ownership, and wealth are empowered as freedoms against social and political democracy."[102]

Turning to Winslow's notion of the catastrophic homology to help explain the formal resonances of fundamentalism and Trumpism, I suggest that it is not simply the case that they share formal points of correspondence with one another, but rather that for many fundamentalist evangelicals the two become nearly indistinguishable from each other. Trumpism is thus itself a kind of economic theology that fashions Trump as a Christ-like redeemer for the marginalized moral-traditionalist and business communities—that faithful remnant of the Judeo-Christian heritage of the United States. This was evidenced by turning to the rhetoric of Stephen Strang, a key piece of the contemporary evangelical-capitalist resonance machine. For Strang, and indeed many others, Trump is foreshadowed in the Old Testament as a preordained instrument of God to summon a spiritual awakening and to combat a demonic globalist agenda that would usurp U.S. sovereignty and enshrine a global Communist state. The embodiment of the white male Christian and corporate person, Trump stands as the final bulwark of the West at the end of history, prophesied to win a second term and save this great nation.

Yet, as we know, Trump would lose the 2020 election. He would incite insurrection against the very system he led. Thousands of radical pro-Trumpers would storm the Capitol building in protest of a Deep State plot, and honestly, for them, how could it be otherwise? If Trump was an earthly manifestation of God's will, a Trump defeat is not simply a defeat for the party or for the nation, but a defeat of a benevolent, omnipotent, and omniscient God. This is the power of the resonance machine's culture of *ressentiment*—it rebounds upon itself and gains strength in its own futility to bend the world to its will. Anything that might stand as evidence of its misguided assumptions or foundations is cast as evidence of its righteousness. In such a Manichean worldview there is to be no compromise. If the rest of the world doesn't conform, damn them all to hell (quite literally). There is no alternative to our present evangelical-neoliberal moment—or so they might tell us. As I move to my conclusion, I want to offer sketches of what an alternative to our present culture of *ressentiment* might look like, beginning with a reformulation of personhood from that of rational mastery and self-ownership to a secularization of the idea of personhood as divine gift.

Conclusion

At present, it seems the cosmic and existential levels of economic theology have come to the surface of our daily politics. As they do so, the folly of our overly economistic view of the person becomes clearer: A culture of existential resentment for this world has become dominant. Apocalyptic rhetorics abound. Environmental degradation continues at rapid speed in the name of shareholder profits. Christianity, which, at its core, preaches that we are all crafted in God's image, is debased in service of a vulgar ethno-nationalism. Embodied vulnerability and precarity, for White men in particular, are to be fended off at all costs even as it means rendering racial, gendered, and sexed others as collateral damage to continued neoliberal policies and systems of state violence.[1] Surely a better world, built upon a more humane humanism and a more complete understanding of personhood, is possible. But how to combat the incipient nihilism of our culture of *ressentiment*?

To answer this question, I want to pose another: what if we were to take embodied vulnerability not as a fact of existential resentment, but rather as a basis for rethinking personhood beyond and outside of possessive individualism? If Trumpism and the culture of *ressentiment* that spawned it are in many ways a fascist response to the futility of (neo)liberalism and its attempt at rational mastery, then might the inherent fragility and vulnerability of life be where we must begin? Here we can perhaps see the one kernel of truth at the heart of traditionalist conservatism: the destructive and limiting nature of liberal conceptions of an overly economistic human nature. Their alternative illiberal vision of this nature, of course, is even more politically harmful in its racial essentialism and justification of organic social hierarchies. What is thus required, I argue, is an emancipatory post-liberal democracy that uses liberalism's language against itself to refashion personhood outside of the grammars of rational self-ownership. This task is particularly significant after four years of Donald Trump and the election of Joe Biden on his promise of a return to normalcy and decency. If this return to normalcy means a return to neoliberal capitalism as we have known it, then we are merely treating the symptoms rather than the cause of our contemporary problems.

What is required is nothing short of what Martin Luther King Jr. in his Riverside Church address deemed a revolution of values from a thing-oriented culture to a person-oriented one. Importantly, I do not take this call as a naive reclamation of an ontologically secure category of personhood; rather, I understand it as a call to recognize personhood as *the* rhetorical site of politics. As King so eloquently proclaimed, such a revolution of values would offer a humane, democratic alternative that combats racism, materialism, and militarism, and argues for the value and dignity of human life.[2] This is the legacy in which the current Black Lives Matter movement dwells, for as Armond Towns has argued, the movement has opened rhetorical space to question the taken-for-granted assumptions of the distinctions between persons and things as well as questions of the value of non-normative bodies.[3] Such a revolution of values demands that we cultivate what Jeremy Engels calls "the arts of gratitude" rather than resentment and come to understand the gift of life.[4] As I conclude, then, I attempt to outline what such an alternative might look like, refashioning and secularizing conceptions of personhood as gift to insist on the inherent value of human life.

To do so we must begin at an existential level, for neoliberalism is as much a political cosmology—a system of economic and theological legitimacy—as it is a political system. As Ned O'Gorman eloquently states, the market under neoliberalism is "a cosmos, a cyclical order of creative destruction that transcends the contingencies of politics, biology, history, and locality. It requires, in stoic fashion, an indifference to the particulars, reserving respect only for the universals."[5] Such a political-economic cosmology thus requires an alternative—one that neither creates an unbridgeable chasm between the transcendent and immanent planes of existence nor collapses one into the other, but rather allows the dynamic interplay of the two to suggest possible political and rhetorical alternatives to neoliberalism and its corporate vision of the person. For even as neoliberalism found its very rationale in the supposed inviolability of the human person before the specters of Communism and the social welfare state, its vision of personhood—as I have argued throughout this book—is inherently limited and ontologically suspect as it only recognizes full personhood as a legal and cultural attribute to be found in the rational market activity of almost exclusively white men.[6] This culture, rather than enshrining the dignity of the person, has in fact subjected the majority of the population to social exclusion and degradation. We must, then, rethink the person beyond (neo) liberalism, offering a new economic theology in its place. This alternative, I suggest, demands a refashioning and secularization of the notion of life as gift.

To be clear, this position does not simply argue that as the market has replaced God and the corporation has become a model for human personhood that we must return to Christian theology in a kind of national reckoning for our collective sins. Nor am I arguing for a simple return to older political theologies of sovereign power as a way of reining in markets and corporate power.[7] Rather, I understand neoliberalism as a governing rationality that directs state action in favor of the market but is not coextensive with the state as such.[8] Indeed, to again paraphrase Mitchell Dean as I did in my introduction, to cut off the king's head—to do away with sovereign power— still leaves us with his empty throne (immanent economic governance) to contend with and is this not what neoliberalism itself wishes? Thus, I seek to include the state as a site of political potential to combat neoliberal governance without being statist in my politics, for to give up the state gives up too much ground to market forces.[9] Likewise, I seek to recuperate humanism and personhood, for to abandon these is also to give up too much

178 | Conclusion

ground to the antihumanism of corporate capitalism and financialization.[10] In the words of Hans Joas, then:

> Our ability to formulate the idea of life as a gift under contemporary conditions in such a way that it also makes sense to the friends of "reason-based argument" is central to achieving a contemporary understanding of human dignity; it is equally important to distinguishing between a universalist sacralization of the person, of all persons, and the self-sacralization of the private individual—in other words, of each person in isolation.[11]

To begin to outline what such a project might look like, I take inspiration from several authors, chief among them William Connolly. Specifically, I take his vision of a nontheistic reverence for life as a starting point for articulating a secular project of human worth and personhood outside of neoliberal logics. Such a position "redraws the line between secularism and religion by refusing either to eliminate reverence or to bind the element of reverence to theism." In this sense, a position of nontheistic reverence demands a different political cosmology and instills a new spiritual ethos into democratic politics. This new cosmology ties reverence not to any traditional notions of God, but rather to a universe that in its infinite expansiveness and general hostility toward human life nevertheless has made possible a world for us to occupy and inhabit. Understanding our position as humans in this way avoids the "ontological narcissism" of traditional liberal or communitarian attempts at rational mastery on the one hand and collective attunement on the other, and instead advocates a tragic frame that recognizes the fragility of the human estate. Relatedly, this cosmology demands a spiritual ethos of deep pluralism—a pluralism that advocates for "agonistic care for difference from the abundance of life that exceeds any particular identity."[12] Difference must be respected then at an ontological level, pushing against static notions of being to recognize the productive, vital force of difference in democratic life.

Beginning with such a renewed political cosmology also demands that we recuperate, even as we move beyond, traditional conceptions of the human. Indeed, noting the unstable position of the human within an unfolding cosmos shatters the liberal notion of a rational, contained, possessive, semi-sovereign individual. The human instead here becomes radically embodied, even as it is rendered vulnerable and porous not only to other individuals but to nonhuman agents and forces that constitute the material world around us.[13] An emphasis on embodied vulnerability as the bedrock of a renewed humanism holds critical insights for rethinking rights and property in a way that challenges corporate personhood and rights.

As Anna Grear forcefully argues, refashioning law, politics, and human rights on the basis of embodied vulnerability points toward the possibility of "a radical politics of interrelationality and compassion" and pushes corporations outside the realm of legal humanity. Likewise, such a position has significant implications for the theory and practice of democratic life, including a rethinking of human subjectivity, a means of reconceptualizing property rights and the limits of corporate privatization, imagining more robust notions of legal equality, and limiting corporate claims to human and constitutional rights.[14]

Flowing from these important contributions, I would suggest, is an inherent argument for the value and dignity of all human life as a collective and not simply as isolated market actors. Indeed, as Grear states, "the body, in its materiality and vulnerability, provides the ultimate figuration of what is most universal and, in the same symbolic moment, most particular to each of us."[15] To think personhood in this way is to call attention to its historical exclusions and to rethink the concept on the basis of these exclusions. This is also the task of critical race theory, Black feminist theory, and decolonial theory that trouble the overly determined nature of Western man.[16] Though mine is not a decolonial project as I do not begin with non-Western discourses or practices, there are, I argue—following Gayatri Spivak—latent traditions within Western thought that may help in this task of a more global, egalitarian picture of human personhood.[17] This brings me back to the notion of personhood as gift, and back to the works of Marcel Mauss.

In her foreword to Mauss's book *The Gift*, Mary Douglas's essay "No Free Gifts" outlines that first and foremost the gift, for Mauss, "is a theory of human solidarity" that stands in contrast to that of capitalist relations of production and consumption.[18] Though Mauss's evolutionary accounting of the history of modern contract from the archaic culture of the gift is orientalizing and problematic both in its heralding of Western societies and

180 | Conclusion

its Comtean positivism, there are important insights in Mauss that must be rescued and fully reckoned with. For as he suggests, "A considerable part of our morality and our lives themselves are still permeated with this same atmosphere of the gift, where obligation and liberty intermingle."[19] In other words, the economic morality of the gift offers a different basis of personhood and society from that of liberal understandings of the social contract—and its attendant notion of the self-possessed individual—yet one that is not entirely alien to its proclaimed desires for equality and liberty. That is to say that it offers a rhetorical means by which we might utilize liberal grammars against themselves and recognize other ways of being in common with one another.

Such a project has been taken up by Jacques Derrida, as the idea of the gift occupies a central and complex position in his ontological metaphysics. Indeed, the gift for Derrida is bound together with concepts of being, time, and event, and represents the impossibility of ethical purity and the ineluctability of metaphysical violence that occur in political and social life. The gift is an impossibility for Derrida as it can only be said to truly emerge in the disruption of the economic circle of the selfsame, yet this gap "is not present anywhere; it resembles an empty word or transcendental illusion."[20] This is to say that for Derrida a true gift is an ontological impossibility, as for a gift to truly be a gift it must not be recognized as such by the donor or the donee, and it must, as such, be delivered without phenomenological intention or instrumental purpose.

And yet, a gift cannot be given from one person to another without intentionality. As Derrida writes, for a gift to exist, "There must be chance, encounter, the involuntary, even unconsciousness or disorder, and there must be intentional freedom, and these two conditions must—miraculously, graciously—agree with each other."[21] An insurmountable ontological impossibility to be sure. Further, Derrida suggests that as soon as I recognize that what I am doing is giving a gift, or the other party recognizes the act as such, the economic circle of debt and exchange is reinscribed—as one of the primary conditions of the gift is that it must be reciprocated. Hence a set of difficult questions arises: can a gift be given freely? Can we be obligated to give a gift, or does obligation imply that it is not a gift at all but rather repayment of a debt? And, finally, might a gift also be a debt or—worse still—a curse, at times, for those who receive them?

Thus, while Mauss saw potential for a more just and moral basis for political economy in the notion of the gift, Derrida notes the impurity of its ethical possibilities and the problems they pose. In the conclusion of his treatise on the gift, for instance, Mauss suggests a kind of golden mean or perfect balance between practices of gift economies and those of contractual, political economy as a way to ensure distributive justice in modern society. Derrida, however, suggests that to institutionalize the logic of the gift into the machinery of political economy returns us to the economic circle rather than disrupts it. As he explains, "Laws, therefore, transform the gift or rather the offering into (distributive) justice, which is economic in the strict sense or the symbolic sense; they transform the alms into exchangist, even contractual circulation."[22] Here we simply return to the scene of metaphysical violence rather than subvert it.

Derrida's challenges to Mauss and his account of the gift are significant, yet raise problems of their own. Namely, if there is no escape from the metaphysical violence of gift and/or economy, what is to be done? Further, does it matter if distributive justice reinscribes the economic circle if, to paraphrase Thomas Paine, we cannot count on nameless or faceless benefactors to dole out charity to ensure equality or justice—particularly when billionaires would rather spend their money on private trips to space than use their fortunes to address the vast social problems we're facing on this planet? When faced with these dilemmas, might not it be best to, as Derrida seems to suggest early in *Given Time*, "give economy its chance"?[23] For ultimately, Derrida's account seemingly replaces politics with ethics, and representation with ontology and metaphysics, leading to significant political impasses.

This is not to say that politics and ethics are not inherently intertwined with one another, or that representation and ontology are not intertwined as well—indeed, I have spent significant portions of this book arguing that they are—but rather that to collapse the distinctions between them (much as with the polarity of the immanent and transcendent) is to escape the difficult rhetorical work of democratic life rather than to face them head-on. As Milbank suggests, Derrida "does not consider that the circle of the *agora* within the wider circle of the *polis* (both evolved from a space marked out by *the circulation of the gift*) might be a sight for judgement, for appropriate partitioning, which can never be simply according to what

182 | Conclusion

appears, but requires mediation by the subjectivity of *phronesis*. A site *for* judgement, not a site *of* an always immanent contractual formalism."[24] In other words, as Mari Lee Mifsud argues, gift culture excavates the possibility for an alternative system of ethics—premised upon friendship, hospitality, and solidarity—that is created in the contact zones between persuasion and invitation, judgment and creation, *techne* and *poiesis*, contract and gift.[25]

Likewise, Derrida's seeming anti-naturalism also renders meaningful political action difficult. As he writes towards the conclusion of *Given Time*, "The gift, if there is any, must go against nature or without nature," and thus, that "There is no nature, only effects of nature: denaturation or naturalization."[26] But what of the very materiality of nature and of the world itself? What if we were to take nature in this sense as the very condition of human life and thus as the very condition of a secular notion of personhood as gift? Indeed, the earth itself is what binds us together in all our manifold differences, for as Jeremy Engels suggests, "At a most basic level, what we share is the sunset."[27] This possibility is briefly explored by Matthias Fritsch, who argues that the "problematic nature of the Rousseauist (or Hobbesian, or Lockean) naturalism, and the many attempts to derive the social contract from the state of nature, should not lead us to overlook the role of the 'natural' in gifts." Indeed, for Fritsch, "The spirit of life or of nature would be seen as the ultimate foundation of social relations. The obligation to return the gift would then also be an obligation to return to nature as the single source of society and normativity."[28] Taking to heart these insights, a reimagining and secularization of personhood as gift, as indicated above, finds human persons indebted not to a divine creator God for their being, but rather to nature and the earth itself for the seeming miracle of human life in a universe so hostile to its very existence. The circle of economic exchange, of credits and debts, may not be purely disrupted as Derrida would desire, but the debt of the gift of personhood is to be paid back to Earth itself—and to other living species and future generations—to ensure that we don't destroy the very conditions of life in the pursuit of rational mastery, self-possession, and corporate profits.

Here, I take Connolly's arguments for immanent naturalism and process philosophy to be a starting point for such a refiguration of Derrida. For Connolly, immanent naturalism "claims that the lawlike image of science lives off the remains of a providential theology that it purports to have left behind," and presumes instead that "if the world is not designed by a god it is apt to be more unruly in its mode of becoming or evolution than can be captured entirely by any set of lawlike statements."[29] From this perspective, life is volatile, surprising, at times chaotic and frightening, and replete with mystery. In terms of its ethical sensibilities, it does not demand a disdain or abuse of this world, as in the case of the evangelical-neoliberal machine, but rather "secretes an ethic of cultivation anchored in care for this world rather than a command authorized by a god, a transcendental subject, or a fictive contract between agents."[30] It demands, then, not a flight from this world or existential grudges regarding the limits of humanity, but rather a strong commitment and attachment to *this* world, finding in its precarity and our own vulnerability sources for political struggle rather than nihilistic flights from politics.

Part of what this necessitates, then, is a refiguration of the dynamic interplay of the transcendent and immanent polarities of power. Writing on this necessity, Connolly suggests "we may need to recraft the long debate between secular, linear, and deterministic images of the world on the one hand and divinely touched, voluntarist, providential, and/or punitive images on the other."[31] This is what Connolly means by a nontheistic position of reverence. In a world in constant becoming, we must be willing and able to accept mystery and chance, to live with and find comfort in uncertainty, and find the beauty of life in these moments. This entails recognizing our very personhood, in all of its limits and vulnerabilities, as a gift rather than a site of existential resentment.

Allow me to provide an example of how this different cosmology might apply to our political world. Rather than reading the COVID-19 pandemic as a preordained and necessary catastrophe for accomplishing God's will for a spiritual awakening, or as a destructive moment ripe for creative entrepreneurial investment, this perspective sees in the pandemic the fatalist presumptions of such teleological evangelical claims as well as the providential claims of creative destruction proffered by neoliberal acolytes. At the same time, the pandemic lays bare the shortcomings of liberal-economic visions of a rational self-possessed personhood. Life is precarious. The earth is not solely ours. Markets are not perfectly rational.

Our physical, ecological, economic, and climatic systems are not subject to our will or limited reason. Our established orders are fragile. To pretend otherwise is ignorant at best and downright deadly at worst.

Rather than continue to invest in an economy premised upon ruthless competition, a position of nontheistic reverence demands an ethos of deep pluralism and enables a collective vision of politics premised upon our embodied vulnerabilities. It does so as it recognizes the need for a wide-ranging coalitional movement of many diverse creeds, faiths, class positions; racial, ethnic, and gender identities; sexual preferences; and political ideologies that, despite their differences and disagreements, share a deep "respect for the earth and care for the future" as crucial to a world premised upon the inherent value of the human person.[32] Importantly, this is not to advocate for an exclusive, limited humanism. It entails rethinking the very concept of humanism and its attendant notion of the person and calls our attention to our ethical responsibilities and debts to the earth, to future generations, and to other species we share this world with. Embodied vulnerability poses inherent possibilities for animal rights and environmental protection, too, yet I maintain that the dehumanizing elements of neoliberalism demand a renewed commitment to human personhood and rights in our current political moment.[33]

Likewise, personhood as gift and its assumed fact of embodied vulnerability provides a way of rethinking property and rights in such ways as to redirect corporate powers, preserving their crucial functions for producing and distributing necessary goods and services required of democracy at a large scale. For example, Grear suggests reimagining property through the idea of common property, arguing that "A re-emphasis on common property . . . could provide an important conceptual mechanism for the curtailment of over-extended exclusory claims by asserting, in effect, the limits of property in the face of other important interests." Common property in this formulation does not forgo the possibility for or even desirability of some forms of private property or the "boundary function of property," but rather establishes limits to what should be commoditized and subjected to private ownership.[34] The concept of property thus becomes closer to notions of propriety, and rights—including rights to property—are fashioned not as natural possessions of economic agents but as what is due to an individual in the calculus of distributive justice in a world of embodied vulnerability.[35]

Also writing on this possibility of refashioning human rights, Ben Golder interrogates Foucault's return to rights discourse in his later works, seeing in this move a "calculated turning of humanism against itself in the name of its exclusions and remainders," using the language of humanism to imagine "a human possibility *contra* the proprieties of orthodox humanism." Rights discourse here becomes a set of "tactical instruments in political struggle," ones that are "imminent and not exterior to" actually existing political relations.[36] By excavating and reclaiming the latent potential of the rhetoric of rights, we might understand differently the relationships between the individual human person and sovereign power in a way that does not delimit but opens spaces of possibility and agency to thinking the person otherwise.

With respect to the corporation, one such possibility is offered by David Ciepley, who argues that we must maintain an analytical and practical distinction between the contractual personhood and rights of corporations granted through statute on the one hand and the constitutional personhood and rights of corporeal persons on the other.[37] Such a distinction corresponds well with Grear's insights regarding embodied vulnerability as the basis for human rights claims, and recognizes the complexity of the corporate form as simultaneously both a discrete legal entity and a creation of the state. It also allows for and grants corporate rights to enter into contracts, to own property, and to sue and be sued in court, for example, while denying them claims to natural rights that would grant them constitutional protections.[38] This might be a first step toward recrafting the corporation within the frame of an affirmative biopolitics.[39]

Such a rethinking of rights also entails a rethinking of responsibilities and obligations that move beyond and depart from a society conceived of as a system of individual market relationships. Such a recasting of responsibility necessitates moving beyond responsibility as simply a casting of blame or liability on individual agents for particular actions or outcomes, and should offer a conception of responsibility as a collective phenomenon that calls into question larger structures, discourses, and collections of persons, implicating the very forces that help shape the terrain in which individuals are formed and act.

One such model is offered by Iris Marion Young in her essay "Responsibility and Global Justice."[40] Drawing from and extending Hannah Arendt's work on collective responsibility after the atrocities of Nazi Germany,

186 | Conclusion

Young articulates a "social connection model" of responsibility that takes into account the often-complex processes that shape social structures in a globalized political economy."[41] Taking into account the structures of social life enables rights claims against structural injustices and demands for collective modes of responsibility. Using anti-sweatshop movements as an example, Young illustrates how responsibility as a legal assignation of blame and redress does not apply in this instance, as injustice here is "a consequence of many individuals and institutions acting in pursuit of their particular goals and interests, within given institutional rules and accepted norms."[42] Implicating a diffuse network of individual and institutional actors, responsibility for justice here is a political and rhetorical act that demands that we act collectively to create a more equitable social order and to preserve and protect the earth.

Elaborating this idea further, Serena Parekh extends Young's work to the context of gender violence and inequality to make claims for a collective and political responsibility for state actors to ameliorate the conditions of gender-based oppression. Adopting such a perspective towards responsibility, as she argues, simultaneously demands a "radical reorientation in how states view their human rights violations," and demands that states move beyond cataloging various rights abuses to actively reconfiguring conditions so that similar abuses will not happen in the future.[43] This orientation would allow for state action to alter political and economic structures that enable a culture of human rights violations and a corporate culture that constrains more humane modes of action in favor of profiteering and exploitation.

When applied to corporations, such a perspective allows us to avoid some of the metaphysical difficulties of identifying an individual agent or coherent theory of the corporation's moral personhood, recognizing instead the ways in which corporate actions are the product of human action and the dense network of social relations that provide them their legal and institutional structures. In this sense, as Dennis Weiser suggests, corporations, like all institutions, "always involve collective responsibility" and demand different ways of conceiving of accountability and the obligations of corporations toward others in a democratic society.[44] Corporations, like state actors, should not be held to standards of individual blame, but should instead be subject to a model of political responsibility that requires efforts to change the cultures and structures within which they operate, and to instill our

Conclusion | **187**

political economy with a new ethos of agonistic respect for difference. This of course requires that corporeal persons and publics engage in collective modes of action and resistance that demand such measures, challenging neoliberal rationality and its epistemology of a corporate society.[45]

As such, this rethinking of rights and responsibility entails a need to rethink the nature of our political obligations. Rather than perceiving them as emerging from the market-based arrangements of a contractual obligation engaged in by atomistic, sovereign, and self-possessing individuals, we might instead understand obligation as coming from our inherent relational interdependency. Young's account of responsibility leads her naturally to a similar conclusion: she writes that "obligations of justice arise between persons by virtue of the social processes that connect them." In this sense, obligations are deeply embedded within dense webs of social relationships and communal belonging. Shaped by the structures, institutions, and processes of civil society, political obligations are in part prescribed by our particular social roles and positionalities within these structures. Demanding that we seek to take responsibility for the social welfare, our obligations must not only be to ourselves, as neoliberalism might ask us to believe, but to adopt a "forward-looking" perspective that seeks to create a more equitable order from existing circumstances.[46]

In part, then, I conclude with a call to recognize our political agency and the power of rhetoric to (re)shape attitudes, opinions, and even the political worlds in which we live. If the case studies in the book demonstrate anything, it is that concerted human effort and rhetorical action cannot only move hearts and minds, but can fundamentally shape and reshape the terra firma of political action. Indeed, freedom is not something one possesses but is rather a practice we engage in, a perspective one takes toward existing relations of power and ways of governing. While agency is unevenly allocated across the field of political action, we must nevertheless recognize, as Karlyn Kohrs Campbell has argued, that agency is a process both promiscuous and protean, allowing for moments of invention, artistic action, and the possibility of social change even within a scene of radical constraint.[47] As Connolly suggests, "*If* we are minor participants in a larger cosmos composed of multiple, interacting force fields that periodically morph, *part* of our experience of attachment to the world may be tied to the experience of vitality and to these small and large moments of real creativity to which it is connected."[48] The vitality of creative rhetorical action is thus part of what makes us most human and part of what shapes our attachment to *this* world. We should not neglect our obligation to and the possibilities for engagement and political action.

Recovering, recognizing, and revitalizing these possibilities for rhetorical action is at once a matter of rational judgment and of affective attunement—of political action and poetic self-fashioning that the ethics of the gift might point us to.[49] Turning to contemporary social movements such as Black Lives Matter, Occupy, #MeToo, and others, Catherine Chaput argues that the significance of these movements lies not only, or even primarily, in their policy orientation but in their capacities to summon different forms of subjectivity.[50] Indeed, as I read them, each movement pushes against the dehumanization that lies at the core of (neo)liberal understandings of personhood, offering new forms of human relationality beyond ownership and contract.[51]

That these movements are already engaging in this work suggests that the means for rhetorical resistance are immanent to the political field. It means recognizing the extant possibilities for vital, creative action from within the dominant grammars of political life. As Barbara Cruikshank argues, this means practicing resistance not in the "hope of a freedom to come," but in the realization that "here and now . . . we are freer than we feel."[52] Indeed, we will not be saved from above. It is our responsibility to recognize our inherent interrelatedness and to pay back the gift of life to future generations, other species, and the planet. Recognizing this fact, we must continue to engage the contested discursive terrain of the person in neoliberal politics, using its own discursive tools against itself to open up alternative ways of living and being together.

Notes

INTRODUCTION

1. This position stands in opposition to that of influential social theorist Jurgen Habermas. See, for example, Jurgen Habermas, *Structural Transformation of the Public Sphere: An Inquiry into a Category of Bourgeois Society* (Cambridge, MA: MIT Press, 1991).
2. Figuring prominently here is the French school of sociology, inaugurated by Emile Durkheim. See Emile Durkheim, *The Elementary Forms of Religious Life*, trans. Karen E. Fields (New York: Free Press, 1995); Louis Dumont, *From Mandeville to Marx: The Genesis and Triumph of Economic Ideology* (Chicago: University of Chicago Press, 1977); Louis Dumont, "A Modified View of Our Origins: The Christian Beginnings of Modern Individualism," in *The Category of the Person: Anthropology, Philosophy, History*, ed. Michael Carrithers, Steven Collins, and Steven Lukes (New York: Cambridge University Press, 1985); Steven Lukes, "Durkheim's 'Individualism and the Intellectuals,'" *Political Studies* 17, no. 1 (1969); Marcel Mauss, "A Category of the Human Mind: The Notion of the Person; The Notion of the Self," trans. W. D. Hallis, in *The Category of*

the Person: Anthropology, Philosophy, History, ed. Michael Carrithers, Steven Collins, and Steven Lukes (New York: Cambridge University Press, 1985). On the political right, see for instance Carl Schmitt, *Political Theology: Four Chapters on the Concept of Sovereignty*, trans. George Schwab, foreword Tracy B. Strong (Chicago: University of Chicago Press, 2006); Richard Weaver, *Ideas Have Consequences* (Chicago: University of Chicago Press, 1948).

3. Giorgio Agamben, *The Kingdom and the Glory: For a Theological Genealogy of Economy and Government*, trans. Lorenzo Chiesa, with Matteo Mandarini (Stanford, CA: Stanford University Press, 2011); Roberto Esposito, *Persons and Things: From the Body's Point of View*, trans. Zakiya Hanafi (Malden, MA: Polity Press, 2015); Dotan Leshem, *The Origins of Neoliberalism: Modeling the Economy from Jesus to Foucault* (New York: Columbia University Press, 2016); Mika Ojakangas, "Apostle Paul and the Profanation of the Law," *Distinktion: Scandinavian Journal of Social Theory* 18 (2009): 47–68; Mika Ojakangas, "On the Pauline Roots of Biopolitics: Apostle Paul in Company with Foucault and Agamben," *Journal for Cultural and Religious Theory* 11, no. 1 (2010): 92–110; Devin Singh, *Divine Currency: The Theological Power of Money in the West* (Stanford, CA: Stanford University Press, 2018); Elettra Stimilli, *The Debt of the Living: Ascesis and Capitalism*, trans. Arianna Bove, foreword by Roberto Esposito (Albany: State University of New York Press, 2017).

4. The prominent and organizing text in this corpus is Agamben's (2011) *The Kingdom and the Glory*.

5. Edwin Black, *Rhetorical Criticism: A Study in Method* (Madison: University of Wisconsin Press, 1965).

6. This point is present throughout much of Burke's writing, but is given a clear formulation in Kenneth Burke, *A Rhetoric of Motives* (Berkeley: University of California Press, 1969).

7. For the original and full account of this perspective toward history, see Friedrich Nietzsche, *On the Genealogy of Morals*, trans. Horace B. Samuel, intro. Costica Bradatan (New York: Barnes and Noble, 2006). See also Michel Foucault, "Nietzsche, Genealogy, History," in *Language, Counter-Memory, Practice*, ed. Donald F. Bouchard (Ithaca, NY: Cornell University Press, 1977). This skepticism of origins is also expressed by Foucault in *The Archaeology of Knowledge*, trans. A. M. Sheridan Smith (New York: Vintage Books, 1972).

8. Foucault, "Nietzsche, Genealogy, History," 154.

9. James Jasinski, "A Constitutive Framework for Rhetorical Historiography:

Toward an Understanding of 'Constitution' in the *Federalist Papers*," in *Doing Rhetorical History: Concepts and Cases*, ed. Kathleen Turner (Tuscaloosa: University of Alabama Press, 1998), 74.

10. For a sampling of literature within rhetorical studies regarding such a perspective, see Deirdre N. McCloskey, *Knowledge and Persuasion in Economics* (New York: Cambridge University Press, 2008); John Poulakos, "Interpreting Sophistical Rhetoric: A Response to Schiappa," *Philosophy and Rhetoric* 23, no. 3 (1990): 218–28; Edward Schiappa, "Neo-Sophistic Rhetorical Criticism or the Historical Reconstruction of Sophistic Doctrine?," *Philosophy and Rhetoric* 23, no. 3 (1990): 192–217; Edward Schiappa, "History and Neo-Sophistic Criticism: A Reply to Poulakos," *Philosophy and Rhetoric* 23, no. 4 (1990): 307–15. This literature is largely informed by the work of Nietzsche, as well as Richard Rorty, *Philosophy and the Mirror of Nature* (Princeton, NJ: Princeton University Press, 1981).

11. E. Culpepper Clark and Raymie E. McKerrow, "The Rhetorical Construction of History," in *Doing Rhetorical History: Concepts and Cases*, ed. Kathleen Turner (Tuscaloosa: University of Alabama Press, 1998), 38.

12. Michelle Ballif, "Writing the Event: The Impossible Possibility for Historiography," *Rhetoric Society Quarterly* 44, no. 3 (2014): 246.

13. On non-Western conceptions of personhood, see for instance Mark Elvin, "Between the Earth and Heaven: Conceptions of the Self in China," in *The Category of the Person: Anthropology, Philosophy, History*, ed. Michael Carrithers, Steven Collins, and Steven Lukes (New York: Cambridge University Press, 1985), 156–89; Godfrey Lienhardt, "Self: Public, Private. Some African Representations," in *The Category of the Person: Anthropology, Philosophy, History*, ed. Michael Carrithers, Steven Collins, and Steven Lukes (New York: Cambridge University Press, 1985), 141–55. On postcolonial approaches to corporate personhood, see Ritu Birla, "Law as Economy: Convention, Corporation, Currency," *UC Irvine Law Review* 1, no. 3 (2011): 1015–37; Ritu Birla, "Maine (and Weber) Against the Grain: Towards a Postcolonial Genealogy of the Corporate Person," *Journal of Law and Society* 40, no. 1 (2013): 92–114.

14. See, in particular, Karma Chavez, "The Body: An Abstract and Actual Rhetorical Concept," *Rhetoric Society Quarterly* 48, no. 3 (2018): 242–50; Samantha Frost, *Biocultural Creatures: Toward a New Theory of the Human* (Durham, NC: Duke University Press, 2016); Allison Rowland, *Zoetropes and the Politics of Humanhood* (Columbus: Ohio State University Press, 2020);

Armond Towns, "Black 'Matter' Lives," *Women's Studies in Communication* 41, no. 4 (2018): 349–58; Alexander Weheliye, *Habeas Viscus: Racializing Assemblages, Biopolitics, and Black Feminist Theories of the Human* (Durham, NC: Duke University Press, 2014); Sylvia Wynter, "Unsettling the Coloniality of Being/Power/Truth/Freedom: Towards the Human, After Man, Its Overrepresentation—An Argument," *CR: The New Centennial Review* 3, no. 3 (2003): 257–337.

15. William E. Connolly, *Capitalism and Christianity, American Style* (Durham, NC: Duke University Press, 2008), 9.

16. See, for instance, John Milbank, *Theology and Social Theory: Beyond Secular Reason*, 2nd ed. (New York: Blackwell Publishing, 2006); and Charles Taylor, *A Secular Age* (Cambridge, MA: Belknap Press of Harvard University Press, 2007).

17. Stuart Hall, "Who Needs Identity?" in *Identity: A Reader*, ed. Paul Du Guy, Jessica Evans, and Peter Redman (New York: Sage, 2000), 15–30.

18. For classic, yet slightly divergent perspectives on the nature and relationships of liberalism and conservatism in the United States, see Louis Hartz, *The Liberal Tradition in America: An Interpretation of American Political Thought since the Revolution* (New York: Harcourt, Brace & World, Inc., 1955); and Clinton Rossiter, *Conservatism in America* (New York: Alfred A. Knopf, 1955).

19. Murray Rothbard, "Life in the Old Right," in *The Paleoconservatives: New Voices on the Old Right*, ed. Joseph Scotchie (New York: Routledge, 1999), 19–30.

20. Friedrich A. Hayek, "Why I Am Not a Conservative," in *The Constitution of Liberty* (Chicago: University of Chicago Press, 1960), https://www.cato.org/sites/cato.org/files/articles/hayek-why-i-am-not-conservative.pdf.

21. See Quinn Slobodian, *Globalists: The End of Empire and the Birth of Neoliberalism* (Cambridge, MA: Harvard University Press, 2018).

22. Michael Lee, *Creating Conservatism: Postwar Words That Made an American Movement* (East Lansing: Michigan State University Press, 2014).

23. Foremost, see Michel Foucault, *The History of Sexuality*, vol. 1, trans. Robert Hurley (New York: Vintage Books, 1978). Though primarily concerned with biopower as opposed to biopolitics, he nevertheless offers the term and a preliminary understanding of the concept here.

24. Michel Foucault, *The Birth of Biopolitics: Lectures at the Collège de France, 1978–1979*, ed. Michel Senellart, François Ewald, Alessandro Fontana, and Arnold I. Davidson, trans. Graham Burchell (New York: Picador, 2008).

25. These ideas are also developed in his lectures *Society Must Be Defended: Lectures*

at the Collège de France, 1975–1976, ed. Maurio Bertani, Alessandro Fontana, and François Ewald, trans. David Macey (New York: Picador, 2003); and *Security, Territory, Population: Lectures at the Collège de France, 1977–1978*, ed. Michel Senellart, François Ewald, Alessandro Fontana, and Arnold I. Davidson, trans. Graham Burchell (New York: Picador, 2007).

26. Miguel Vatter, *The Republic of the Living: Biopolitics and the Critique of Civil Society* (New York: Fordham University Press, 2014).

27. Thomas Lemke, *Biopolitics: An Advanced Introduction* (New York: New York University Press, 2011), 31.

28. For instance, note Marx's commitment to, even if in inverted form, Smithian notions of classical political economy and his reworking of the labor theory of value. See Duncan K. Foley, *Adam's Fallacy: A Guide to Economic Theology* (Cambridge, MA: Belknap Press of Harvard University Press, 2006).

29. Mitchell Dean and Kaspar Villadsen, *State Phobia and Civil Society: The Political Legacy of Michel Foucault* (Stanford, CA: Stanford University Press, 2016).

30. Foucault, *The Birth of Biopolitics*, 282.

31. Agamben, *The Kingdom and the Glory*, 51.

32. For instance, see Mitchell Dean, *The Signature of Power: Sovereignty, Governmentality and Biopolitics* (New York: Sage, 2013); Phillip Goodchild, *Credit and Faith* (Lanham, MD: Rowman and Littlefield, 2019); Adam Kotsko, *Neoliberalism's Demons: On the Political Theology of Late Capital* (Stanford, CA: Stanford University Press, 2018); Leshem, *The Origins of Neoliberalism*; Singh, *Divine Currency*.

33. See Robert Asen, "Knowledge, Communication, and Anti-Critical Publicity: The Friedmans' Market Public," *Communication Theory* 31, no. 2 (2021): 169–89; Catherine Chaput and Joshua Hanan, "Economic Rhetoric as *Taxis*: Neoliberal Governmentality and the Dispositif of Freakonomics," *Journal of Cultural Economy* 8, no. 1 (2014): 42–61; Catherine Chaput, *Market Affect and the Rhetoric of Political Economic Debates* (Columbia: University of South Carolina Press, 2019); Ned O'Gorman, *The Iconoclastic Imagination: Image, Catastrophe, and Economy in America from the Kennedy Assassination to September 11* (Chicago: University of Chicago Press, 2016).

34. Chaput, *Market Affect*; Catherine Chaput and Joshua Hanan, "Rhetorical Hegemony: Transactional Ontologies and the Reinvention of Material Infrastructures," *Philosophy & Rhetoric* 52, no. 4 (2019): 339–65.

35. Dennis K. Mumby, "What's Cooking in Organizational Discourse Studies? A

Response to Alvesson and Karreman," *Human Relations* 64, no. 9 (2011): 1147–61; see also Matthew Koschmann and James McDonald, "Organizational Rituals, Communication, and the Question of Agency," *Management Communication Quarterly* 29, no. 2 (2015): 229–56; Kate Lockwood Harris, "Feminist Dilemmatic Theorizing: New Materialism in Communication Studies," *Communication Theory* 26, no. 2 (2016): 150–70; David R. Novak, "Democratic Work at an Organization-Society Boundary: Sociomateriality and the Communicative Instantiation," *Management Communication Quarterly* 30, no. 2 (2016): 218–44; Consuelo Vasquez and Ruben Dittus Benavente, "Revisiting Autopoiesis: Studying the Constitutive Dynamics of Organization as a System of Narratives," *Management Communication Quarterly* 30, no. 2 (2016): 269–74.

36. Timothy Kuhn, Karen Lee Ashcraft, and François Cooren, *The Work of Communication: Relational Perspectives on Working and Organizing in Contemporary Capitalism* (New York: Routledge, 2019).

37. Nicholas Paliewicz, "How Trains Became People: Southern Pacific Railroad Co.'s Networked Rhetorical Culture and the Dawn of Corporate Personhood," *Journal of Communication Inquiry* 43, no. 2 (2019): 207.

38. See Timothy D. Peters, "Corporations, Sovereignty, and the Religion of Neoliberalism," *Law and Critique* 29 (2018): 271–92.

39. Roberto Esposito, "The Dispositif of the Person," *Law, Culture and the Humanities* 8, no. 1 (2012): 17–30; Roberto Esposito, *Third Person*, trans. Zakiya Hanafi (Malden, MA: Polity, 2012); Esposito, *Persons and Things*.

40. Roland Marchand, Creating the Corporate Soul: The Rise of Public Relations and Corporate Imagery in American Big Business (Berkeley: University of California Press, 2001).

41. Kotsko, *Neoliberalism's Demons*, 112.

42. Luke Winslow, *American Catastrophe: Fundamentalism, Climate Change, Gun Rights, and the Rhetoric of Donald J. Trump* (Columbus: Ohio State University Press, 2020).

43. Dean, *Signature of Power*, 194.

44. See Jacob Taubes, *Occidental Eschatology*, trans. David Ratmoko (Stanford, CA: Stanford University Press, 2009).

45. For literature regarding the gift, see Jacques Derrida, *Given Time*, vol. 1, *Counterfeit Money*, trans. Peggy Kamuf (Chicago: University of Chicago Press, 1992); Marcel Mauss, *The Gift: The Form and Reason for Exchange in Archaic Societies*, trans. W. D. Halls, foreword by Mary Douglas (New York: Norton,

1990); Mari Lee Mifsud, *Rhetoric and the Gift: Ancient Rhetorical Theory and Contemporary Communication* (Pittsburgh, PA: Duquesne University Press, 2015). On personhood and the logic of the gift, see Melinda Cooper, *Life as Surplus: Biotechnology and Capitalism in the Neoliberal Era* (Seattle: University of Washington Press, 2008), specifically chapter 6; Hans Joas, *The Sacredness of the Person: A New Genealogy of Human Rights*, trans. Alec Skinner (Washington, DC: Georgetown University Press, 2013).

46. The specifics of these arguments will be developed in the conclusion. I draw these claims from several sources, including James W. Bernauer, SJ, ed., *Amor Mundi: Explorations in the Faith and Thought of Hannah Arendt* (Boston: Martinus Nijhoff Publisher, 1987); William E. Connolly, *Identity/Difference: Democratic Negotiations of Political Paradox*, expanded ed. (Minneapolis: University of Minnesota Press, 2002); William E. Connolly, *The Fragility of Things: Self-Organizing Processes, Neoliberal Fantasies, and Democratic Activism* (Durham, NC: Duke University Press, 2013); Anna Grear, *Redirecting Human Rights: Facing the Challenge of Corporate Legal Humanity* (New York: Palgrave Macmillan, 2010), among others.

47. Mifsud, *Rhetoric and the Gift.*

CHAPTER ONE. GENEALOGIES OF THE PERSON

1. Martin Hollis, "Of Masks and Men," in *The Category of the Person: Anthropology, Philosophy, History*, ed. Michael Carrithers, Steven Collins, and Steven Lukes (New York: Cambridge University Press, 1985), 220.

2. Steven Lukes, "Conclusion," in *The Category of the Person: Anthropology, Philosophy, History*, ed. Michael Carrithers, Steven Collins, and Steven Lukes (New York: Cambridge University Press, 1985), 285.

3. Jeffrey Bussolini, "What Is a Dispositive?" *Foucault Studies* 10 (2010): 85–107.

4. Catherine Chaput and Joshua Hanan, "Economic Rhetoric as *Taxis*: Neoliberal Governmentality and the Dispositif of Freakonomics," *Journal of Cultural Economy* 8, no. 1 (2014): 42–61.

5. See Michel Foucault, *The Birth of Biopolitics: Lectures at the Collège de France, 1978–1979*, ed. Michel Senellart, François Ewald, Alessandro Fontana, and Arnold I. Davidson, trans. Graham Burchell (New York: Picador, 2008).

6. Chaput and Hanan, "Economic Rhetoric as *Taxis*."

7. Roberto Esposito, "The Dispositif of the Person," *Law, Culture and the Humanities* 8, no. 1 (2012): 17–30.

8. Roberto Esposito, *Third Person: Politics of Life and Philosophy of the Impersonal*, trans. Zakiya Hanafi (Malden, MA: Polity Press, 2012).

9. On this history, see Frederick Hallis, *Corporate Personality: A Study in Jurisprudence* (London: Oxford University Press, 1930). See also Roberto Esposito, *Persons and Things: From the Body's Point of View*, trans. Zakiya Hanafi (Malden, MA: Polity Press, 2015).

10. Esposito, *Third Person*.

11. Esposito, *Persons and Things*, 25.

12. See, for instance, Judith Butler, *Frames of War: When Is Life Grievable?* (New York: Verso, 2009).

13. Lisa Marie Cacho, *Social Death: Racialized Rightlessness and the Criminalization of the Unprotected* (New York: New York University Press, 2012).

14. For a more radical take on the social death thesis and anti-Blackness, see Calvin Warren, *Ontological Terror: Blackness, Nihilism, and Emancipation* (Durham, NC: Duke University Press, 2018).

15. Chaput and Hanan, "Economic Rhetoric as *Taxis*," 56.

16. See Joshua Barkan, *Corporate Sovereignty: Law and Government under Capitalism* (Minneapolis: University of Minnesota Press, 2013). The ideas in this book build upon his earlier essays, including "Roberto Esposito's Political Biology and Corporate Forms of Life," *Law, Culture and the Humanities* 8, no. 1 (2012): 84–101.

17. Dotan Leshem, *The Origins of Neoliberalism: Modeling the Economy from Jesus to Foucault* (New York: Columbia University Press, 2017), 14.

18. Leshem, *The Origins of Neoliberalism*, 15.

19. Angela Mitropoulos, *Contract and Contagion: From Biopolitics to Oikonomia* (Minor Compositions, 2012), 55.

20. Leshem, *The Origins of Neoliberalism*, 15, 16.

21. Leshem, *The Origins of Neoliberalism*, 17.

22. For an excellent treatment of the shifting understandings of rhetoric in the classical period, see George A. Kennedy, *Classical Rhetoric and Its Christian and Secular Tradition from Ancient to Modern Times* (Chapel Hill: University of North Carolina Press, 1980).

23. Leshem, *The Origins of Neoliberalism*, 21, 22.

24. Esposito, "The Dispositif of the Person," 17–30.

Notes | **197**

25. Esposito, *Persons and Things*, 29.
26. Orlando Patterson, *Slavery and Social Death: A Comparative Study* (Cambridge, MA: Harvard University Press, 1982), 28.
27. Patterson, *Slavery and Social Death*, 31.
28. Patterson, *Slavery and Social Death*, 5.
29. It is worth noting that it is Patterson's theory of social death that Cacho extends to the carceral system in the United States.
30. Marcel Mauss, "A Category of the Human Mind: The Notion of the Person; The Notion of the Self," trans. W. D. Hallis, in *The Category of the Person: Anthropology, Philosophy, History*, ed. Michael Carrithers, Steven Collins, and Steven Lukes (New York: Cambridge University Press, 1985), 20.
31. Esposito, *Persons and Things*, 35.
32. Louis Dumont, "A Modified View of Our Origins: The Christian Beginnings of Modern Individualism," in *The Category of the Person: Anthropology, Philosophy, History*, ed. Michael Carrithers, Steven Collins, and Steven Lukes (New York: Cambridge University Press, 1985), 119.
33. Elettra Stimilli, *The Debt of the Living: Ascesis and Capitalism*, trans. Ariana Bove, foreword by Roberto Esposito (Albany: State University of New York Press, 2017), 70.
34. Leshem, *The Origins of Neoliberalism*, 155.
35. Ernst Kantorowicz, *The King's Two Bodies: A Study in Medieval Political Theology* (Princeton, NJ: Princeton University Press, 2016), 87.
36. It is from this heritage that the phrase "the king is dead, long live the king" is derived.
37. Kantorowicz, *King's Two Bodies*, 209.
38. Here, Kantorowicz illustrates a hierarchy of such forms, created via a blend of Augustinian and Aristotelian thought. This hierarchy is composed as such: household, neighborhood, city, kingdom, and universe. See specifically p. 209.
39. Otto Von Gierke, *Political Theories of the Middle Age*, trans. Frederic William Maitland (Cambridge: Cambridge University Press, 1951), 87.
40. See also Hallis, *Corporate Personality*; Harold Laski, "The Personality of Associations," *Harvard Law Review* 29, no. 4 (1916): 404–26.
41. Thomas Hobbes, *Leviathan*, ed. Edwin Curley (Indianapolis, IN: Hackett Publishing Company, 1994).
42. Hobbes, *Leviathan*, 101.
43. Hobbes, *Leviathan*, 102–3. Indeed, in a sense, for Hobbes we are all artificial

Notes

persons as our personhood is authored by the power of an absolute sovereign person—that of the state. This is, of course, a secularization of earlier Christian doctrine in which our personhood is granted by God.

44. Barkan, *Corporate Sovereignty*, 38.

45. Hobbes, *Leviathan*, 217–18.

46. Rather than cracking the edifice of sovereign power from within, however, the corporation in many ways strengthened the purview of state power by diffusing and extending its territorial reach. For more on this point see Barkan, *Corporate Sovereignty*.

47. Phillip J. Stern, *The Company-State: Corporate Sovereignty and the Early-Modern Foundations of the British Empire in India* (Oxford: Oxford University Press, 2012).

48. C. B. MacPherson, *The Political Theory of Possessive Individualism: Hobbes to Locke* (Oxford: Oxford University Press, 1962).

49. MacPherson, *The Political Theory of Possessive Individualism*, 210.

50. Benjamin M. Friedman, *Religion and the Rise of Capitalism* (New York: Alfred A. Knopf, 2021): 44–49, 133–45.

51. MacPherson, *The Political Theory of Possessive Individualism*, 261.

52. Armond Towns, "Black 'Matter' Lives," *Women's Studies in Communication* 41, no. 4 (2018): 351; see also Alexander Weheliye, *Habeas Viscus: Racializing Assemblages, Biopolitics, and Black Feminist Theories of the Human* (Durham, NC: Duke University Press, 2014).

53. Anna Grear, *Redirecting Human Rights: Facing the Challenge of Corporate Legal Humanity* (New York: Palgrave Macmillan, 2010), 44.

54. Grear, *Redirecting Human Rights*, 66 and chapter 3.

55. See for instance H. W. Brands, *American Colossus: The Triumph of Capitalism, 1865–1900* (New York: Anchor Books, 2010); Duncan K. Foley, *Adam's Fallacy: A Guide to Economic Theology* (Cambridge, MA: Belknap Press of Harvard University Press, 2006).

56. Friedman, *Religion and the Rise of Capitalism*, 166.

57. Foley, *Adam's Fallacy*, 3.

58. Friedman, *Religion and the Rise of Capitalism*.

59. Scott R. Bowman, *The Modern Corporation and American Political Thought: Law, Power, Ideology* (University Park: Pennsylvania State University Press, 1996), 7.

60. Bowman, *Modern Corporation*; David Ciepley, "Beyond Public and Private: Toward a Political Theory of the Corporation," *American Political Science Review*

107, no. 1 (2013): 139–58.

61. See Friedman, *Religion and the Rise of Capitalism*, specifically chapter 10, "The Clerical Economists."

62. Jeffrey Sklansky, *The Soul's Economy: Market Society and Selfhood in American Thought, 1820–1920* (Chapel Hill: University of North Carolina Press, 2002), 23.

63. Sklansky, *The Soul's Economy*, 15.

64. Bowman, *Modern Corporation*, 3, 8.

65. Bowman, *Modern Corporation*; Ciepley, "Beyond Public and Private"; Ralph Nader and Mark Green, eds., *Corporate Power in America: Ralph Nader's Conference on Corporate Accountability* (New York: Grossman Publishers, 1971).

66. Terrett v. Taylor, 9 Cranch 43 (1815).

67. Bowman, *Modern Corporation*, 43.

68. Bowman, *Modern Corporation*, 43.

69. Dartmouth College v. Woodward, 4 Wheaton 518 (1819).

70. Dartmouth College v. Woodward, 4 Wheaton 518 (1819).

71. Sean Wilentz, *Andrew Jackson* (New York: Times Books, 2005), 78.

72. Robert V. Remini, *Andrew Jackson* (New York: Twayne Publishers, 1966), 141.

73. Nader and Green, *Corporate Power in America*.

74. Thorstein Veblen, *Absentee Ownership and Business Enterprise in Recent Times: The Case of America* (New York: Viking Press, 1938).

75. Alfred Dupont Chandler, *The Visible Hand: The Managerial Revolution in American Business* (Cambridge, MA: Harvard University Press, 1977), 36–49.

76. Chandler, *Visible Hand*, 75.

77. Mansel G. Blackford and K. Austin Kerr, *Business Enterprise in American History*, 3rd ed. (Boston: Houghton Mifflin Company, 1994), 125.

78. Chandler, *Visible Hand*, 108.

79. Chandler, *Visible Hand*, 90.

80. Charles Sellers, *The Market Revolution: Jacksonian America, 1815–1846* (New York: Oxford University Press, 1991).

81. For a powerful indictment of such tendencies in Germanic historicism, see Deirdre N. McCloskey, *The Bourgeois Virtues: Ethics for an Age of Commerce* (Chicago: University of Chicago Press, 2006).

CHAPTER TWO. BODY

1. "Incorporation, n.1," OED Online, September 2018, Oxford University Press, http://www.oed.com.ezproxy.library.wisc.edu/view/Entry/93966?redirectedFrom=incorporation#eid.
2. Karma Chavez, "The Body: An Abstract and Actual Rhetorical Concept," *Rhetoric Society Quarterly* 48, no. 3 (2018): 246.
3. Alan Trachtenberg, *The Incorporation of America: Culture and Society in the Gilded Age*, 25th anniversary ed. (New York: Hill and Wang, 2007).
4. Paul Kens, *Justice Stephen Field: Shaping Liberty from the Gold Rush to the Gilded Age* (Lawrence: University of Kansas Press, 1997).
5. See Joshua A. Lynn, *Preserving the White Man's Republic: Jacksonian Democracy, Race, and the Transformation of American Conservatism* (Charlottesville: University of Virginia Press, 2019).
6. Arthur Schlesinger Jr., *The Age of Jackson* (Boston: Little, Brown and Co., 1953).
7. Sean Wilentz, *Andrew Jackson* (New York: Times Books, 2005), 82.
8. Theodore Sedgwick, *What Is a Monopoly?; or Some Considerations upon the Subject of Corporations and Currency* (New York: George P. Scott and Co., 1835); for further explication of this phenomenon, see Joshua Barkan, *Corporate Sovereignty: Law and Government under Capitalism* (Minneapolis: University of Minnesota Press, 2013).
9. Alex Zakaras, "Nature, Religion, and the Market in Jacksonian Political Thought," *Journal of the Early Republic* 39, no. 1 (2019): 125.
10. Charles Sellers, *The Market Revolution: Jacksonian America, 1815–1846* (New York: Oxford University Press, 1991), 203.
11. Wilentz, *Andrew Jackson*, 83.
12. Schlesinger, *Age of Jackson*, 353.
13. Kens, *Justice Stephen Field*.
14. On O'Sullivan and the Democratic Party, see Adam Gomez, "Deus Vult: John L. O'Sullivan, Manifest Destiny, and American Democratic Messianism," *American Political Thought* 1, no. 2 (2012): 236–62; Lynn, *Preserving the White Man's Republic*; Schlesinger, *Age of Jackson*.
15. See Benjamin M. Friedman, *Religion and the Rise of Capitalism* (New York: Alfred A. Knopf, 2021), 281.
16. Reginald Horsman, *Race and Manifest Destiny: The Origins of American Racial Anglo-Saxonism* (Cambridge, MA: Harvard University Press, 1981), 160.

17. Gomez, "Deus Vult," 239.

18. Gomez, "Deus Vult"; Horsman, *Race and Manifest Destiny*.

19. Lyon Rathbun, "The Debate over Annexing Texas and the Emergence of Manifest Destiny," *Rhetoric and Public Affairs* 4, no. 3 (2001): 474.

20. Rathbun, "The Debate over Annexing Texas," 474.

21. Horsman, *Race and Manifest Destiny*, 205.

22. Gomez, "Deus Vult," 241.

23. Lynn, *Preserving the White Man's Republic*.

24. Schlesinger, *The Age of Jackson*, 286.

25. Lynn, *Preserving the White Man's Republic*, 67.

26. Lynn, *Preserving the White Man's Republic*, 59.

27. Lynn, *Preserving the White Man's Republic*, 6.

28. Zakaras, "Nature, Religion, and the Market," 126.

29. Carl Brent Swisher, *Stephen J. Field: Craftsman of the Law* (Washington, DC: Brookings Institution, 1930); see also Kens, *Justice Stephen Field*.

30. See Christopher Childers, *The Failure of Popular Sovereignty: Slavery, Manifest Destiny, and the Radicalization of Southern Politics* (Lawrence: University of Kansas Press, 2012).

31. Kens, *Justice Stephen Field*, 97.

32. Swisher, *Stephen J. Field*, 239; see also Kens, *Justice Stephen Field*.

33. Schlesinger, *The Age of Jackson*, 337.

34. Carey Federman, "Constructing Types of Persons in 1886: Corporate and Criminal," *Law and Critique* 14 (May 2003): 181–82.

35. Jay Howard Graham, *Everyman's Constitution: Historical Essays on the Fourteenth Amendment, the "Conspiracy Theory," and American Constitutionalism* (Madison: University of Wisconsin Press, 1968), 112–13.

36. Monroe Berger, *Equality by Statute: The Revolution in Civil Rights*, rev. ed. (Garden City, NY: Anchor Books, 1968); Kens, *Justice Stephen Field*.

37. Kens, *Justice Stephen Field*, 119–20, 124; see also chapter 8.

38. Kens, *Justice Stephen Field*, 123, 128.

39. Berger, *Equality by Statute*, 80.

40. Benjamin Quarles, *The Negro in the Making of America*, 3rd ed., new intro. by V. P. Franklin (New York: Simon and Schuster, 1996).

41. Charles A. Beard and Mary R. Beard, *The Rise of American Civilization*, new ed. revised and enlarged (New York: Macmillan, 1956).

42. Graham, *Everyman's Constitution*. Here, Graham levies a harsh criticism against

Notes

the conspiracy theory offered by the Beards, claiming that their work assumes a linear causality and an organized collection of interests on behalf of industrial capital capable of orchestrating a concerted effort to change the Constitution that does not hold up to historical scrutiny.

43. Graham, *Everyman's Constitution*; see also Thom Hartmann, *Unequal Protection: How Corporations Became "People"—And How You Can Fight Back*, 2nd ed, revised and expanded (San Francisco: Berrett-Koehler Publishers, 2010).

44. Kens, *Justice Stephen Field*; Graham, *Everyman's Constitution*, 137, 392.

45. John Norton Pomeroy, *Some Account of the Work of Stephen J. Field as a State Judge, and Judge of the Supreme Court of the United States* (Chauncey and Black, 1881), 384.

46. Pomeroy, *Work of Stephen J. Field*; on logics of infection Chinese immigration discourse, see Nayan Shah, *Contagious Divides: Epidemics and Race in San Francisco's Chinatown* (Berkeley: University of California Press, 2001).

47. Neil Larry Shumsky, *The Evolution of Political Protest and the Workingmen's Party of California* (Columbus: Ohio State University Press, 1991).

48. Andrew Gyory, *Closing the Gate: Race, Politics, and the Chinese Exclusion Act* (Chapel Hill: University of North Carolina Press, 1998), 112.

49. Shumsky, *Evolution of Political Protest*, 166.

50. Edlie L. Wong, *Racial Reconstruction: Black Inclusion, Chinese Exclusion and the Fictions of Citizenship* (New York: New York University Press, 2015), 124.

51. Alexander Saxton, *The Indispensable Enemy: Labor and the Anti-Chinese Movement in California* (Berkeley: University of California Press, 1995), 101.

52. Indeed, a historian as astute as Graham reads Field in such a way.

53. Kens, *Justice Stephen Field*, 195.

54. Pomeroy, *Work of Stephen J. Field*, 390; emphasis added.

55. Wong, *Racial Reconstruction*, 144.

56. Swisher, *Stephen J. Field*, 239; see also Kens, *Justice Stephen Field*, chapter 6.

57. Quoted in Graham, *Everyman's Constitution*, 105.

58. Saxton, *Indispensable Enemy*, 120, 128.

59. Paul Kens, "Civil Liberties, Chinese Laborers, and Corporations," in *Law in the Western United States*, ed. Gordon Morris Bakken (Norman: University of Oklahoma Press, 2000), 499.

60. Najia Aarim-Heriot, *Chinese Immigrants, African Americans, and Racial Anxiety in the United States, 1848–82* (Urbana: University of Illinois Press, 2003), 192.

61. Graham, *Everyman's Constitution*, 571.

Notes | **203**

62. Saxton, *Indispensable Enemy*, 155.

63. Kens, "Civil Liberties," 499, 500.

64. David M. Jordan, *Roscoe Conkling of New York: Voice in the Senate* (Ithaca, NY: Cornell University Press, 1971).

65. Jordan, *Roscoe Conkling of New York*.

66. Graham, *Everyman's Constitution*, 31.

67. This description of the corporate person is Graham's.

68. For Field as a political conservative, see Robert G. McCloskey, *Conservatism in the Age of Enterprise: A Study of William Graham Sumner, Stephen J. Field, and Andrew Carnegie* (Cambridge, MA: Harvard University Press, 1951).

69. Graham, *Everyman's Constitution*.

70. *In re* Tiburcio Parrott, 1 Fed. 481 (C. C. D. Cal 1880), http://law.resource.org/pub/us/case/reporter/F/0001/0001.f.0481.pdf.

71. *In re* Tiburcio Parrott, 1 Fed. 481 (C. C. D. Cal 1880), 21.

72. *In re* Tiburcio Parrott, 1 Fed. 481 (C. C. D. Cal 1880), 30.

73. David Roediger, *The Wages of Whiteness: Race and the Making of the American Working Class*, new ed., intro. Kathleen Cleaver (New York: Verso, 2007).

74. Giorgio Agamben, *Homo Sacer: Sovereign Power and Bare Life*, trans. Daniel Heller-Roazen (Stanford, CA: Stanford University Press, 1998).

75. William Rodney Herring and Mark Garrett Longaker, "Wishful, Rational, and Political Thinking: The Labor Theory of Value as Rhetoric," *Argumentation and Advocacy* 50, no. 4 (2014): 157.

76. *In re* Tiburcio Parrott, 1 Fed. 481 (C. C. D. Cal 1880), 21.

77. Perhaps unsurprisingly, it was Judge Sawyer who, in the 1878 case of *In re Ah Yup*, ruled that the Chinese were not fit to be considered legally white; see Ian Haney-Lopez, *White by Law: The Legal Construction of Race* (New York: New York University Press, 1996).

78. K. C. Councilor, "Feeding the Body Politic: Metaphors of Digestion in Progressive Era US Immigration Discourse," *Communication and Critical/Cultural Studies* 14, no. 2 (2016): 149.

79. Thomas Hobbes, *Leviathan*, ed. Edwin Curley (Indianapolis, IN: Hackett Publishing Company, 1994), 218.

80. Kens, *Justice Stephen Field*.

81. Graham, *Everyman's Constitution*.

82. The Railroad Tax Case: County of San Mateo v. Southern Pacific Railroad Co. Opinions of Justice Field and Judge Sawyer, Delivered in the US Circuit Court at

204 | Notes

San Francisco, September 25, 1882.

83. County of San Mateo v. Southern Pacific Railroad, 17, 22.

84. On various theories of corporate personality, see Frederick Hallis, *Corporate Personality: A Study in Jurisprudence* (London: Oxford University Press, 1930); see also Barkan, *Corporate Sovereignty*.

85. Giorgio Agamben, *The Kingdom and the Glory: For a Theological Genealogy of Economy and Government*, trans. Lorenzo Chiesa, with Matteo Mandarini (Stanford, CA: Stanford University Press, 2011).

86. County of San Mateo v. Southern Pacific Railroad, 37, 38.

87. On this point, see Nicholas Paliewicz, "How Trains Became People: Southern Pacific Railroad Co.'s Networked Rhetorical Culture and the Dawn of Corporate Personhood," *Journal of Communication Inquiry* 43, no. 2 (2019): 194–213.

88. County of San Mateo v. Southern Pacific Railroad, 39, 52–53.

89. County of San Mateo v. Southern Pacific Railroad, 33.

90. For a similar point, see Trachtenberg, *Incorporation of America*, chapter 1.

91. Nikolas Rose, *Inventing Our Selves: Psychology, Power, and Personhood* (Cambridge: Cambridge University Press, 1996), 26, 99.

92. On the Cartesian roots of liberal subjectivity, see Hannah Arendt, *The Human Condition*, 2nd ed. (Chicago: University of Chicago Press, 1998).

93. County of San Mateo v. Southern Pacific Railroad, 75.

94. County of San Mateo v. Southern Pacific Railroad, 84.

95. On this point see Jurgen Habermas, *Structural Transformation of the Public Sphere: An Inquiry into a Category of Bourgeois Society* (Cambridge, MA: MIT Press, 1991).

96. See Waite's footnote attached to the decision of Santa Clara County v. Southern Pacific Railroad Co., 118 US 394 (1886).

97. Federman, "Creating Types of Persons in 1886," 188.

98. Lynn, *Preserving the White Man's Republic*, 278.

99. See Mark Hulliung, *The Social Contract in America: From the Revolution to the Present Age* (Lawrence: University Press of Kansas, 2007).

CHAPTER THREE. SOUL

1. Robert G. McCloskey, *Conservatism in the Age of Enterprise: A Study of William Graham Sumner, Stephen J. Field, and Andrew Carnegie* (Cambridge, MA:

Harvard University Press, 1951), 3.

2. T. J. Jackson Lears, *Rebirth of a Nation: The Making of Modern America, 1877–1920* (New York: Harper Perennial, 2010).

3. Robert Crunden, *Ministers of Reform: The Progressives' Achievement in American Civilization, 1889–1920* (Urbana: University of Illinois Press, 1982).

4. Richard Hofstadter, *The Age of Reform: From Bryan to FDR* (New York: Vintage Books, 1955), 214.

5. Alfred Dupont Chandler, *The Visible Hand: The Managerial Revolution in American Business* (Cambridge, MA: Harvard University Press, 1977).

6. Thorstein Veblen, *Absentee Ownership and Business Enterprise in Recent Times: The Case of America* (New York: Viking Press, 1938).

7. Adolf Berle and Gardiner C. Means, *The Modern Corporation and Private Property* (New York: Commerce Clearing House, Loose leaf service division of the Corporation Trust Company, 1932), 1, 45–46.

8. Roland Marchand, *Creating the Corporate Soul: The Rise of Public Relations and Corporate Imagery in American Big Business* (Berkeley: University of California Press, 2001), 8.

9. Richard Tedlow, *Keeping the Corporate Image: Public Relations and Business, 1900–1950* (Greenwich, CT: JAI Press, 1979), 19.

10. Inger Stole, *Advertising on Trial: Consumer Activism and Corporate Public Relations in the 1930s* (Urbana: University of Illinois Press, 2006).

11. Daniel Pope, *The Making of Modern Advertising* (New York: Basic Books, 1983), 31.

12. Pope, *Making of Modern Advertising*, 31.

13. Pope, *Making of Modern Advertising*, 42–58.

14. See Pamela Walker Laird, *Advertising Progress: American Business and the Rise of Consumer Marketing* (Baltimore, MD: Johns Hopkins University Press, 2001), specifically chapter 5.

15. Pope, *Making of Modern Advertising*, 78, 80–84, 94.

16. Laird, *Advertising Progress*, 115, 133.

17. Walter Lippmann, *Drift and Mastery: An Attempt to Diagnose the Current Unrest* (Englewood Cliffs, NJ: Prentice-Hall, 1961); Roland Marchand, *Advertising the American Dream: Making Way for Modernity, 1920–1940* (Berkeley: University of California Press, 1986).

18. Marchand, *Advertising the American Dream*, 358.

19. Timothy Gloege, *Guaranteed Pure: The Moody Bible Institute, Business, and the*

Making of Modern Evangelicalism (Chapel Hill: University of North Carolina Press, 2015), 117.

20. Laird, *Advertising Progress*, 255.

21. Marchand, *Advertising the American Dream*, 358.

22. Tedlow, *Keeping the Corporate Image*, 196.

23. Stuart Ewen, *PR! A Social History of Spin* (New York: Basic Books, 1996), 64.

24. Jeffrey R. Lustig, *Corporate Liberalism: The Origins of Modern American Political Theory, 1890–1920* (Berkeley: University of California Press, 1982), 153.

25. Lustig, *Corporate Liberalism*; Ewen, *PR!*.

26. Ewen, *PR!*, 84–85.

27. Ewen, *PR!*, 91, 11.

28. Marchand, *Creating the Corporate Soul*, 4.

29. This point is made clear in part 3, "The Pagan and Masculine Virtues: Courage, with Temperance," in Deirdre N. McCloskey, *The Bourgeois Virtues: Ethics for an Age of Commerce* (Chicago: University of Chicago Press, 2006).

30. Morrell Heald, *The Social Responsibilities of Business: Company and Community, 1900–1960* (Cleveland, OH: Press of Case Western Reserve University, 1970), 87.

31. Laird, *Advertising Progress*.

32. T. J. Jackson Lears, "From Salvation to Self-Realization: Advertising and the Therapeutic Roots of the Consumer Culture, 1880–1930," in *The Culture of Consumption: Critical Essays in American History, 1880–1980*, ed. Richard Wrightman Fox and T. J. Jackson Lears (New York: Pantheon Books, 1983), 17.

33. Michel Foucault, *Security, Territory, Population: Lectures at the Collège de France, 1977–1978*, ed. Michel Senellart, François Ewald, Alessandro Fontana, and Arnold I. Davidson, trans. Graham Burchell (New York: Picador, 2007); Michel Foucault, "The Subject and Power," in *Michel Foucault: Beyond Structuralism and Hermeneutics*, ed. Hubert L. Dreyfus and Paul Rabinow (Chicago: University of Chicago Press, 1982), 208–26.

34. Foucault, *Security, Territory, Population*, 127.

35. Brian Kaylor, "Sheep without a Shepherd (but with an Archbishop): Foucault's Pastoral Power and the Denying of Communion," *Atlantic Journal of Communication* 19 (2011): 154.

36. Foucault, "Subject and Power," 214.

37. John Durham Peters, *Speaking into the Air: A History of the Idea of Communication* (Chicago: University of Chicago Press, 1999), 52.

38. Kaylor, "Sheep without a Shepherd," 163.

39. Marchand, *Advertising the American Dream*, 207.

40. Marchand, *Advertising the American Dream*, 222, 223.

41. Gloege, *Guaranteed Pure*, 148.

42. Marchand, *Advertising the American Dream*; M. M. Manring, *Slave in a Box: The Strange Career of Aunt Jemima* (Charlottesville: University Press of Virginia, 1998).

43. Manring, *Slave in a Box*, 115.

44. Vincent Jude Miller, *Consuming Religion: Christian Faith and Practice in a Consumer Culture* (New York: Continuum, 2005).

45. Miller, *Consuming Religion*.

46. Richard Ellsworth Day, *Breakfast Table Autocrat: The Life Story of Henry Parsons Crowell* (Chicago: Moody Press, 1946).

47. Day, *Breakfast Table Autocrat*, 28; Joe Musser, *Cereal Tycoon: Henry Parsons Crowell, Founder of the Quaker Oats Company* (Chicago: Moody Publishers, 2002), 13.

48. Day, *Breakfast Table Autocrat*, 36.

49. Max Weber, *The Protestant Ethic and the Spirit of Capitalism*, trans. Talcott Parsons, foreword by R. H. Tawney (New York: Scribner, 1930).

50. Weber, *The Protestant Ethic*, 113–14, 115.

51. James Calvin Davis and Charles Mathewes, "Saving Grace and Moral Striving: Thrift in Puritan Theology," in *Thrift and Thriving in America: Capitalism and Moral Order from the Puritans to the Present*, ed. Joshua J. Yates and James Davison Hunter (New York: Oxford University Press, 2011), 101.

52. Musser, *Cereal Tycoon*, 5.

53. Quoted in Day, *Breakfast Table Autocrat*, 58.

54. Day, *Breakfast Table Autocrat*, 59.

55. Musser, *Cereal Tycoon*, 82–83.

56. Arthur F. Marquette, *Brands, Trademarks, and Good Will: The Story of the Quaker Oats Company* (New York: McGraw-Hill, 1967), 6.

57. Marquette, *Brands, Trademarks, and Good Will*, 8.

58. Harrison John Thornton, *The History of the Quaker Oats Company* (Chicago: University of Chicago Press, 1933).

59. Thornton, *History of Quaker Oats*, 93–95.

60. Thornton, *History of Quaker Oats*, 69–70, and chapter 3.

61. Marquette, *Brands, Trademarks, and Good Will*, 50–51.

62. Thornton, *History of Quaker Oats*, 251.

Notes

63. Both Day, *Breakfast Table Autocrat*, 157, and Musser, *Cereal Tycoon*, 120, note this as a crucial turning point for Crowell.

64. Day, *Breakfast Table Autocrat*, 174.

65. Gloege, *Guaranteed Pure*, 163, 169.

66. See Gloege, *Guaranteed Pure*, 177.

67. Day, *Breakfast Table Autocrat*, 179.

68. Day, *Breakfast Table Autocrat*, 155.

69. Day, *Breakfast Table Autocrat*, 160–61, 199.

70. Day, *Breakfast Table Autocrat*, 205.

71. President's Message; "Dedication Program, The Moody Bible Institute of Chicago, Feb. 4th, 1939"; Crowell, Henry P. CBC953; Moody Bible Institute, Chicago; June 20, 2016.

72. Day, *Breakfast Table Autocrat*, 266–68.

73. Gloege, *Guaranteed Pure*.

74. T. J. Jackson Lears, "The Modernization of Thrift," in *Thrift and Thriving in America: Capitalism and Moral Order from the Puritans to the Present*, ed. Joshua J. Yates and James Davison Hunter (New York: Oxford University Press, 2011), 209–41.

75. Lears, "The Modernization of Thrift," 211.

76. James Davison Hunter, "Thrift and Moral Formation," in *Thrift and Thriving in America: Capitalism and Moral Order from the Puritans to the Present*, ed. Joshua J. Yates and James Davison Hunter (New York: Oxford University Press, 2011), 254.

77. Lears, "The Modernization of Thrift," 221.

78. Hunter, "Thrift and Moral Formation," 253.

79. Jennifer Scanlon, "Thrift and Advertising," in *Thrift and Thriving in America: Capitalism and Moral Order from the Puritans to the Present*, ed. Joshua J. Yates and James Davison Hunter (New York: Oxford University Press, 2011), 290, 285.

80. Obituary in the *Chicago Tribune*, October 24, 1944; "Henry Crowell, Head of Quaker Oats, Dies at 89"; Crowell, Henry P. CBC953; Moody Bible Institute, Chicago; June 20, 2016.

81. Obituary in the *Daily News*, October 24, 1944; "H. P. Crowell Dies; Leader in Quaker Oats Co."; Crowell, Henry P. CBC953; Moody Bible Institute, Chicago; June 20, 2016.

82. Article in *Chicago Tribune*, November 11, 1944; "Crowell Will Leaves Fortune to Church Work"; Crowell, Henry P. CBC953; Moody Bible Institute, Chicago; June 20, 2016.

83. *Church Builders*, June 2001; Bernard R. DeRemer "A Superb Steward"; Crowell, Henry P. CVC953; Moody Bible Institute, Chicago; June 20, 2016.

84. Musser, *Cereal Tycoon*, 5.

85. *Church Builders*, June 2001; Bernard R. DeRemer "A Superb Steward"; Crowell, Henry P. CVC953; Moody Bible Institute, Chicago; June 20, 2016.

86. Richard Fried, *The Man Everybody Knew: Bruce Barton and the Making of Modern America* (Chicago: Ivan R. Dee, 2005), 12.

87. Fried, *The Man Everybody Knew*, 10.

88. Leo P. Ribuffo, "Jesus Christ as Business Statesman: Bruce Barton and the Selling of Corporate Capitalism," *American Quarterly* 33, no. 2 (1981): 209.

89. Fried, *The Man Everybody Knew*, 13, 17.

90. Fried, *The Man Everybody Knew*, 19.

91. Ribuffo, "Jesus Christ as Business Statesman"; see also Fried, *The Man Everybody Knew*.

92. Fried, *The Man Everybody Knew*, 28.

93. Fried, *The Man Everybody Knew*, 26.

94. Fried, *The Man Everybody Knew*, 32–33.

95. Ribuffo, "Jesus Christ as Business Statesman," 212; Fried, *The Man Everybody Knew*, 32–33.

96. Ribuffo, "Jesus Christ as Business Statesman," 214.

97. On the role of evangelical senses of capitalism in YMCA media, see Ronald Walter Greene, "Y Movies: Film and the Modernization of Pastoral Power," *Communication and Critical/Cultural Studies* 2, no. 1 (2005): 20–36.

98. Fried, *The Man Everybody Knew*. For a history of the CPI see Stephen Vaughn, *Holding Fast the Inner Lines: Democracy, Nationalism, and the Committee on Public Information* (Chapel Hill: University of North Carolina Press, 1980).

99. Fried, *The Man Everybody Knew*, 49.

100. Fried, *The Man Everybody Knew*, 57.

101. Bruce Barton, "Calls Advertising Power to Keep Business Striving for High Ideals," *New York Evening Post*, January 3, 1928, Bruce Barton Papers, box 102, State Historical Society of Wisconsin.

102. Marchand, *Creating the Corporate Soul*, 133, 134. "Forger of institutional souls" is Marchand's description of Barton.

103. Fried, *The Man Everybody Knew*, 62.

104. Marchand, *Creating the Corporate Soul*, 142–43, 146.

105. Fried, *The Man Everybody Knew*, 86.

106. Bruce Barton, "And There Arose a New King Which Knew Not Joseph," Bruce Barton Papers, box 122, State Historical Society of Wisconsin.

107. Barton, *The Man and the Book Nobody Knows* (Indianapolis, IN: Bobbs-Merrill, 1959).

108. Barton, "And There Arose a New King."

109. Barton, "And There Arose a New King."

110. Ribuffo, "Jesus Christ as Business Statesman," 218.

111. Barton, *The Man and the Book Nobody Knows*, 12.

112. Barton, *The Man and the Book Nobody Knows*, 24–29, 115.

113. Ribuffo, "Jesus Christ as Business Statesman," 220.

114. Barton, *The Man and the Book Nobody Knows*, 65.

115. Barton, *The Man and the Book Nobody Knows*, 72.

116. See Kenneth Burke, *A Rhetoric of Motives* (Berkeley: University of California Press, 1969).

117. Barton, *The Man and the Book Nobody Knows*, 79, 80.

118. Barton, *The Man and the Book Nobody Knows*, 88, 89.

119. Barton, *The Man and the Book Nobody Knows*, 93, 94, 97.

120. Peters, *Speaking into the Air*.

121. Kevin Musgrave, "A Battle for Hearts and Minds: Evangelical Capitalism and Pastoral Power in Bruce Barton's 'The Public,'" *Rhetoric and Public Affairs* 20, no. 1 (2017): 133–60.

122. Bruce Barton, "The Public," *Vital Speeches of the Day* 2, no. 6 (1935): 175.

123. Walter Lippmann, *The Phantom Public* (New Brunswick, NJ: Transaction Publishers, 1993).

124. See, for instance, Marchand, *Creating the Corporate Soul*.

125. Barton, "The Public," 175.

126. Majia Holmer Nadesan, "The Discourses of Corporate Spiritualism and Evangelical Capitalism," *Management Communication Quarterly* 13 (1999): 3–42.

127. Stuart Ewen, *Captains of Consciousness: Advertising and the Social Roots of the Consumer Culture* (New York: McGraw-Hill, 1976).

128. "Trade Heads Challenge Raw Deal," *New York Journal*, December 4, 1935, Bruce Barton Papers, box 60, State Historical Society of Wisconsin.

129. See Fried, *The Man Everybody Knew*.

130. "Barton Lists 39 'Roosevelt Emergencies,'" *Herald-Tribune*, March 17, 1939, Bruce Barton Papers, box 60, State Historical Society of Wisconsin.

131. Fried, *The Man Everybody Knew*, 190.

132. Charles E. Adams to Mr. D. L. Chambers of The Bobbs-Merrill Co., April 14, 1925, Bruce Barton Papers, box 107, State Historical Society of Wisconsin.
133. William Robert Catton to The Bobbs-Merrill Company, April 25, 1925, Bruce Barton Papers, box 107, State Historical Society of Wisconsin.
134. Fried, *The Man Everybody Knew*, 100, 52. Indeed, Barton spent time in his youth working several odd jobs outside of the publishing industry, including building bridges.
135. T. J. Jackson Lears, "From Salvation to Self-Realization," 31, 37.
136. Gloege, *Guaranteed Pure*, 10.

CHAPTER FOUR. VOICE

1. Jonathan P. Herzog, *The Spiritual-Industrial Complex: America's Religious Battle against Communism in the Early Cold War* (New York: Oxford University Press, 2011).
2. See Edmund A. Opitz, *Religion and Capitalism: Allies Not Enemies* (New Rochelle, NY: Arlington House, 1970).
3. George Nash, *The Conservative Intellectual Movement in America since 1945* (New York: Basic Books, 1976), 4.
4. Herzog, *The Spiritual-Industrial Complex*, 5–6.
5. Friedrich A. Hayek, *The Road to Serfdom*, 50th anniversary ed., intro. Milton Friedman (Chicago: University of Chicago Press, 1994), 70–78.
6. See Quinn Slobodian, *Globalists: The End of Empire and the Birth of Neoliberalism* (Cambridge, MA: Harvard University Press, 2018); and Mitchell Dean, *The Signature of Power: Sovereignty, Governmentality and Biopolitics* (Los Angeles: Sage, 2013).
7. Pierre Dardot and Christian Laval, *The New Way of the World: On Neoliberal Society*, trans. Gregory Elliott (New York: Verso, 2017), 6, 63.
8. The literature on neoliberalism, its origins, its scope, and its aims is massive. Though there is much disagreement among competing camps of scholars—notably between more traditional Marxist interpretations of neoliberalism as a backlash of capital against the state, and Foucauldian approaches to neoliberalism as a cultural logic and regime of governance—one thing seems clear: neoliberalism is diverse and multifarious in its spread across the globe. On the flexibility of neoliberalism see Aiwha Ong, *Neoliberalism as Exception:*

Mutations in Citizenship and Sovereignty (Durham, NC: Duke University Press, 2006); Jamie Peck, *Constructions of Neoliberal Reason* (New York: Oxford University Press, 2010). On the fissures between key neoliberal thinkers, see Javier Aranzadi, *Liberalism against Liberalism: Theoretical Analysis of the Works of Ludwig von Mises and Gary Becker* (New York: Routledge, 2006). For accounts that trace neoliberalism to the Mont Pelerin Society and its forerunner, the Lippmann Colloquium, see Dardot and Laval, *The New Way of the World*; Philip Mirowski and Dieter Plehwe, eds., *The Road from Mont Pelerin: The Making of the Neoliberal Thought Collective* (Cambridge, MA: Harvard University Press, 2009); David Harvey, *A Brief History of Neoliberalism* (New York: Oxford University Press, 2007); Naomi Klein, *The Shock Doctrine: The Rise of Disaster Capitalism* (New York: Picador, 2008). Others trace its origins to Germanic ordoliberalism; notable here is Mitchell Dean, *The Signature of Power: Sovereignty, Governmentality, and Biopolitics* (New York: Sage, 2013); Michel Foucault, *The Birth of Biopolitics: Lectures at the Collège de France, 1978–1979*, ed. Michel Senellart, François Ewald, Alessandro Fontana, and Arnold I. Davidson, trans Graham Burchell (New York: Picador, 2008). Still others trace its roots to U.S. Cold War mathematical and computational advancements. For instance, see S. M. Amadae, *Rationalizing Capitalist Democracy: The Cold War Origins of Rational Choice Liberalism* (Chicago: University of Chicago Press, 2003); S. M. Amadae, *Prisoners of Reason: Game Theory and Neoliberal Political Economy* (Cambridge: Cambridge University Press, 2016). Many scholars find the uniqueness of neoliberalism in its refiguring of subjectivity. See Wendy Brown, *Undoing the Demos: Neoliberalism's Stealth Revolution* (Cambridge, MA: Zone Books, 2015). A smaller body of scholarship, yet one that is compelling, finds neoliberalism's uniqueness in its accommodation to and governing for the corporation. See Carolyn Hardin, "Finding the 'Neo' in Neoliberalism," *Cultural Studies* 28, no. 2 (2012): 199–221; Rob Van Horn, "Reinventing Monopoly and the Role of Corporations: The Roots of Chicago Law and Economics," in *The Road from Mont Pelerin: The Making of the Neoliberal Thought Collective*, ed. Philip Mirowski and Dieter Plehwe (Cambridge, MA: Harvard University Press, 2009), 204–37. For a good compilation of essays that deals with many of these themes, see Sanford F. Schram and Marianna Pavlovskaya, eds., *Rethinking Neoliberalism: Resisting the Disciplinary Regime* (New York: Routledge, 2018).

9. Milton Friedman, *Capitalism and Freedom*, with the assistance of Rose D. Friedman (Chicago: University of Chicago Press, 1962), 25, 201.

10. Michael Lee, *Creating Conservatism: Postwar Words That Made an American Movement* (East Lansing: Michigan State University Press, 2014), 43, 50–63.

11. For Kirk's thoughts on the rootedness of political life on the bedrock of transcendent truths, see his *The Conservative Mind: From Burke to Santayana* (Chicago: Henry Regnery Company, 1953), his *The Roots of American Order* (LaSalle, IL: Open Court Press, 1974), and his essay "The Question of Tradition," in *The Paleoconservatives: New Voices of the Old Right*, ed. Joseph Scotchie (New York: Routledge, 1999), 59–78.

12. This phrase became something of a clarion call for conservatives throughout the twentieth century. This point is noted by both Lee, *Creating Conservatism*, and Nash, *The Conservative Intellectual Movement*.

13. Richard Weaver, *Ideas Have Consequences* (Chicago: University of Chicago Press, 1948); see chapters 7, 8, and 9 for his restorative vision for the West.

14. Weaver, *Ideas Have Consequences*, 133–34; emphasis added.

15. Weaver, *Ideas Have Consequences*, 181, 165, 172.

16. See Herzog, *The Spiritual-Industrial Complex*; Lee, *Creating Conservatism*.

17. Lee, *Creating Conservatism*, 166.

18. Herzog, *The Spiritual-Industrial Complex*, 39, 42, 44.

19. Lee, *Creating Conservatism*; Nash, *The Conservative Intellectual Movement*.

20. Kevin Kruse, *One Nation Under God: How Corporate America Invented Christian America* (New York: Basic Books, 2015), xv.

21. Kruse, *One Nation Under God*, 7, 15–16.

22. Nash, *The Conservative Intellectual Movement*, 24. Here, Nash was quoting John Chamberlain.

23. Opitz, *Capitalism and Christianity*. For a brilliant and illuminating elucidation of this insight regarding the ineffability of the market and the iconoclastic logic of neoliberal rhetoric, see Ned O'Gorman, *The Iconoclastic Imagination: Image, Catastrophe, and Economy in America from the Kennedy Assassination to September 11* (Chicago: University of Chicago Press, 2015).

24. Opitz, *Capitalism and Christianity*, 25–26, 33.

25. T. Jeremy Gunn, *Spiritual Weapons: The Cold War and the Forging of an American National Religion* (Westport, CT: Praeger, 2009), 7–11, 24.

26. Herzog, *The Spiritual-Industrial Complex*, 160–68.

27. O'Gorman, *The Iconoclastic Imagination*, 167.

28. Herzog, *The Spiritual-Industrial Complex*, 91; O'Gorman, *The Iconoclastic Imagination*, 167.

214 | Notes

29. Herzog, *The Spiritual-Industrial Complex*, 91.

30. Kruse, *One Nation Under God*.

31. Kruse, *One Nation Under God*, 68.

32. Herzog, *The Spiritual-Industrial Complex*, 95–96, 97.

33. Lee, *Creating Conservatism*, 78.

34. James Gilbert, *Another Chance: Postwar America, 1945–1985*, 2nd ed. (Chicago: Dorsey Press, 1986).

35. Jason Stahl, *Right Moves: The Conservative Think Tank in American Political Culture since 1945* (Chapel Hill: University of North Carolina Press, 2016), 11.

36. Paul Gottfried and Thomas Fleming, *The Conservative Movement* (Woodbridge, CT: Twayne Publishers, 1988), 30, 41.

37. See for instance Richard A. Viguerie, *America's Right Turn: How Conservatives Used New and Alternative Media to Take Power* (Chicago: Bonus Books, 2004); on the different connotations of "New Right" in Europe and the United States see David G. Green, *The New Right: The Counter-Revolution in Political, Economic and Social Thought* (London: Wheatsheaf Books, 1987); Desmond S. King, *The New Right: Politics, Markets, and Citizenship* (London: Macmillan Education, 1987).

38. David M. Ricci, *The Transformation of American Politics: The New Washington and the Rise of Think Tanks* (New Haven, CT: Yale University Press, 1993).

39. Todd Gitlin, *The Whole World Is Watching: Mass Media in the Making and Unmaking of the New Left* (Berkeley: University of California Press, 1980), 25.

40. For the ubiquity of this language both historically and in contemporary scholarship, one need only give a cursory glance at social movement literature in rhetorical studies. See, for instance, Charles E. Morris III and Stephen Howard Browne, eds., *Readings on the Rhetoric of Social Protest*, 2nd ed. (State College, PA: Strata Publishing, 2001); John Waite Bowers and Donovan J. Ochs, *The Rhetoric of Agitation and Control* (Reading, MA: Addison-Wesley Publishing Company, 1971).

41. Daniel Bell, *The End of Ideology: On the Exhaustion of Political Ideas in the Fifties*, rev. ed. (New York: Free Press, 1965).

42. Corey Robin, *The Reactionary Mind: Conservatism from Edmund Burke to Sarah Palin* (New York: Oxford University Press), 13.

43. Stahl, *Right Moves*, 14, 35.

44. Smith, *Idea Brokers*, 177.

45. Irving Kristol, *Two Cheers for Capitalism* (New York: Basic Books, 1978); see also

Ricci, *The Transformation of American Politics*; Smith, *Idea Brokers*.

46. Kim Phillips-Fein, *Invisible Hands: The Making of the Conservative Movement from the New Deal to Reagan* (New York: W.W. Norton and Co., 2009), 154.

47. Russell Kirk, "The Inhumane Businessman," *Fortune* 55 (May 1957): 160–61, 248, https://kirkcenter.org/education/the-inhumane-businessman/.

48. See Harvey, *A Brief History of Neoliberalism*; John Nichols and Robert W. McChesney, *Dollarocracy: How the Money-and-Media Election Complex Is Destroying America* (New York: Nation Books, 2013).

49. Nichols and McChesney, *Dollarocracy*, 71.

50. Earl M. Maltz, "The Triumph of the Southern Man: Dowell, Shelby County, and the Jurisprudence of Justice Lewis F. Powell, Jr.," *Duke Journal of Constitutional Law & Public Policy* 14 (2019): 171.

51. John C. Jeffries, *Justice Lewis F. Powell, Jr.* (New York: Charles F. Scribner's Sons, 1994), 42.

52. Jeffries, *Justice Lewis F. Powell, Jr.*; John N. Jacob, *The Lewis F. Powell, Jr. Papers: A Guide* (Lexington, VA: Washington and Lee University School of Law, 1997).

53. Jeffries, *Justice Lewis F. Powell, Jr.*, 42, 43.

54. Anders Walker, *The Burning House: Jim Crow and the Making of Modern America* (New Haven, CT: Yale University Press, 2018), 173.

55. See Slobodian, *Globalists*.

56. Stahl, *Right Moves*, 63.

57. Nichols and McChesney, *Dollarocracy*, 72.

58. Jeffries, *Justice Lewis F. Powell, Jr.*, 210–11.

59. See Walker, *The Burning House*, 168.

60. See Maltz, "The Triumph of the Southern Man"; Walker, *The Burning House*, 169.

61. Lewis F. Powell Jr., "Education on Communism: What the Bar Can Do," speech delivered to the Connecticut State Bar Association, October 4, 1962, *Washington and Lee University School of Law Scholarly Commons*.

62. Lewis F. Powell Jr. "Prayer Breakfast, American Bar Association, San Francisco, CA," *Washington and Lee University School of Law Scholarly Commons*.

63. Lewis F. Powell Jr., "A Lawyer Looks at Civil Disobedience," *Washington and Lee Law Review* 23, no. 2 (1966): 205.

64. Powell, "A Lawyer Looks at Civil Disobedience," 230.

65. Walker, *The Burning House*.

216 | Notes

66. Jeffries, *Justice Lewis F. Powell, Jr.*, 219.

67. M. Kelly Carr, *The Rhetorical Invention of Diversity: Supreme Court Opinions, Public Argument, and Affirmative Action* (East Lansing: Michigan State University Press, 2018), 109.

68. Walker, *The Burning House*, 4, 194.

69. Walker, *The Burning House*, 184.

70. Carr, *The Rhetorical Invention of Diversity*, 111, and particularly her conclusion.

71. Carr, *The Rhetorical Invention of Diversity*.

72. For a slightly different historical take on the "literalization" of the market of ideas, see Lisa Siraganian, *Modernism and the Meaning of Corporate Persons* (Oxford: Oxford University Press, 2021). For differing interpretations of the metaphor of the marketplace of ideas in free-speech law, see James Arnt Aune, "Justice Holmes's Rhetoric and the Progressive Path of the Law," in *Rhetoric and Reform in the Progressive Era*, vol. 6, *Rhetorical History of the United States*, ed. J. Michael Hogan (East Lansing: Michigan State University Press, 2003); Marouf Hasian Jr., "The Rhetorical Turn in First Amendment Scholarship: A Case Study of Holmes and the 'Marketplace of Ideas,'" *Free Speech Yearbook* 31, no. 1 (1993): 42–65; David Rabban, *Free Speech in Its Forgotten Years* (New York: Cambridge University Press, 1998), specifically chapter 8.

73. Lewis F. Powell Jr., "Attack on American Free Enterprise System," *Snail Darter Documents*, Paper 79, http://lawdigitalcommons.bc.edu/darter_materials/79 (1971), 1, 2.

74. Powell, "Attack on American Free Enterprise System," 2.

75. Friedman, *Capitalism and Freedom*.

76. Powell, "Attack on American Free Enterprise System," 3.

77. Powell, "Attack on American Free Enterprise System," 7, 8.

78. Powell, "Attack on American Free Enterprise System," 9.

79. Powell, "Attack on American Free Enterprise System," 10.

80. Powell, "Attack on American Free Enterprise System," 10.

81. Powell, "Attack on American Free Enterprise System," 11.

82. Powell, "Attack on American Free Enterprise System," 18, 13.

83. Powell, "Attack on American Free Enterprise System," 20.

84. Spiro T. Agnew, "Television News Coverage," in *Words of a Century: The Top 100 American Speeches, 1900–1999*, ed. Stephen E. Lucas and Martin J. Medhurst (New York: Oxford University Press, 2009), 496–503.

85. Powell, "Attack on American Free Enterprise System," 21.

86. Powell, "Attack on American Free Enterprise System," 22.

87. Oscar H. Gandy Jr., *Beyond Agenda Setting: Information Subsidies and Public Policy* (Ann Arbor: University of Michigan Press, 1982), 61, 62.

88. Both the Chamber of Commerce and political think tanks are registered 501(c)(3) nonprofit organizations.

89. Powell, "Attack on American Free Enterprise System," 24.

90. Importantly, this line of argument was not exclusive to the right, as a similar claim was famously made by former American Political Science Association president and political theorist Theodore Lowi in *The End of Liberalism: The Second Republic of the United States*, 2nd ed. (New York: W.W. Norton & Co., 1979).

91. Powell, "Attack on American Free Enterprise System," 24–25.

92. Philip Wander, "The Third Persona: An Ideological Turn in Rhetorical Theory," *Central States Speech Journal* 35, no. 4 (1984): 197–216.

93. Robert Asen, "Ideology, Materiality, and Counterpublicity: William E. Simon and the Rise of a Conservative Counterintelligentsia," *Quarterly Journal of Speech* 95, no. 3 (2009): 263–88.

94. Powell, "Attack on American Free Enterprise System," 26.

95. Nichols and McChesney, *Dollarocracy*, 78.

96. William E. Simon, *A Time for Truth* (New York: McGraw Hill, 1978); Asen, "Ideology, Materiality, and Counterpublicity."

97. Jean Stefancic and Richard Delgado, *No Mercy: How Conservative Think Tanks and Foundations Changed America's Social Agenda* (Philadelphia: Temple University Press, 1996).

98. Shanto Iyengar, *Media Politics: A Citizen's Guide*, 3rd ed. (New York: W.W. Norton, 2015).

99. Smith, *Idea Brokers*, 215.

100. First National Bank of Boston v. Bellotti, 435 U.S. 765 (1978), 4.

101. First National Bank of Boston v. Bellotti, 435 U.S. 765 (1978), 9.

102. Kerr, *The Corporate Free Speech Movement*, 46.

103. Laura Stein, *Speech Rights in America: The First Amendment, Democracy, and the Media* (Urbana: University of Illinois Press, 2006), 16.

104. Seyla Benhabib, "Models of Public Space: Hannah Arendt, the Liberal Tradition, and Jurgen Habermas," in *Habermas and the Public Sphere*, ed. Craig Calhoun (Cambridge, MA: MIT Press, 1992), 83.

105. First National Bank of Boston v. Bellotti, 435 U.S. 765 (1978), 7, 9.

218 | Notes

106. First National Bank of Boston v. Bellotti, 435 U.S. 765 (1978), 11, 27, 8.

107. Aune, *Selling the Free Market*.

108. Bethany Moreton, *To Serve God and Wal-Mart: The Making of Christian Free Enterprise* (Cambridge, MA: Harvard University Press, 2009).

CHAPTER FIVE. CONSCIENCE

1. William Connolly, *Capitalism and Christianity, American Style* (Durham, NC: Duke University Press, 2008), see particularly page 39.

2. Robin West, "Freedom of the Church and Our Endangered Civil Rights: Exiting the Social Contract," in *The Rise of Corporate Religious Liberty*, ed. Micah Schwarzman, Chad Flanders, and Zoe Robinson (New York: Oxford University Press, 2016), 402–3.

3. Connolly, *Capitalism and Christianity*, 44.

4. Jamie Peck refers to the Reagan (and Thatcher) eras as the neoliberal vanguard. Likewise, Will Davies suggests that at this moment neoliberalism was a "self-conscious insurgency" that was largely combative rather than normative. That neoliberalism became the new way of the world, as Pierre Dardot and Christian Laval suggest, was largely the product of these formative years. See Jamie Peck, *Constructions of Neoliberal Reason* (New York: Oxford University Press, 2013); Will Davies, "The New Neoliberalism," *New Left Review* 101 (September–October 2016): 121–34; Pierre Dardot and Christian Laval, *The New Way of the World: On Neoliberal Society*, trans. Gregory Elliott (New York: Verso, 2017).

5. Corey Robin, *The Reactionary Mind: Conservatism from Edmund Burke to Sarah Palin* (New York: Oxford University Press).

6. For instance, see again Emile Durkheim, *The Elementary Forms of Religious Life*, trans. Karen E. Fields (New York: Free Press, 1995); Louis Dumont, *From Mandeville to Marx: The Genesis and Triumph of Economic Ideology* (Chicago: University of Chicago Press, 1977); Louis Dumont, "A Modified View of Our Origins: The Christian Beginnings of Modern Individualism," in *The Category of the Person: Anthropology, Philosophy, History*, ed. Michael Carrithers, Steven Collins, and Steven Lukes (New York: Cambridge University Press, 1985); Steven Lukes, "Durkheim's 'Individualism and the Intellectuals,'" *Political Studies* 17, no. 1 (1969); Marcel Mauss, "A Category of the Human Mind: The Notion of the Person; The Notion of the Self," trans. W. D. Hallis, in *The Category of the*

Person: Anthropology, Philosophy, History, ed. Michael Carrithers, Steven Collins, and Steven Lukes (New York: Cambridge University Press, 1985).

7. Connolly, *Capitalism and Christianity*, 48–49.
8. Connolly, *Capitalism and Christianity*, 49.
9. Philip Gorski, "Christianity and Democracy after Trump," *Political Theology Network*, July 26, 2018, https://politicaltheology.com/christianity-and-democracy-after-trump/.
10. Jeffrey W. Robbins, "The White Christian Nationalist Hustle," in *Doing Theology in the Age of Trump: A Critical Report on Christian Nationalism*, ed. Jeffrey W. Robbins and Clayton Crockett (Eugene, OR: Cascade Press, 2018).
11. See Lawrence Grossberg, *Under the Cover of Chaos: Trump and the Battle for the American Right* (London: Pluto Press, 2018).
12. "Influential Evangelicals," *Time* magazine, February 7, 2005.
13. The literature on Reagan in rhetorical studies is quite large. I will not attempt to broach this corpus here as it is not necessary for the attenuated task at hand, yet here is a small sampling of this literature: Amos Kiewe and Davis Houck, *A Shining City on a Hill: Ronald Reagan's Economic Rhetoric, 1951–1989* (New York: Praeger, 1991); Mary E. Stuckey, *Playing the Game: The Presidential Rhetoric of Ronald Reagan* (New York: Praeger, 1990); Martin J. Medhurst, "LBJ, Reagan, and the American Dream: Competing Visions of Liberty," *Presidential Studies Quarterly* 46, no. 1 (2016): 98–124; Robert C. Rowland and John M. Jones, "Reagan's Farewell Address: Redefining the American Dream," *Rhetoric & Public Affairs* 20, no. 4 (2017): 635–66; David Zarefsky, C. Miller-Tutzauer, and Frank Tutzauer, "Reagan's Safety Net for the Truly Needy: The Rhetorical Use of Definition," *Central States Speech Journal* 35 (1984): 113–19.
14. Craig R. Smith, "Ronald Reagan's Rhetorical Re-invention of Conservatism," *Quarterly Journal of Speech* 103, no. 1–2 (2017): 42.
15. Meg Kunde, "Making the Free Market Moral: Ronald Reagan's Covenantal Economy," *Rhetoric & Public Affairs* 22, no. 2 (2019): 217–52.
16. A phrase Reagan borrowed from Puritan John Winthrop. See Kiewe and Houck, *A Shining City on a Hill*, for more on this metaphor.
17. Kunde, "Making the Free Market Moral," 225, 232.
18. Kunde, "Making the Free Market Moral," 234, emphasis added.
19. Kunde, "Making the Free Market Moral," 236.
20. Tim Christiaens, "Hayek's Vicarious Secularization of Providential Theology," *Philosophy and Social Criticism* 45, no. 1 (2018): 9, 15.

Notes

21. See Lars Cornelissen, "The Secularization of Providential Order: F. A. Hayek's Political-Economic Theology," *Political Theology* 18, no. 8 (2017), on the shift from a naturalistic liberalism to the secular ontology of Hayek.

22. Grossberg, *Under the Cover of Chaos*, 64.

23. On the complexities of historical views of Reagan, particularly with regard to his Evil Empire address, see Robert C. Rowland and John M. Jones, "Reagan's Strategy for the Cold War and the Evil Empire Address," *Rhetoric & Public Affairs* 19, no. 3 (2016): 427–63.

24. Michael J. Lee, "WFB: The Gladiatorial Style and the Politics of Provocation," *Rhetoric & Public Affairs* 13, no. 2 (2010): 217–50.

25. Robert C. Rowland and John A. Jones, "Entelechial and Reformative Symbolic Trajectories in Contemporary Conservatism: A Case Study of Reagan and Buchanan in Houston and Beyond," *Rhetoric & Public Affairs* 4, no. 1 (2001): 60.

26. Rowland and Jones, "Entelechial and Reformative Strategies," 74.

27. Luke Winslow, *American Catastrophe: Fundamentalism, Climate Change, Gun Rights, and the Rhetoric of Donald J. Trump* (Columbus: Ohio State University Press, 2020), 123.

28. Richard A. Viguerie, *Conservatives Betrayed: How George W. Bush and Other Big Government Republicans Hijacked the Conservative Cause* (Los Angeles: Bonus Books, 2006).

29. Winslow, *American Catastrophe*, 123, 124.

30. Joseph Scotchie, "Introduction: Paleoconservatism as the Opposition Party," in *The Paleoconservatives: New Voices on the Old Right*, ed. Joseph Scotchie (New York: Routledge, 1999), 1.

31. For more on the Rockford Institute, see Paul Gottfried and Thomas Fleming, *The Conservative Movement* (Woodbridge, CT: Twayne Publishers, 1988).

32. Murray Rothbard, "Life in the Old Right," in *The Paleoconservatives: New Voices on the Old Right*, ed. Joseph Scotchie (New York: Routledge, 1999), 21.

33. See Scotchie, "Introduction," 6.

34. Scotchie, "Introduction," 10.

35. Quinn Slobodian, *Globalists: The End of Empire and the Birth of Neoliberalism* (Cambridge, MA: Harvard University Press, 2018).

36. Patrick Buchanan, *The Great Betrayal: How American Sovereignty and Social Justice Are Being Sacrificed to the Gods of the Global Economy* (New York: Little, Brown, 1998), 113.

37. Buchanan, *The Great Betrayal*, 54, 55, 113.

38. See David Ciepley, "Beyond Public and Private: Toward a Political Theory of the Corporation," *American Political Science Review* 107, no. 1 (2013) on this biological metaphor.

39. On Brimelow and VDare, see Jeffrey Tischauser and Kevin Musgrave, "Far-Right Media as Imitated Counterpublicity: A Discourse Analysis on Racial Meaning and Identity on Vdare.com," *Howard Journal of Communications* 31, no. 3 (2020): 282–96.

40. Peter Brimelow, *Alien Nation: Common Sense about America's Immigration Disaster* (New York: Harper Perennial, 1996), xix, 10.

41. On the linkages of this conspiratorial thinking among paleoconservatives, the alt-right, and Donald Trump, see Kevin Musgrave and Jeffrey Tischauser, "Radical Traditionalism, Metapolitics, and Identitarianism: The Rhetoric of Richard Spencer," *b2o: an online journal*, special issue: The New Extremism (September 1, 2019).

42. Paul Gottfried, *Multiculturalism and the Politics of Guilt: Towards a Secular Theocracy* (Columbia: University of Missouri Press, 2002), 56, 59.

43. Paul Gottfried, *After Liberalism: Mass Democracy in the Managerial State* (Princeton, NJ: Princeton University Press, 1999), 95.

44. Gottfried, *Multiculturalism and the Politics of Guilt*, 9, 88.

45. Gottfried, *After Liberalism*, 117.

46. Sam Francis, *Revolution from the Middle* (Raleigh, NC: Middle American Press, 1997), 27.

47. Darrell Enck-Wanzer, "Barack Obama, the Tea Party, and the Threat of Race: On Racial Neoliberalism and Born Again Racism," *Communication, Culture & Critique* 4, no. 1 (2011): 23–30.

48. See Goran Dahl, *Radical Conservatism and the Future of Politics* (London: Sage, 1999).

49. See, for instance, the Pew Research Center's data on the 2016 election: Jessica Martinez and Gregory A. Smith, "How the Faithful Voted: A Preliminary 2016 Analysis," Pew Research Center (November 9, 2016), https://www.pewresearch.org/fact-tank/2016/11/09/how-the-faithful-voted-a-preliminary-2016-analysis/.

50. Kurt Eichenwald, "Donald Trump's God Problem," *Newsweek*, September 2, 2016.

51. "GOP Mystery: Why Do Many Evangelicals Back Donald Trump?" *NPR Morning Edition*, March 14, 2016.

52. Alex Morris, "False Idol—Why the Christian Right Worships Donald Trump,"

Rolling Stone, December 2, 2019, https://www.rollingstone.com/politics/politics-features/christian-right-worships-donald-trump-915381/.

53. Christopher Lane, "The True Mission of Donald Trump's Pastor," *Daily Beast*, January 15, 2017.

54. Winslow, *American Catastrophe*, 9, 7.

55. See Winslow, *American Catastrophe*, 9–15; on the prophetic rhetorical tradition, the authoritative text is James Darsey, *The Prophetic Tradition and Radical Rhetoric in America* (New York: NYU Press, 1999).

56. Winslow, *American Catastrophe*, 35–36.

57. Winslow, *American Catastrophe*, 46.

58. Winslow, *American Catastrophe*, 52, 59.

59. Adam Kotsko, *Neoliberalism's Demons: On the Political Theology of Late Capital* (Stanford, CA: Stanford University Press, 2018), 112–13.

60. See also Wendy Brown, *In the Ruins of Neoliberalism: The Rise of Antidemocratic Politics in the West* (New York: Columbia University Press, 2019).

61. Kotsko, *Neoliberalism's Demons*.

62. Kotsko, *Neoliberalism's Demons*, 115.

63. See Connolly, *Capitalism and Christianity, American Style*.

64. Joshua Gunn, *Political Perversion: Rhetorical Aberration in the Time of Trumpeteering* (Chicago: University of Chicago Press, 2020), 75; see also Jennifer Mercieca, *Demagogue for President: The Rhetorical Genius of Donald Trump* (College Station: Texas A&M University Press, 2020).

65. Gunn, *Political Perversion*, 75.

66. See also Winslow, *American Catastrophe*, on this point.

67. Gunn, *Political Perversion*, 79; see also Eric King Watts, "Postracial Fantasies, Blackness, and Zombies," *Communication and Critical/Cultural Studies* 14, no. 4 (2017): 317–33.

68. Donovan O. Schaefer, "Whiteness and Civilization: Shame, Race, and the Rhetoric of Donald Trump," *Communication and Critical/Cultural Studies* 17, no. 1 (2019): 2–3.

69. See, too, Paul Elliott Johnson, "The Art of Masculine Victimhood: Donald Trump's Demagoguery," *Women's Studies in Communication* 40, no. 3 (2017): 229–50.

70. Casey Ryan Kelly, "Donald J. Trump and the Rhetoric of *Ressentiment*," *Quarterly Journal of Speech* 106, no. 1 (2020): 3.

71. Connolly, *Capitalism and Christianity*, 28.

72. See Brown, *In the Ruins of Neoliberalism*, 174–75, and particularly chapter 4.
73. William E. Connolly, *The Fragility of Things: Self-Organizing Processes, Neoliberal Fantasies, and Democratic Activism* (Durham, NC: Duke University Press, 2013), 136.
74. See Melinda Cooper, *Life as Surplus: Biotechnology and Capitalism in the Neoliberal Era* (Seattle: University of Washington Press, 2008).
75. Connolly, *The Fragility of Things*, 171.
76. Kelly, "Donald J. Trump and the Rhetoric of *Ressentiment*," 18.
77. See Grossberg, *Under the Cover of Chaos*.
78. Clayton Crockett, "Christian Kingship and the Empire's New Clothes," in *Doing Theology in the Age of Trump: A Critical Report on Christian Nationalism*, ed. Jeffrey W. Robbins and Clayton Crockett (Eugene, OR: Cascade Press, 2018), 41.
79. Stephen E. Strang, *God, Trump, and the 2020 Election: Why He Must Win and What's at Stake for Christians If He Loses* (Lake Mary, FL: FrontLine, 2020), 53, 141.
80. Winslow, *American Catastrophe*, 10, 11.
81. For a fuller depiction of the right's understanding of so-called cultural Marxism, see Paul M. Weyrich and William S. Lind, *The Next Conservatism* (South Bend, IN: St. Augustine Press, 2009).
82. Stephen E. Strang, *God and Donald Trump* (Lake Mary, FL: FrontLine, 2017), 53.
83. Stephen E. Strang, *Trump Aftershock: The President's Seismic Impact on Culture and Faith in America* (Lake Mary, FL: FrontLine, 2018), 118.
84. Strang, *Trump Aftershock*, 119, 148.
85. Stephen E. Strang, *God, Trump, and COVID-19: How the Pandemic Is Affecting Christians, the World, and America's 2020 Election* (Lake Mary, FL: FrontLine, 2020), 78.
86. Strang, *God, Trump, and COVID-19*, 45; emphasis added.
87. Kelly, "Donald J. Trump and the Rhetoric of *Ressentiment*," 3, 11. On the affective power and constitutive functions of suffering to evangelical identity, see Christian Lundberg, "Enjoying God's Death: *The Passion of the Christ* and the Practices of an Evangelical Public," *Quarterly Journal of Speech* 95, no. 4 (2009): 387–411.
88. Quoted in Strang, *God and Donald Trump*, 174.
89. Strang, *Trump Aftershock*, 175, 197–98.
90. Brown, *In the Ruins of Neoliberalism*, 173, 174.
91. Strang, *God, Trump, and the 2020 Election*, 16–24.

92. Jerry Falwell Jr., "Foreword," in Stephen E. Strang, *Trump Aftershock: The President's Seismic Impact on Culture and Faith in America* (Lake Mary, FL: FrontLine, 2018), x.

93. Strang, *God, Donald Trump, and the 2020 Election*, 16–24.

94. Winslow, *American Catastrophe*, 14.

95. Strang, *God, Trump, and COVID-19*, 71–76.

96. Brown, *In the Ruins of Neoliberalism*, 125.

97. Strang, *God, Trump, and COVID-19*, 78, 94, 96.

98. Winslow, *American Catastrophe*, 14.

99. Edwin Black, "The Second Persona," *Quarterly Journal of Speech* 56, no. 2 (1970): 109–19.

100. Winslow, *American Catastrophe*, 153.

101. Brown, *In the Ruins of Neoliberalism*, 130.

102. Brown, *In the Ruins of Neoliberalism*, 160.

CONCLUSION

1. Zygmunt Bauman, *Collateral Damage: Social Inequalities in a Global Age* (London: Polity, 2011).

2. Martin Luther King Jr., "Speech at Riverside Church," in *Words of a Century: The Top 100 American Speeches, 1900–1999*, ed. Stephen E. Lucas and Martin J. Medhurst (New York: Oxford University Press, 2009), 453–63.

3. Armond Towns, "Black 'Matter' Lives," *Women's Studies in Communication* 41, no. 4 (2018): 349–58. On the linkages of King's legacy and BLM, see too Andre E. Johnson, "Dislocations and Shutdowns: MLK, BLM, and the Rhetoric of Confrontation," *Journal of Contemporary Rhetoric* 8, no. 3 (2018): 137–45; and see Barbara A. Biesecker, "From General History to Philosophy: Black Lives Matter, Late Neoliberal Molecular Biopolitics, and Rhetoric," *Philosophy & Rhetoric* 50, no. 4 (2017): 409–30, on BLM and a rhetoric of copossibility. I also want to thank Amy Young for her insights during the Q and A period of a panel during NCA's (virtual) conference.

4. Jeremy Engels, *The Art of Gratitude* (Albany, NY: SUNY Press, 2018).

5. Ned O'Gorman, *The Iconoclastic Imagination: Image, Catastrophe, and Economy in America from the Kennedy Assassination to September 11* (Chicago: University of Chicago Press, 2016), 194.

Notes | **225**

6. O'Gorman, too, notes the inviolability of the human person as the ontological basis—a "lodestar" of Lippmann's neoliberalism in his *The Iconoclastic Imagination*.

7. Melinda Cooper, *Life as Surplus: Biotechnology and Capitalism in the Neoliberal Era* (Seattle: University of Washington Press, 2008), 16. Nor am I advocating, to paraphrase Ron Greene during our panel on neoliberalism, rhetoric, and economic theology at the 2019 NCA convention in Baltimore, that we follow the Benedictine Option of the Rod Drehers of the world. See Rod Dreher, *The Benedict Option: A Strategy for Christians in a Post-Christian Nation* (New York: Sentinel, 2017).

8. Mitchell Dean and Kaspar Villadsen, *State Phobia and Civil Society: The Political Legacy of Michel Foucault* (Stanford, CA: Stanford University Press, 2016).

9. See William E. Connolly, *The Fragility of Things: Self-Organizing Processes, Neoliberal Fantasies, and Democratic Activism* (Durham, NC: Duke University Press, 2013).

10. See J. Paul Narkunas, *Reified Life: Speculative Capital and the Ahuman Condition* (New York: Fordham University Press, 2018).

11. Hans Joas, *The Sacredness of the Person: A New Genealogy of Human Rights*, trans. Alex Skinner (Washington, DC: Georgetown University Press, 2013), 159.

12. William E. Connolly, *Identity/Difference: Democratic Negotiations of Political Paradox*, expanded ed. (Minneapolis: University of Minnesota Press, 2002), 82, 30, 10.

13. See Connolly, *The Fragility of Things*. This point is also made, from a slightly different vantage, in Samantha Frost's *Biocultural Creatures: Toward a New Theory of the Human* (Durham, NC: Duke University Press, 2016).

14. Anna Grear, *Redirecting Human Rights: Facing the Challenge of Corporate Legal Humanity* (New York: Palgrave Macmillan, 2010), 163, 205.

15. Grear, *Redirecting Human Rights*, 205.

16. Alexander G. Weheliye, *Habeas Viscus: Racializing Assemblages, Biopolitics, and Black Feminist Theories of the Human* (Durham, NC: Duke University Press, 2014), 8; for an excellent collection of essays on Sylvia Wynter's notion of genres of the human and its impact on decolonial theory, see Katherine McKittrick's edited volume *Sylvia Wynter: On Being Human as Praxis* (Durham, NC: Duke University Press, 2015); for an application of these insights in rhetorical studies, see Allison L. Rowland, *Zoetropes and the Politics of Humanhood* (Columbus: Ohio State University Press, 2020).

226 | Notes

17. I take such a reading of Western thought against itself to resonate with what Gayatri Spivak called the "ab-use" of its history and precepts. See Gayatri Chakravorty Spivak, *An Aesthetic Education in the Era of Globalization* (Cambridge, MA: Harvard University Press, 2013).

18. Mary Douglas, "Foreword: No Free Gifts," in Marcel Mauss, *The Gift: The Form and Reason for Exchange in Archaic Societies*, trans. W. D. Halls (New York: W.W. Norton, 2000), x.

19. Marcel Mauss, *The Gift: The Form and Reason for Exchange in Archaic Societies*, trans. W. D. Halls (New York: W.W. Norton, 2000), 65.

20. Jacques Derrida, *Given Time: 1. Counterfeit Money*, trans. Peggy Kamuf (Chicago: University of Chicago Press, 1992), 29.

21. Derrida, *Given Time*, 123.

22. Derrida, *Given Time*, 138.

23. Derrida, *Given Time*, 30.

24. John Milbank, "Can a Gift Be Given? Prolegomena to a Future Trinitarian Metaphysic," *Modern Theology* 11, no. 1 (1995): 151.

25. Mari Lee Mifsud, *Rhetoric and the Gift: Ancient Rhetorical Theory and Contemporary Communication* (Pittsburgh, PA: Duquesne University Press, 2015), 17.

26. Derrida, *Given Time*, at 162 and 170.

27. Engels, *Art of Gratitude*, 155.

28. Matthias Fritsch, "The Gift of Nature in Mauss and Derrida," *Oxford Literary Review* 37, no. 1 (2015): 16, 8.

29. William E. Connolly, *Capitalism and Christianity, American Style* (Durham, NC: Duke University Press, 2008), 80.

30. Connolly, *Capitalism and Christianity*, 84.

31. Connolly, *Fragility of Things*, 149.

32. Connolly, *Capitalism and Christianity*, 7.

33. Grear, *Redirecting Human Rights*, 163.

34. Grear, *Redirecting Human Rights*, 186.

35. For more, see Grear's elucidation in chapter eight of her *Redirecting Human Rights*.

36. Benjamin Golder, *Foucault and the Politics of Rights* (Stanford, CA: Stanford University Press, 2015), 82, 6.

37. David Ciepley, "Beyond Public and Private: Toward a Political Theory of the Corporation," *American Political Science Review* 107, no. 1 (2013): 139–58; David

Ciepley, "Neither Persons nor Associations: Against Constitutional Rights for Corporations," *Journal of Law and Courts* 1, no. 2 (2013): 221–45.

38. Ciepley, "Neither Persons nor Associations," 221–45.

39. Joshua Barkan, *Corporate Sovereignty: Law and Government under Capitalism* (Minneapolis: University of Minnesota Press, 2013). While Grossberg argues for the possible necessity of thinking capitalism without the corporation as a way to combat our cultural predicament, I would argue that we need to think the corporation outside of and beyond liberal capitalism. See Lawrence Grossberg, *Under the Cover of Chaos: Trump and the Battle for the American Right* (London: Pluto Press, 2018).

40. Iris Marion Young, "Responsibility and Global Justice: A Social Connection Model," *Social Policy and Philosophy Foundation* 23, no. 1 (2006): 102–30.

41. See Hannah Arendt, "Collective Responsibility," in *Amor Mundi: Explorations in the Faith and Thought of Hannah Arendt*, ed. James W. Bernauer (Boston: Martinus Nijhoff Publishers, 1987), 43–50.

42. Young, "Responsibility and Global Justice," 102–30.

43. Serena Parekh, "Getting to the Root of Gender Inequality: Structural Injustice and Political Responsibility," *Hypatia* 26, no. 4 (2011): 683.

44. Dennis Weiser, "Two Concepts of Communication as Criteria for Collective Responsibility," *Journal of Business Ethics* 7, no. 10 (1988): 735–44, 741.

45. See Carolyn Hardin, "Finding the 'Neo' in Neoliberalism," *Cultural Studies* 28, no. 2 (2012): 199–221.

46. Young, "Responsibility and Global Justice," 102, 123.

47. Karlyn Kohrs Campbell, "Agency: Promiscuous and Protean," *Communication and Critical/Cultural Studies* 2, no. 1 (2005): 1–19; see too Judith Butler, *Undoing Gender* (New York: Routledge, 2004).

48. Connolly, *The Fragility of Things*, 147.

49. Sonja Foss, "Rhetorical Criticism as Synecdoche for Agency," *Rhetoric Review* 25, no. 4 (2006): 375–79; Mifsud, *Rhetoric and the Gift*.

50. Catherine Chaput, *Market Affect and the Rhetoric of Political Economic Debates* (Columbia: University of South Carolina Press, 2019).

51. See too Freya Thimsen, "The People Against Corporate Personhood: Doxa and Dissensual Democracy," *Quarterly Journal of Speech* 101, no. 3 (2015): 485–508.

52. Barbara Cruikshank, "Neoliberalism: Towards a Critical Counter-Conduct," in *Rethinking Neoliberalism: Resisting the Disciplinary Regime*, ed. Sanford F. Schram and Marianna Pavlovskaya (New York: Routledge, 2018), 253.

Bibliography

Aarim-Heriot, Najia. *Chinese Immigrants, African Americans, and Racial Anxiety in the United States, 1848–82*. Urbana: University of Illinois Press, 2003.

Abraham, Felicia. "CHARISMA Digital Ranks among 'Top 5' Digital Magazines." *Charisma*. https://www.charismamag.com/site-archives/570-news/featured-news/12170-charisma-digital-ranks-among-top-5-digital-magazines.

Agamben, Giorgio. *Homo Sacer: Sovereign Power and Bare Life*. Translated by Daniel Heller-Roazen. Stanford, CA: Stanford University Press, 1998.

———. *The Kingdom and the Glory: For a Theological Genealogy of Economy and Government*. Translated by Lorenzo Chiesa, with Matteo Mandarini. Stanford, CA: Stanford University Press, 2011.

Agnew, Spiro T. "Television News Coverage." In *Words of a Century: The Top 100 American Speeches, 1900–1999*, edited by Stephen E. Lucas and Martin J. Medhurst, 496–503. New York: Oxford University Press, 2009.

Amadae, S. M. *Prisoners of Reason: Game Theory and Neoliberal Political Economy*. Cambridge: Cambridge University Press, 2016.

———. *Rationalizing Capitalist Democracy: The Cold War Origins of Rational Choice Liberalism*. Chicago: University of Chicago Press, 2003.

Bibliography

Aranzadi, Javier. *Liberalism against Liberalism: Theoretical Analysis of the Works of Ludwig von Mises and Gary Becker*. New York: Routledge, 2006.

Arendt, Hannah. "Collective Responsibility." In *Amor Mundi: Explorations in the Faith and Thought of Hannah Arendt*, edited by James W. Bernauer, 43–50. Boston: Martinus Nijhoff Publishers, 1987.

———. *The Human Condition*. 2nd ed. Chicago: University of Chicago Press, 1998.

Asen, Robert. "Ideology, Materiality, and Counterpublicity: William E. Simon and the Rise of a Conservative Counterintelligentsia." *Quarterly Journal of Speech* 95, no. 3 (2009): 263–88.

———. "Knowledge, Communication, and Anti-Critical Publicity: The Friedmans' Market Public." *Communication Theory* 31, no. 2 (2021): 169–89.

Aune, James Arnt. "Justice Holmes's Rhetoric and the Progressive Path of the Law." In *Rhetoric and Reform in the Progressive Era*, vol. 6, *Rhetorical History of the United States*, edited by J. Michael Hogan, 145–84. East Lansing: Michigan State University Press, 2003.

———. *Selling the Free Market: The Rhetoric of Economic Correctness*. New York: Guilford Press, 2001.

Ballif, Michelle. "Writing the Event: The Impossible Possibility for Historiography." *Rhetoric Society Quarterly* 44, no. 3 (2014): 243–55.

Barkan, Joshua. *Corporate Sovereignty: Law and Government under Capitalism*. Minneapolis: University of Minnesota Press, 2013.

———. "Roberto Esposito's Political Biology and Corporate Forms of Life." *Law, Culture and the Humanities* 8, no. 1 (2012): 84–101.

Barton, Bruce. "And There Arose a New King Which Knew Not Joseph." Bruce Barton Papers, box 122, State Historical Society of Wisconsin.

———. "Calls Advertising Power to Keep Business Striving for High Ideals." *New York Evening Post*, January 3, 1928. Bruce Barton Papers, box 102, State Historical Society of Wisconsin.

———. *The Man and the Book Nobody Knows*. Indianapolis, IN: Bobbs-Merrill, 1959.

———. "The Public." *Vital Speeches of the Day* 2, no. 6 (1935).

"Barton Lists 39 'Roosevelt Emergencies.'" *Herald-Tribune*, March 17, 1939. Bruce Barton Papers, box 60, State Historical Society of Wisconsin.

Bauman, Zygmunt. *Collateral Damage: Social Inequalities in a Global Age*. London: Polity, 2011.

Beard, Charles A., and Mary R. Beard. *The Rise of American Civilization*. New ed., revised and enlarged. New York: Macmillan, 1956.

Bell, Daniel. *The End of Ideology: On the Exhaustion of Political Ideas in the Fifties.* Revised ed. New York: Free Press, 1965.

Benhabib, Seyla. "Models of Public Space: Hannah Arendt, the Liberal Tradition, and Jurgen Habermas." In *Habermas and the Public Sphere*, edited by Craig Calhoun, 73–98. Cambridge, MA: MIT Press, 1992.

Berger, Monroe. *Equality by Statute: The Revolution in Civil Rights.* Revised ed. Garden City, NY: Anchor Books, 1968.

Berle, Adolf, and Gardiner C. Means. *The Modern Corporation and Private Property.* New York: Commerce Clearing House (Loose leaf service division of the Corporation Trust Company), 1932.

Bernauer, James W., SJ, ed. *Amor Mundi: Explorations in the Faith and Thought of Hannah Arendt.* Boston: Martinus Nijhoff Publishers, 1987.

Biesecker, Barbara A. "From General History to Philosophy: Black Lives Matter, Late Neoliberal Molecular Biopolitics, and Rhetoric." *Philosophy & Rhetoric* 50, no. 4 (2017): 409–30.

Birla, Ritu. "Law as Economy: Convention, Corporation, Currency." *UC Irvine Law Review* 1, no. 3 (2011): 1015–37.

———. "Maine (and Weber) Against the Grain: Towards a Postcolonial Genealogy of the Corporate Person." *Journal of Law and Society* 40, no. 1 (2013): 92–114.

Black, Edwin. *Rhetorical Criticism: A Study in Method.* Madison: University of Wisconsin Press, 1965.

———. "The Second Persona." *Quarterly Journal of Speech* 56, no. 2 (1970): 109–19.

Blackford, Mansel G., and K. Austin Kerr. *Business Enterprise in American History.* 3rd ed. Boston: Houghton Mifflin Company, 1994.

Bowers, John Waite, and Donovan J. Ochs. *The Rhetoric of Agitation and Control.* Reading, MA: Addison-Wesley Publishing Company, 1971.

Bowman, Scott R. *The Modern Corporation and American Political Thought: Law, Power, Ideology.* University Park: Pennsylvania State University Press, 1996.

Brands, H. W. *American Colossus: The Triumph of Capitalism, 1865–1900.* New York: Anchor Books, 2010.

Brimelow, Peter. *Alien Nation: Common Sense about America's Immigration Disaster.* New York: Harper Perennial, 1996.

Brown, Wendy. *In the Ruins of Neoliberalism: The Rise of Antidemocratic Politics in the West.* New York: Columbia University Press, 2019.

———. *Undoing the Demos: Neoliberalism's Stealth Revolution.* Cambridge, MA: Zone Books, 2015.

232 | Bibliography

Buchanan, Patrick. *The Great Betrayal: How American Sovereignty and Social Justice Are Being Sacrificed to the Gods of the Global Economy.* New York: Little, Brown & Co., 1998.

Burke, Kenneth. *A Rhetoric of Motives.* Berkeley: University of California Press, 1969.

Bussolini, Jeffrey. "What Is a Dispositive?" *Foucault Studies* 10 (2010): 85–107.

Butler, Judith. *Frames of War: When Is Life Grievable?* New York: Verso, 2009.

———. *Undoing Gender.* New York: Routledge, 2004.

Cacho, Lisa Marie. *Social Death: Racialized Rightlessness and the Criminalization of the Unprotected.* New York: New York University Press, 2012.

Campbell, Karlyn Kohrs. "Agency: Promiscuous and Protean." *Communication and Critical/Cultural Studies* 2, no. 1 (2005): 1–19.

Carr, Kelly M. *The Rhetorical Invention of Diversity: Supreme Court Opinions, Public Argument, and Affirmative Action.* East Lansing: Michigan State University Press, 2018).

Chandler, Alfred Dupont. *The Visible Hand: The Managerial Revolution in American Business.* Cambridge, MA: Harvard University Press, 1977.

Chaput, Catherine. *Market Affect and the Rhetoric of Political Economic Debates.* Columbia: University of South Carolina Press, 2019.

Chaput, Catherine, and Joshua Hanan. "Economic Rhetoric as *Taxis*: Neoliberal Governmentality and the *Dispositif* of Freakonomics." *Journal of Cultural Economy* 8, no. 1 (2015): 42–61.

———. "Rhetorical Hegemony: Transactional Ontologies and the Reinvention of Material Infrastructures." *Philosophy & Rhetoric* 52, no. 4 (2019): 339–65.

Charles E. Adams to Mr. D. L. Chambers of The Bobbs-Merrill Co., April 14, 1925. Bruce Barton Papers, box 107, State Historical Society of Wisconsin.

Chavez, Karma. "The Body: An Abstract and Actual Rhetorical Concept." *Rhetoric Society Quarterly* 48, no. 3 (2018): 242–50.

Childers, Christopher. *The Failure of Popular Sovereignty: Slavery, Manifest Destiny, and the Radicalization of Southern Politics.* Lawrence: University of Kansas Press, 2012.

Christiaens, Tim. "Hayek's Vicarious Secularization of Providential Theology." *Philosophy and Social Criticism* 45, no. 1 (2018): 71–95.

Church Builders, June 2001; Bernard R. DeRemer "A Superb Steward"; Crowell, Henry P. CVC953; Moody Bible Institute, Chicago; June 20, 2016.

Ciepley, David. "Beyond Public and Private: Toward a Political Theory of the

Corporation." *American Political Science Review* 107, no. 1 (2013): 139–58.

Clark, E. Culpepper, and Raymie E. McKerrow. "The Rhetorical Construction of History." In *Doing Rhetorical History: Concepts and Cases*, edited by Kathleen Turner, 33–46. Tuscaloosa: University of Alabama Press, 1998.

Connolly, William E. *Capitalism and Christianity, American Style*. Durham, NC: Duke University Press, 2008.

———. *The Fragility of Things: Self-Organizing Processes, Neoliberal Fantasies, and Democratic Activism*. Durham, NC: Duke University Press, 2013.

———. *Identity/Difference: Democratic Negotiations of Political Paradox*. Expanded ed. Minneapolis: University of Minnesota Press, 2002.

Cooper, Melinda. *Life as Surplus: Biotechnology and Capitalism in the Neoliberal Era*. Seattle: University of Washington Press, 2008.

Cornelissen, Lars. "The Secularization of Providential Order: F. A. Hayek's Political-Economic Theology." *Political Theology* 18, no. 8 (2017): 660–76.

Councilor, K. C. "Feeding the Body Politic: Metaphors of Digestion in Progressive Era US Immigration Discourse." *Communication and Critical/Cultural Studies* 14, no. 2 (2016): 139–57.

Crockett, Clayton. "Christian Kingship and the Empire's New Clothes." In *Doing Theology in the Age of Trump: A Critical Report on Christian Nationalism*, edited by Jeffrey W. Robbins and Clayton Crockett, 39–42. Eugene, OR: Cascade Press, 2018.

"Crowell Will Leaves Fortune to Church Work." *Chicago Tribune*, November 11, 1944.

Crowell, Henry P. CBC953, Moody Bible Institute, Chicago, June 20, 2016.

Cruikshank, Barbara. "Neoliberalism: Towards a Critical Counter-Conduct." In *Rethinking Neoliberalism: Resisting the Disciplinary Regime*, edited by Sanford F. Schram and Marianna Pavlovskaya, 236–55. New York: Routledge, 2018.

Crunden, Robert. *Ministers of Reform: The Progressives' Achievement in American Civilization, 1889–1920*. Urbana: University of Illinois Press, 1982.

Dahl, Goran. *Radical Conservatism and the Future of Politics*. London: Sage, 1999.

Dardot, Pierre, and Christian Laval. *The New Way of the World: On Neoliberal Society*. Translated by Gregory Elliott. New York: Verso, 2017.

Darsey, James. *The Prophetic Tradition and Radical Rhetoric in America*. New York: NYU Press, 1999.

Dartmouth College v. Woodward, 4 Wheaton 518 (1819).

Davis, James Calvin, and Charles Mathewes. "Saving Grace and Moral Striving: Thrift in Puritan Theology." In *Thrift and Thriving in America: Capitalism and*

Moral Order from the Puritans to the Present, edited by Joshua J. Yates and James Davison Hunter, 88–116. New York: Oxford University Press, 2011.

Davies, Will. "The New Neoliberalism." *New Left Review* 101 (September–October 2016): 121–34.

Day, Richard Ellsworth. *Breakfast Table Autocrat: The Life Story of Henry Parsons Crowell*. Chicago: Moody Press, 1946.

Dean, Mitchell. *The Signature of Power: Sovereignty, Governmentality and Biopolitics*. New York: Sage, 2013.

Dean, Mitchell, and Kaspar Villadsen. *State Phobia and Civil Society: The Political Legacy of Michel Foucault*. Stanford, CA: Stanford University Press, 2016.

Derrida, Jacques. *Given Time: 1. Counterfeit Money*. Translated by Peggy Kamuf. Chicago: University of Chicago Press, 1992.

Douglas, Mary. "Foreword: No Free Gifts." In Marcel Mauss, *The Gift: The Form and Reason for Exchange in Archaic Societies*, translated by W. D. Halls, vii–xviii. New York: W.W. Norton, 2000.

Dreher, Rod. *The Benedict Option: A Strategy for Christians in a Post-Christian Nation*. New York: Sentinel, 2017.

Dumont, Louis. "A Modified View of Our Origins: The Christian Beginnings of Modern Individualism." In *The Category of the Person: Anthropology, Philosophy, History*, edited by Michael Carrithers, Steven Collins, and Steven Lukes, 93–122. New York: Cambridge University Press, 1985.

———. *From Mandeville to Marx: The Genesis and Triumph of Economic Ideology*. Chicago: University of Chicago Press, 1977.

Durkheim, Emile. *The Elementary Forms of Religious Life*. Translated by Karen E. Fields. New York: Free Press, 1995.

Eichenwald, Kurt. "Donald Trump's God Problem." *Newsweek*, September 2, 2016.

Elvin, Mark. "Between the Earth and Heaven: Conceptions of the Self in China." In *The Category of the Person: Anthropology, Philosophy, History*, edited by Michael Carrithers, Steven Collins, and Steven Lukes, 156–89. New York: Cambridge University Press, 1985.

Enck-Wanzer, Darrell. "Barack Obama, the Tea Party, and the Threat of Race: On Racial Neoliberalism and Born Again Racism." *Communication, Culture & Critique* 4, no. 1 (2011): 23–30.

Engels, Jeremy. *The Art of Gratitude*. Albany, NY: SUNY Press, 2018.

Esposito, Roberto. "The Dispositif of the Person." *Law, Culture and the Humanities* 8, no. 1 (2012): 17–30.

———. *Persons and Things: From the Body's Point of View*. Translated by Zakiya Hanafi. Malden, MA: Polity, 2015.

———. *Third Person: Politics of Life and Philosophy of the Impersonal*. Translated by Zakiya Hanafi. Malden, MA: Polity, 2012.

Ewen, Stuart. *Captains of Consciousness: Advertising and the Social Roots of the Consumer Culture*. New York: McGraw-Hill, 1976.

———. *PR! A Social History of Spin*. New York: Basic Books, 1996.

Falwell, Jerry, Jr. "Foreword." In Stephen E. Strang, *Trump Aftershock: The President's Seismic Impact on Culture and Faith in America*, xi–xii. Lake Mary, FL: FrontLine, 2018.

Federman, Carey. "Constructing Types of Persons in 1886: Corporate and Criminal." *Law and Critique* 14 (May 2003): 167–89.

First National Bank of Boston v. Bellotti, 435 U.S. 765 (1978).

Foley, Duncan K. *Adam's Fallacy: A Guide to Economic Theology*. Cambridge, MA: Belknap Press of Harvard University Press, 2006.

Foss, Sonja. "Rhetorical Criticism as Synecdoche for Agency." *Rhetoric Review* 25, no. 4 (2006): 375–79.

Foucault, Michel. *The Archaeology of Knowledge*. Translated by A. M. Sheridan Smith. New York: Vintage Books, 1972.

———. *The Birth of Biopolitics: Lectures at the Collège de France, 1978–1979*. Edited by Michel Senellart, François Ewald, Alessandro Fontana, and Arnold I. Davidson. Translated by Graham Burchell. New York: Picador, 2008.

———. *The History of Sexuality*. Vol. 1. Translated by Robert Hurley. New York: Vintage Books, 1978.

———. "Nietzsche, Genealogy, History." In *Language, Counter-Memory, Practice*, edited by Donald F. Bouchard. Ithaca, NY: Cornell University Press, 1977.

———. *Security, Territory, Population: Lectures at the Collège de France, 1977–1978*. Edited by Michel Senellart, François Ewald, Alessandro Fontana, and Arnold I. Davidson. Translated by Graham Burchell. New York: Picador, 2007.

———. *Society Must Be Defended: Lectures at the Collège de France, 1975–1976*. Edited by Maurio Bertani, Alessandro Fontana, and François Ewald. Translated by David Macey. New York: Picador, 2003.

———. "The Subject and Power." In *Michel Foucault: Beyond Structuralism and Hermeneutics*, edited by Hubert L. Dreyfus and Paul Rabinow, 208–26. Chicago: University of Chicago Press, 1982.

Francis, Sam. *Revolution from the Middle*. Raleigh, NC: Middle American Press, 1997.

Bibliography

Fried, Richard. *The Man Everybody Knew: Bruce Barton and the Making of Modern America*. Chicago: Ivan R. Dee, 2005.

Friedman, Benjamin M. *Religion and the Rise of Capitalism*. New York: Alfred A. Knopf, 2021.

Friedman, Milton. *Capitalism and Freedom*. With the assistance of Rose D. Friedman. Chicago: University of Chicago Press, 1962.

Fritsch, Matthias. "The Gift of Nature in Mauss and Derrida." *Oxford Literary Review* 37, no. 1 (2015): 1–23.

Frost, Samantha. *Biocultural Creatures: Toward a New Theory of the Human*. Durham, NC: Duke University Press, 2016.

Gandy, Oscar H., Jr. *Beyond Agenda Setting: Information Subsidies and Public Policy*. Ann Arbor: University of Michigan Press, 1982.

Gierke, Otto Von. *Political Theories of the Middle Age*. Translated by Frederic William Maitland. Cambridge: Cambridge University Press, 1951.

Gilbert, James. *Another Chance: Postwar America, 1945–1985*. 2nd ed. Chicago: Dorsey Press, 1986.

Gitlin, Todd. *The Whole World Is Watching: Mass Media in the Making and Unmaking of the New Left*. Berkeley: University of California Press, 1980.

Gloege, Timothy. *Guaranteed Pure: The Moody Bible Institute, Business, and the Making of Modern Evangelicalism*. Chapel Hill: University of North Carolina Press, 2015.

Golder, Ben. *Foucault and the Politics of Rights*. Stanford, CA: Stanford University Press, 2015.

Gomez, Adam. "Deus Vult: John L. O'Sullivan, Manifest Destiny, and American Democratic Messianism." *American Political Thought* 1, no. 2 (2012): 236–62.

Goodchild, Philip. *Credit and Faith*. Lanham, MD: Rowman and Littlefield, 2019.

"GOP Mystery: Why Do Many Evangelicals Back Donald Trump?" *NPR Morning Edition*, March 14, 2016.

Gorski, Philip. "Christianity and Democracy after Trump." *Political Theology Network*, July 18, 2018. https://politicaltheology.com/christianity-and-democracy-after-trump/.

Gottfried, Paul. *After Liberalism: Mass Democracy in the Managerial State*. Princeton, NJ: Princeton University Press, 1999.

———. *Multiculturalism and the Politics of Guilt: Towards a Secular Theocracy*. Columbia: University of Missouri Press, 2002.

Gottfried, Paul, and Thomas Fleming. *The Conservative Movement*. Woodbridge, CT:

Twayne Publishers, 1988.

Graham, Jay Howard. *Everyman's Constitution: Historical Essays on the Fourteenth Amendment, the "Conspiracy Theory," and American Constitutionalism*. Madison: University of Wisconsin Press, 1968.

Grear, Anna. *Redirecting Human Rights: Facing the Challenge of Corporate Legal Humanity*. New York: Palgrave Macmillan, 2010.

Green, David G. *The New Right: The Counter-Revolution in Political, Economic and Social Thought*. London: Wheatsheaf Books, 1987.

Greene, Ronald Walter. "Y Movies: Film and the Modernization of Pastoral Power." *Communication and Critical/Cultural Studies* 2, no. 1 (2005): 20–36.

Grossberg, Lawrence. *Under the Cover of Chaos: Trump and the Battle for the American Right*. London: Pluto Press, 2018.

Gunn, Joshua. *Political Perversion: Rhetorical Aberration in the Time of Trumpeteering*. Chicago: University of Chicago Press, 2020.

Gunn, T. Jeremy. *Spiritual Weapons: The Cold War and the Forging of an American National Religion*. Westport, CT: Praeger, 2009.

Gyory, Andrew. *Closing the Gate: Race, Politics, and the Chinese Exclusion Act*. Chapel Hill: University of North Carolina Press, 1998.

Habermas, Jurgen. *Structural Transformation of the Public Sphere: An Inquiry into a Category of Bourgeois Society*. Cambridge, MA: MIT Press, 1991.

Hall, Stuart. "Who Needs Identity?" In *Identity: A Reader*, edited by Paul Du Guy, Jessica Evans, and Peter Redman. New York: Sage, 2000.

Hallis, Frederick. *Corporate Personality: A Study in Jurisprudence*. London: Oxford University Press, 1930.

Haney-Lopez, Ian. *White by Law: The Legal Construction of Race*. New York: New York University Press, 1996.

Hardin, Carolyn. "Finding the 'Neo' in Neoliberalism." *Cultural Studies* 28, no. 2 (2012): 199–221.

Harris, Kate Lockwood. "Feminist Dilemmatic Theorizing: New Materialism in Communication Studies." *Communication Theory* 26, no. 2 (2016): 150–70.

Hartmann, Thom. *Unequal Protection: How Corporations Became "People"—And How You Can Fight Back*. 2nd ed., revised and expanded. San Francisco: Berrett-Koehler Publishers, 2010.

Hartz, Louis. *The Liberal Tradition in America: An Interpretation of American Political Thought since the Revolution*. New York: Harcourt, Brace & World, Inc., 1955.

Bibliography

Harvey, David. *A Brief History of Neoliberalism*. New York: Oxford University Press, 2007.

Hasian, Marouf, Jr. "The Rhetorical Turn in First Amendment Scholarship: A Case Study of Holmes and the 'Marketplace of Ideas.'" *Free Speech Yearbook* 31, no. 1 (1993): 42–65.

Hayek, Friedrich A. *The Road to Serfdom*. 50th anniversary ed. Introduction by Milton Friedman. Chicago: University of Chicago Press, 1994.

———. "Why I Am Not a Conservative." In *The Constitution of Liberty*. Chicago: University of Chicago Press, 1960.

Heald, Morrell. *The Social Responsibilities of Business: Company and Community, 1900–1960*. Cleveland, OH: Press of Case Western Reserve University, 1970.

Herring, William Rodney, and Mark Garrett Longaker. "Wishful, Rational, and Political Thinking: The Labor Theory of Value as Rhetoric." *Argumentation and Advocacy* 50, no. 4 (2014): 193–209.

Herzog, Jonathan P. *The Spiritual-Industrial Complex: America's Religious Battle against Communism in the Early Cold War*. New York: Oxford University Press, 2011.

Hobbes, Thomas. *Leviathan*. Edited by Edwin Curley. Indianapolis, IN: Hackett Publishing Company, 1994.

Hofstadter, Richard. *The Age of Reform: From Bryan to FDR*. New York: Vintage Books, 1955.

Hollis, Martin. "Of Masks and Men." In *The Category of the Person: Anthropology, Philosophy, History*, edited by Michael Carrithers, Steven Collins, and Steven Lukes, 217–33. New York: Cambridge University Press, 1985.

Horsman, Reginald. *Race and Manifest Destiny: The Origins of American Racial Anglo-Saxonism*. Cambridge, MA: Harvard University Press, 1981.

Hulliung, Mark. *The Social Contract in America: From the Revolution to the Present Age*. Lawrence: University Press of Kansas, 2007.

Hunter, James Davison. "Thrift and Moral Formation." In *Thrift and Thriving in America: Capitalism and Moral Order from the Puritans to the Present*, edited by Joshua J. Yates and James Davison Hunter, 242–63. New York: Oxford University Press, 2011.

In re Tiburcio Parrott, 1 Fed. 481 (C. C. D. Cal 1880). http://law.resource.org/pub/us/case/reporter/F/0001/0001.f.0481.pdf.

Iyengar, Shanto. *Media Politics: A Citizen's Guide*. 3rd ed. New York: W.W. Norton, 2015.

Jackson Lears, T. J. "From Salvation to Self-Realization: Advertising and the Therapeutic Roots of the Consumer Culture, 1880–1930." In *The Culture of Consumption: Critical Essays in American History, 1880–1980*, edited by Richard Wrightman Fox and T. J. Jackson Lears, 1–38. New York: Pantheon Books, 1983.

———. "The Modernization of Thrift." In *Thrift and Thriving in America: Capitalism and Moral Order from the Puritans to the Present*, edited by Joshua J. Yates and James Davison Hunter, 209–41. New York: Oxford University Press, 2011.

———. *Rebirth of a Nation: The Making of Modern America, 1877–1920*. New York: Harper Perennial, 2010.

Jacob, John N. *The Lewis F. Powell, Jr. Papers: A Guide*. Lexington, VA: Washington and Lee University School of Law, 1997.

Jasinski, James. "A Constitutive Framework for Rhetorical Historiography: Toward an Understanding of 'Constitution' in the *Federalist Papers*." In *Doing Rhetorical History: Concepts and Cases*, edited by Kathleen Turner, 72–92. Tuscaloosa: University of Alabama Press, 1998.

Jeffries, John C., Jr. *Justice Lewis F. Powell, Jr*. New York: Charles F. Scribner's Sons, 1994.

Joas, Hans. *The Sacredness of the Person: A New Genealogy of Human Rights*. Translated by Alec Skinner. Washington, DC: Georgetown University Press, 2013.

Johnson, Andre E. "Dislocations and Shutdowns: MLK, BLM, and the Rhetoric of Confrontation." *Journal of Contemporary Rhetoric* 8, no. 3 (2018): 137–45.

Johnson, Paul Elliott. "The Art of Masculine Victimhood: Donald Trump's Demagoguery." *Women's Studies in Communication* 40, no. 3 (2017): 229–50.

Jordan, David M. *Roscoe Conkling of New York: Voice in the Senate*. Ithaca, NY: Cornell University Press, 1971.

Kantorowicz, Ernst. *The King's Two Bodies: A Study in Medieval Political Theology*. Princeton, NJ: Princeton University Press, 2016.

Kaylor, Brian. "Sheep without a Shepherd (but with an Archbishop): Foucault's Pastoral Power and the Denying of Communion." *Atlantic Journal of Communication* 19 (2011): 152–68.

Kelly, Casey Ryan. "Donald J. Trump and the Rhetoric of *Ressentiment*." *Quarterly Journal of Speech* 106, no. 1 (2020): 2–24.

Kennedy, George A. *Classical Rhetoric and Its Christian and Secular Tradition from Ancient to Modern Times*. Chapel Hill: University of North Carolina Press, 1980.

Kens, Paul. "Civil Liberties, Chinese Laborers, and Corporations." In *Law in the*

Western United States, edited by Gordon Morris Bakken, 499–502. Norman: University of Oklahoma Press, 2000.

———. *Justice Stephen Field: Shaping Liberty from the Gold Rush to the Gilded Age*. Lawrence: University of Kansas Press, 1997.

Kerr, Robert L. *The Corporate Free Speech Movement: Cognitive Feudalism and the Endangered Marketplace of Ideas*. El Paso, TX: LFB Press, 2008.

Kiewe, Amos, and Davis Houck. *A Shining City on a Hill: Ronald Reagan's Economic Rhetoric, 1951–1989*. New York: Praeger, 1991.

King, Desmond S. *The New Right: Politics, Markets, and Citizenship*. London: Macmillan Education, 1987.

King, Martin Luther, Jr. "Speech at Riverside Church." In *Words of a Century: The Top 100 American Speeches, 1900–1999*, edited by Stephen E. Lucas and Martin J. Medhurst, 453–63. New York: Oxford University Press, 2009.

Kirk, Russell. *The Conservative Mind: From Burke to Santayana*. Chicago: Henry Regnery Company, 1953.

———. "The Inhumane Businessman." *Fortune* 55 (1957): 160–61, 248. http:// kirkcenter.org/education/the-inhumane-businessman/.

———. "The Question of Tradition." In *The Paleoconservatives: New Voices of the Old Right*, edited by Joseph Scotchie, 59–78. New York: Routledge, 1999.

———. *The Roots of American Order*. LaSalle, IL: Open Court Press, 1974.

Klein, Naomi. *The Shock Doctrine: The Rise of Disaster Capitalism*. New York: Picador, 2008.

Koschmann, Matthew A., and James McDonald. "Organizational Rituals, Communication, and the Question of Agency." *Management Communication Quarterly* 29, no. 2 (2015): 229–56.

Kotsko, Adam. *Neoliberalism's Demons: On the Political Theology of Late Capital*. Stanford, CA: Stanford University Press, 2018.

Kristol, Irving. *Two Cheers for Capitalism*. New York: Basic Books, 1978.

Kruse, Kevin. *One Nation Under God: How Corporate America Invented Christian America*. New York: Basic Books, 2015.

Kuhn, Timothy, Karen Ashcraft, and François Cooren. *The Work of Communication: Relational Perspectives on Working and Organizing in Contemporary Capitalism*. New York: Routledge, 2019.

Kunde, Meg. "Making the Free Market Moral: Ronald Reagan's Covenantal Economy." *Rhetoric & Public Affairs* 22, no. 2 (2019): 217–52.

Laird, Pamela Walker. *Advertising Progress: American Business and the Rise of*

Consumer Marketing. Baltimore, MD: Johns Hopkins University Press, 2001.

Lane, Christopher. "The True Mission of Donald Trump's Pastor." *Daily Beast,* January 15, 2017.

Laski, Harold. "The Personality of Associations." *Harvard Law Review* 29, no. 4 (1916): 404–26.

Lee, Michael J. *Creating Conservatism: Postwar Words That Made an American Movement.* East Lansing: Michigan State University Press, 2014.

———. "WFB: The Gladiatorial Style and the Politics of Provocation." *Rhetoric & Public Affairs* 13, no. 2 (2010): 217–50.

Lemke, Thomas. *Biopolitics: An Advanced Introduction.* New York: New York University Press, 2011.

Lienhardt, Godfrey. "Self: Public, Private. Some African Representations." In *The Category of the Person: Anthropology, Philosophy, History,* edited by Michael Carrithers, Steven Collins, and Steven Lukes, 141–55. New York: Cambridge University Press, 1985.

Leshem, Dotan. *The Origins of Neoliberalism: Modeling the Economy from Jesus to Foucault.* New York: Columbia University Press, 2017.

Lippmann, Walter. *Drift and Mastery: An Attempt to Diagnose the Current Unrest.* Englewood Cliffs, NJ: Prentice-Hall, 1961.

———. *The Phantom Public.* New Brunswick, NJ: Transaction Publishers, 1993.

Lowi, Theodore. *The End of Liberalism: The Second Republic of the United States.* 2nd ed. New York: W.W. Norton & Company, 1979.

Lukes, Steven. "Conclusion." In *The Category of the Person: Anthropology, Philosophy, History,* edited by Michael Carrithers, Steven Collins, and Steven Lukes, 282–301. New York: Cambridge University Press, 1985.

———. "Durkheim's 'Individualism and the Intellectuals.'" *Political Studies* 17, no. 1 (1969): 14–30.

Lundberg, Christian. "Enjoying God's Death: *The Passion of the Christ* and the Practices of an Evangelical Public." *Quarterly Journal of Speech* 95, no. 4 (2009): 387–411.

Lustig, Jeffrey R. *Corporate Liberalism: The Origins of Modern American Political Theory, 1890–1920.* Berkeley: University of California Press, 1982.

Lynn, Joshua A. *Preserving the White Man's Republic: Jacksonian Democracy, Race, and the Transformation of American Conservatism.* Charlottesville: University of Virginia Press, 2019.

MacPherson, C. B. *The Political Theory of Possessive Individualism: Hobbes to Locke.*

Oxford: Oxford University Press, 1962.

Maltz, Earl M. "The Triumph of the Southern Man: *Dowell, Shelby County*, and the Jurisprudence of Justice Lewis F. Powell, Jr." *Duke Journal of Constitutional Law & Public Policy* 14 (2019): 169–232.

Manring, M. M. *Slave in a Box: The Strange Career of Aunt Jemima*. Charlottesville: University Press of Virginia, 1998).

Marchand, Roland. *Advertising the American Dream: Making Way for Modernity, 1920–1940*. Berkeley: University of California Press, 1986.

———. *Creating the Corporate Soul: The Rise of Public Relations and Corporate Imagery in American Big Business*. Berkeley: University of California Press, 2001.

Marquette, Arthur F. *Brands, Trademarks, and Good Will: The Story of the Quaker Oats Company*. New York: McGraw-Hill, 1967.

Martinez, Jessica, and Gregory A. Smith. "How the Faithful Voted: A Preliminary 2016 Analysis." Pew Research Center (November 9, 2016). https://www.pewresearch.org/fact-tank/2016/11/09/how-the-faithful-voted-a-preliminary-2016-analysis/.

Mauss, Marcel. "A Category of the Human Mind: The Notion of the Person; The Notion of the Self." Translated by W. D. Hallis. In *The Category of the Person: Anthropology, Philosophy, History*, edited by Michael Carrithers, Steven Collins, and Steven Lukes, 1–25. New York: Cambridge University Press, 1985.

———. *The Gift: The Form and Reason for Exchange in Archaic Societies*. Translated by W. D. Halls. New York: W.W. Norton, 2000.

McCloskey, Deirdre N. *The Bourgeois Virtues: Ethics for an Age of Commerce*. Chicago: University of Chicago Press, 2006.

———. *Knowledge and Persuasion in Economics*. New York: Cambridge University Press, 2008.

McCloskey, Robert G. *Conservatism in the Age of Enterprise: A Study of William Graham Sumner, Stephen J. Field, and Andrew Carnegie*. Cambridge, MA: Harvard University Press, 1951.

McKittrick, Katherine, ed. *Sylvia Wynter: On Being Human as Praxis*. Durham, NC: Duke University Press, 2015.

Medhurst, Martin J. "LBJ, Reagan, and the American Dream: Competing Visions of Liberty." *Presidential Studies Quarterly* 46, no. 1 (2016): 98–124.

Mercieca, Jennifer. *Demagogue for President: The Rhetorical Genius of Donald Trump*. College Station: Texas A&M University Press, 2020.

Mifsud, Mari Lee. *Rhetoric and the Gift: Ancient Rhetorical Theory and Contemporary*

Communication. Pittsburgh, PA: Duquesne University Press, 2015.

Milbank, John. "Can a Gift Be Given? Prolegomena to a Future Trinitarian Metaphysic." *Modern Theology* 11, no. 1 (1995): 120–61.

———. *Theology and Social Theory: Beyond Secular Reason.* 2nd ed. New York: Blackwell Publishing.

Miller, Vincent Jude. *Consuming Religion: Christian Faith and Practice in a Consumer Culture.* New York: Continuum, 2005.

Mirowski, Philip, and Dieter Plehwe, eds. *The Road from Mont Pelerin: The Making of the Neoliberal Thought Collective.* Cambridge, MA: Harvard University Press, 2009.

Mitropoulos, Angela. *Contract and Contagion: From Biopolitics to Oikonomia.* Brooklyn, NY: Minor Compositions, 2012.

Moreton, Bethany. *To Serve God and Wal-Mart: The Making of Christian Free Enterprise.* Cambridge, MA: Harvard University Press, 2009.

Morris, Alex. "False Idol—Why the Christian Right Worships Donald Trump." *Rolling Stone,* December 2, 2019. https://www.rollingstone.com/politics/politics-features/christian-right-worships-donald-trump-915381/.

Morris, Charles E., III, and Stephen Howard Browne, eds. *Readings on the Rhetoric of Social Protest.* 2nd ed. State College, PA: Strata Publishing, 2001.

Mumby, Dennis K. "What's Cooking in Organizational Discourse Studies? A Response to Alvesson and Karreman." *Human Relations* 64, no. 9 (2011): 1147–61.

Musgrave, Kevin. "A Battle for Hearts and Minds: Evangelical Capitalism and Pastoral Power in Bruce Barton's 'The Public.'" *Rhetoric and Public Affairs* 20, no. 1 (2017): 133–60.

Musgrave, Kevin, and Jeffrey Tischauser. "Radical Traditionalism, Metapolitics, and Identitarianism: The Rhetoric of Richard Spencer." *b2o: an online journal,* special issue: The New Extremism (September 1, 2019).

Musser, Joe. *Cereal Tycoon: Henry Parsons Crowell, Founder of the Quaker Oats Company.* Chicago: Moody Publishers, 2002.

Nader, Ralph, and Mark Green, eds. *Corporate Power in America: Ralph Nader's Conference on Corporate Accountability.* New York: Grossman Publishers, 1971.

Nadesan, Majia Holmer. "The Discourses of Corporate Spiritualism and Evangelical Capitalism." *Management Communication Quarterly* 13 (1999): 3–42.

Narkunas, J. Paul. *Reified Life: Speculative Capital and the Ahuman Condition.* New York: Fordham University Press, 2018.

Nash, George. *The Conservative Intellectual Movement in America since 1945.* New York: Basic Books, 1976.

244 | Bibliography

Nichols, John, and Robert W. McChesney. *Dollarocracy: How the Money-and-Media Election Complex Is Destroying America.* New York: Nation Books, 2013.

Nietzsche, Friedrich. *On the Genealogy of Morals.* Translated by Horace B. Samuel. Introduction by Costica Bradatan. New York: Barnes and Noble, 2006.

Novak, David R. "Democratic Work at an Organization-Society Boundary: Sociomateriality and the Communicative Instantiation." *Management Communication Quarterly* 20, no. 2 (2016): 218–44.

Obituary in the *Chicago Tribune,* October 24, 1944; "Henry Crowell, Head of Quaker Oats, Dies at 89"; Crowell, Henry P. CBC953; Moody Bible Institute, Chicago; June 20, 2016.

Obituary in the *Daily News,* October 24, 1944; "[H. P.] Crowell Dies; Leader in Quaker Oats Co."; Crowell, Henry P. CBC953; Moody Bible Institute, Chicago; June 20, 2016.

O'Gorman, Ned. *The Iconoclastic Imagination: Image, Catastrophe, and Economy in America from the Kennedy Assassination to September 11.* Chicago: University of Chicago Press, 2016.

Ojakangas, Mika. "Apostle Paul and the Profanation of the Law." *Distinktion: Scandinavian Journal of Social Theory* 18 (2009): 47–68.

———. "On the Pauline Roots of Biopolitics: Apostle Paul in Company with Foucault and Agamben." *Journal for Cultural and Religious Theory* 11, no. 1 (2010): 92–110.

Ong, Aiwha. *Neoliberalism as Exception: Mutations in Citizenship and Sovereignty.* Durham, NC: Duke University Press, 2006.

Opitz, Edmund A. *Religion and Capitalism: Allies, Not Enemies.* New Rochelle, NY: Arlington House, 1970.

Paliewicz, Nicholas. "How Trains Became People: Southern Pacific Railroad Co.'s Networked Rhetorical Culture and the Dawn of Corporate Personhood." *Journal of Communication Inquiry* 43, no. 2 (2019): 194–213.

Parekh, Serena. "Getting to the Root of Gender Inequality: Structural Injustice and Political Responsibility." *Hypatia* 26, no. 4 (2011): 672–89.

Patterson, Orlando. *Slavery and Social Death: A Comparative Study.* Cambridge, MA: Harvard University Press, 1982.

Peck, Jamie. *Constructions of Neoliberal Reason.* New York: Oxford University Press, 2010.

Peters, John Durham. *Speaking into the Air: A History of the Idea of Communication.* Chicago: University of Chicago Press, 1999.

Peters, Timothy D. "Corporations, Sovereignty, and the Religion of Neoliberalism." *Law and Critique* 29 (2018): 271–92.

Phillips-Fein, Kim. *Invisible Hands: The Making of the Conservative Movement from the New Deal to Reagan.* New York: W.W. Norton and Company, 2009.

Pomeroy, John Norton. *Some Account of the Work of Stephen J. Field as a State Judge, and Judge of the Supreme Court of the United States.* Chauncey and Black, 1881.

Pope, Daniel. *The Making of Modern Advertising.* New York: Basic Books, 1983.

Poulakos, John. "Interpreting Sophistical Rhetoric: A Response to Schiappa." *Philosophy and Rhetoric* 23, no. 3 (1990): 218–28.

Powell, Lewis F., Jr. "Attack on American Free Enterprise System." *Snail Darter Documents*, Paper 79. http://lawdigitalcommons.bc.edu/darter_materials/79 (1971).

———. "Education on Communism: What the Bar Can Do." Speech delivered to the Connecticut State Bar Association, October 4, 1962. *Washington and Lee University School of Law Scholarly Commons.* https://scholarlycommons.law.wlu.edu.

———. "A Lawyer Looks at Civil Disobedience." *Washington and Lee Law Review* 23, no. 2 (1966): 205–31.

———. "Prayer Breakfast, American Bar Association, San Francisco, CA." *Washington and Lee University School of Law Scholarly Commons.* https://scholarlycommons.law.wlu.edu.

President's Message; "Dedication Program, The Moody Bible Institute of Chicago, Feb. 4th, 1939"; Crowell, Henry P. CBC953; Moody Bible Institute, Chicago; June 20, 2016.

Quarles, Benjamin. *The Negro in the Making of America.* 3rd ed. New introduction by V. P. Franklin. New York: Simon and Schuster, 1996.

Rabban, David. *Free Speech in Its Forgotten Years.* New York: Cambridge University Press, 1998.

Rathbun, Lyon. "The Debate over Annexing Texas and the Emergence of Manifest Destiny." *Rhetoric and Public Affairs* 4, no. 3 (2001): 459–93.

Remini, Robert V. *Andrew Jackson.* New York: Twayne Publishers, 1966.

Ribuffo, Leo P. "Jesus Christ as Business Statesman: Bruce Barton and the Selling of Corporate Capitalism." *American Quarterly* 33, no. 2 (1981): 206–31.

Ricci, David M. *The Transformation of American Politics: The New Washington and the Rise of Think Tanks.* New Haven, CT: Yale University Press, 1993.

Robbins, Jeffrey W. "The White Christian Nationalist Hustle." In *Doing Theology in the Age of Trump: A Critical Report on Christian Nationalism*, edited by Jeffrey W. Robbins and Clayton Crockett, 30–34. Eugene, OR: Cascade Press, 2018.

Robin, Corey. *The Reactionary Mind: Conservatism from Edmund Burke to Sarah Palin*. New York: Oxford University Press.

Roediger, David. *The Wages of Whiteness: Race and the Making of the American Working Class*. New ed. Introduction by Kathleen Cleaver. New York: Verso, 2007.

Rorty, Richard. *Philosophy and the Mirror of Nature*. Princeton, NJ: Princeton University Press, 1981.

Rose, Nikolas. *Inventing Our Selves: Psychology, Power, and Personhood*. Cambridge: Cambridge University Press, 1996.

Rossiter, Clinton. *Conservatism in America*. New York: Alfred A. Knopf, 1955.

Rothbard, Murray. "Life in the Old Right." In *The Paleoconservatives: New Voices on the Old Right*, edited by Joseph Scotchie, 19–30. New York: Routledge, 1999.

Rowland, Allison L. *Zoetropes and the Politics of Humanhood*. Columbus: Ohio State University Press, 2020.

Rowland, Robert C., and John A. Jones. "Entelechial and Reformative Symbolic Trajectories in Contemporary Conservatism: A Case Study of Reagan and Buchanan in Houston and Beyond." *Rhetoric & Public Affairs* 4, no. 1 (2001): 55–84.

Rowland, Robert C., and John M. Jones. "Reagan's Farewell Address: Redefining the American Dream." *Rhetoric & Public Affairs* 20, no. 4 (2017): 635–66.

———. "Reagan's Strategy for the Cold War and the Evil Empire Address." *Rhetoric & Public Affairs* 19, no. 3 (2016): 427–63.

Santa Clara County v. Southern Pacific Railroad Co., 118 U.S. 394 (1886).

Saxton, Alexander. *The Indispensable Enemy: Labor and the Anti-Chinese Movement in California*. Berkeley: University of California Press, 1995.

Scanlon, Jennifer. "Thrift and Advertising." In *Thrift and Thriving in America: Capitalism and Moral Order from the Puritans to the Present*, edited by Joshua J. Yates and James Davison Hunter, 284–306. New York: Oxford University Press, 2011.

Schaefer, Donovan O. "Whiteness and Civilization: Shame, Race, and the Rhetoric of Donald Trump." *Communication and Critical/Cultural Studies* 17, no. 1 (2019): 1–18.

Schiappa, Edward. "History and Neo-Sophistic Criticism: A Reply to Poulakos." *Philosophy and Rhetoric* 23, no. 4 (1990): 307–15.

———. "Neo-Sophistic Rhetorical Criticism or the Historical Reconstruction of

Sophistic Doctrine?" *Philosophy and Rhetoric* 23, no. 3 (1990): 192–217.

Schlesinger, Arthur, Jr. *The Age of Jackson*. Boston: Little, Brown and Company, 1953.

Schmitt, Carl. *Political Theology: Four Chapters on the Concept of Sovereignty*. Translated by George Schwab. Foreword by Tracy B. Strong. Chicago: University of Chicago Press, 2006.

Schram, Sanford F., and Marianna Pavlovskaya, eds. *Rethinking Neoliberalism: Resisting the Disciplinary Regime*. New York: Routledge, 2018.

Scotchie, Joseph. "Introduction: Paleoconservatism as the Opposition Party." In *The Paleoconservatives: New Voices on the Old Right*, edited by Joseph Scotchie, 1–18. New York: Routledge, 1999.

Sedgwick, Theodore. *What Is a Monopoly?; or Some Considerations upon the Subject of Corporations and Currency*. New York: George P. Scott and Co., 1835.

Sellers, Charles. *The Market Revolution: Jacksonian America, 1815–1846*. New York: Oxford University Press, 1991.

Shah, Nayan. *Contagious Divides: Epidemics and Race in San Francisco's Chinatown*. Berkeley: University of California Press, 2001.

Shumsky, Neil Larry. *The Evolution of Political Protest and the Workingmen's Party of California*. Columbus: Ohio State University Press, 1991.

Simon, William E. *A Time for Truth*. New York: McGraw Hill, 1978.

Singh, Devin. *Divine Currency: The Theological Power of Money in the West*. Stanford, CA: Stanford University Press, 2018.

Siraganian, Lisa. *Modernism and the Meaning of Corporate Persons*. Oxford: Oxford University Press, 2021.

Sklansky, Jeffrey. *The Soul's Economy: Market Society and Selfhood in American Thought, 1820–1920*. Chapel Hill: University of North Carolina Press, 2002.

Slobodian, Quinn. *Globalists: The End of Empire and the Birth of Neoliberalism*. Cambridge, MA: Harvard University Press, 2018.

Smith, Craig R. "Ronald Reagan's Rhetorical Re-invention of Conservatism." *Quarterly Journal of Speech* 103, no. 1–2 (2017): 33–65.

Smith, James Allen. *The Idea Brokers: Think Tanks and the Rise of the New Policy Elite*. New York: Free Press, 1991.

Spivak, Gayatri Chakravorty. *An Aesthetic Education in the Era of Globalization*. Cambridge, MA: Harvard University Press, 2013.

Stahl, Jason. *Right Moves: The Conservative Think Tank in American Political Culture since 1945*. Chapel Hill: University of North Carolina Press, 2016.

248 | Bibliography

Stefancic, Jean, and Richard Delgado. *No Mercy: How Conservative Think Tanks and Foundations Changed America's Social Agenda.* Philadelphia: Temple University Press, 1996.

Stein, Laura. *Speech Rights in America: The First Amendment, Democracy, and the Media.* Urbana: University of Illinois Press, 2006.

Stern, Phillip J. *The Company-State: Corporate Sovereignty and the Early-Modern Foundations of the British Empire in India.* Oxford: Oxford University Press, 2012.

Stimilli, Elettra. *The Debt of the Living: Ascesis and Capitalism.* Translated by Ariana Bove. Foreword by Roberto Esposito. Albany: State University of New York Press, 2017.

Stole, Inger. *Advertising on Trial: Consumer Activism and Corporate Public Relations in the 1930s.* Urbana: University of Illinois Press, 2006.

Strang, Stephen E. *God and Donald Trump.* Lake Mary, FL: FrontLine, 2017.

———. *God, Trump, and COVID-19: How the Pandemic Is Affecting Christians, the World, and America's 2020 Election.* Lake Mary, FL: FrontLine, 2020.

———. *God, Trump, and the 2020 Election: Why He Must Win and What's at Stake for Christians If He Loses.* Lake Mary, FL: FrontLine, 2020.

———. *Trump Aftershock: The President's Seismic Impact on Culture and Faith in America.* Lake Mary, FL: FrontLine, 2018.

Stuckey, Mary E. *Playing the Game: The Presidential Rhetoric of Ronald Reagan.* New York: Praeger, 1990.

Swisher, Carl Brent. *Stephen J. Field: Craftsman of the Law.* Washington, DC: Brookings Institution, 1930.

Taubes, Jacob. *Occidental Eschatology.* Translated with a preface by David Ratmoko. Stanford, CA: Stanford University Press, 2009.

Taylor, Charles. *A Secular Age.* Cambridge, MA: Belknap Press of Harvard University Press, 2007.

Tedlow, Richard. *Keeping the Corporate Image: Public Relations and Business, 1900–1950.* Greenwich, CT: JAI Press, 1979.

Terrett v. Taylor, 9 Cranch 43 (1815).

The Railroad Tax Case: County of San Mateo v. Southern Pacific Railroad Co. Opinions of Justice Field and Judge Sawyer. Delivered in the U.S. Circuit Court at San Francisco, September 25, 1882.

Thimsen, Freya. "The People against Corporate Personhood: Doxa and Dissensual Democracy." *Quarterly Journal of Speech* 101, no. 3 (2015): 485–508.

Thornton, Harrison John. *The History of the Quaker Oats Company.* Chicago:

University of Chicago Press, 1933.

Tischauser, Jeffrey, and Kevin Musgrave. "Far-Right Media as Imitated Counterpublicity: A Discourse Analysis on Racial Meaning and Identity on Vdare. com." *Howard Journal of Communications* 31, no. 3 (2020): 282–96.

Towns, Armond. "Black 'Matter' Lives." *Women's Studies in Communication* 41, no. 4 (2018): 349–58.

Trachtenberg, Alan. *The Incorporation of America: Culture and Society in the Gilded Age*. 25th anniversary ed. New York: Hill and Wang, 2007.

"Trade Heads Challenge Raw Deal." *New York Journal*, December 4, 1935. Bruce Barton Papers, box 60, State Historical Society of Wisconsin.

Van Horn, Rob. "Reinventing Monopoly and the Role of Corporations: The Roots of Chicago Law and Economics." In *The Road from Mont Pelerin: The Making of the Neoliberal Thought Collective*, edited by Philip Mirowski and Dieter Plehwe, 204–37. Cambridge, MA: Harvard University Press, 2009.

Vasquez, Consuelo, and Ruben Dittus Benavente. "Revisiting Autopoiesis: Studying the Constitutive Dynamics of Organization as a System of Narratives." *Management Communication Quarterly* 30, no. 2 (2016): 269–74.

Vatter, Miguel. *The Republic of the Living: Biopolitics and the Critique of Civil Society*. New York: Fordham University Press, 2014.

Vaughn, Stephen. *Holding Fast the Inner Lines: Democracy, Nationalism, and the Committee on Public Information*. Chapel Hill: University of North Carolina Press, 1980.

Veblen, Thorstein. *Absentee Ownership and Business Enterprise in Recent Times: The Case of America*. New York: Viking Press, 1938.

Viguerie, Richard A. *America's Right Turn: How Conservatives Used New and Alternative Media to Take Power*. Chicago: Bonus Books, 2004.

———. *Conservatives Betrayed: How George W. Bush and Other Big Government Republicans Hijacked the Conservative Cause*. Los Angeles: Bonus Books, 2006.

Walker, Anders. *The Burning House: Jim Crow and the Making of Modern America*. New Haven: Yale University Press, 2018.

Wander, Philip. "The Third Persona: An Ideological Turn in Rhetorical Theory." *Central States Speech Journal* 35, no. 4 (1984): 197–216.

Warren, Calvin. *Ontological Terror: Blackness, Nihilism, and Emancipation*. Durham, NC: Duke University Press, 2018.

Watts, Eric King. "Postracial Fantasies, Blackness, and Zombies." *Communication and Critical/Cultural Studies* 14, no. 4 (2017): 317–33.

Weaver, Richard. *Ideas Have Consequences*. Chicago: University of Chicago Press, 1948.

Weber, Max. *The Protestant Ethic and the Spirit of Capitalism*. Translated by Talcott Parsons. Foreword by R. H. Tawney. New York: Scribner, 1930.

Weheliye, Alexander G. *Habeas Viscus: Racializing Assemblages, Biopolitics, and Black Feminist Theories of the Human*. Durham, NC: Duke University Press, 2014.

Weiser, Dennis. "Two Concepts of Communication as Criteria for Collective Responsibility." *Journal of Business Ethics* 7, no. 10 (1988): 735–44.

West, Robin. "Freedom of the Church and Our Endangered Civil Rights: Exiting the Social Contract." In *The Rise of Corporate Religious Liberty*, edited by Micah Schwarzman, Chad Flanders, and Zoe Robinson, 399–418. New York: Oxford University Press, 2016.

Weyrich, Paul M., and William S. Lind. *The Next Conservatism*. South Bend, IN: St. Augustine Press, 2009.

Wilentz, Sean. *Andrew Jackson*. New York: Times Books, 2005.

William Robert Catton to The Bobbs-Merrill Company, April 25, 1925. Bruce Barton Papers, box 107, State Historical Society of Wisconsin.

Winslow, Luke. *American Catastrophe: Fundamentalism, Climate Change, Gun Rights, and the Rhetoric of Donald J. Trump*. Columbus: Ohio State University Press, 2020.

———. *Economic Injustice and the Rhetoric of the American Dream*. Lanham, MD: Lexington Books, 2017.

Wong, Edlie L. *Racial Reconstruction: Black Inclusion, Chinese Exclusion and the Fictions of Citizenship*. New York: New York University Press, 2015.

Wynter, Sylvia. "Unsettling the Coloniality of Being/Power/Truth/Freedom: Towards the Human, After Man, Its Overrepresentation—An Argument," *CR: The New Centennial Review* 3, no. 3 (2003): 257-337.

Young, Iris Marion. "Responsibility and Global Justice: A Social Connection Model." *Social Policy and Philosophy Foundation* 23, no. 1 (2006): 102–30.

Zakaras, Alex. "Nature, Religion, and the Market in Jacksonian Political Thought." *Journal of the Early Republic* 39, no. 1 (2019): 123–33.

Zarefsky, David, C. Miller-Tutzauer, and Frank Tutzauer. "Reagan's Safety Net for the Truly Needy: The Rhetorical Use of Definition." *Central States Speech Journal* 35 (1984): 113–19.

Index

A

advertising, 62, 64, 71, 75, 81, 87, 88, 90; as apostles of modernity, 59; as benevolent force, 82; and corporate moral legitimacy, 63; evangelical functions of, 85, 92; history of, 57, 58, 60; as manipulative, 86; parables of, 66, 84; and pastoral power, 64, 83; white male composition of, 67

Agamben, Giorgio, xxii, xxiii, 2, 43

agency, xvi, 12, 65, 67, 185, 187; collective, 68; perceived loss of, 34; public, 90; rhetorical, 128

Anglo-Saxonism, 21, 28

Arendt, Hannah, 5, 185

assemblage, xviii; Christian capitalist assemblage, xxx, 160; of Jacksonian personhood, 30. See also *dispositif*

atheism, 101; of Communism, 96, 156, 163; of political economy, xxii

B

Barton, Bruce, xxvii, 63, 68, 78–82, 85–93, 96, 111; and *The Man Nobody Knows*, 83, 84, 91

Batten, Barton, Durstine, and Osborne (BBDO), xxvii, 63, 68, 81, 82

biopolitics, xx, xxi, xxv; affirmative, 185; biopolitical theory, 2; of race, 42; and rhetoric, 3

body, xxvi, 8, 9, 14, 23, 24; and biopolitics, 3, 5; bodily capacity, 42; Chinese, 43; civil bodies, 8; corporate, xxvii, 47, 149; of corporation, 32, 48; duality of mind and, 49; human and nonhuman, 2; of laborer, xxvii; and metonymy, 33, 52; of nation, xxvii, 25, 29, 30, 37, 44; political bodies, 45; quasi-disembodiment, 13, 16; white, masculine, able-body, xxvii, 13, 24, 29, 51, 52

Buckley v. Valeo, xxviii, 129, 130, 131

251

Buckley, William F., 108, 109, 125, 140, 144

C

California, 24, 27, 28, 31, 35, 36, 47; state constitution, 38, 40, 41, 46; state tax law, 39

capitalism: Calvinist ethos of, 70, 77; Christian, 68, 105, 165, 168; as civilizing force, 48; consumer, 63, 67; corporate, 85, 93, 178; and creative destruction, 156; and democracy, 20, 21; entrepreneurial, 56; and evangelicalism, 135, 139; humanization of, 60; industrial, 134; liberal, xv, xxvi, 96, 115; logic of, xvi, xxi; and monopoly, 44, 100; moral, 80; and neoliberalism, xxiv, 138, 159, 160, 176; right-wing critics of, 148; self-regulating, 81; and Trumpism, 141, 161, 162; versus Communism, 102, 107, 142, 144; Western, 122. *See also* evangelical capitalism

catastrophic homology, xxix, 154, 155, 163, 164, 173; rhetoric of, xxviii

Chambers, Whittaker, 101, 102, 106, 144

Chinese: Burlingame Treaty, 36, 38, 41, 42, 44; exclusion, 44, 46, 49, 50; immigration, 35, 43, 45; labor, 24, 34, 39, 40; personhood of, 42

Christianity, xiii, xiv, xv, xix, xxv, 8, 92; and capitalism, 96, 105, 135, 138, 139, 165, 168; Catholicism, 14; Charismatic Pentecostal, 141, 162; and civilization, 112; debasement of, 152, 175; and doctrine of common grace, 167, 168; evangelicalism, xxviii, xxix; and founding fathers, 166; fundamentalism, 75, 155, 158, 169, 170; and Gnosticism, 99; and industry, 53; and media, 162; and nationalism, 95, 163, 166; non-Christian, 44; and nondenominational orthodoxy, 73; and political economy, 14, 15; and Progressivism, 55, 56, 68, 77; Protestantism, 20, 63, 65, 85, 154; secularization of, 78, 79, 93, 149; social gospel, 80, 103; and society, 52; and state power, xviii, 42, 106, 143; and Trumpism, xxviii, 154, 156, 169, 173; values of, 69, 70; and work ethic, 70, 74

Citizens United, xv, 135, 137, 138, 140

civil society, xx, xxiii, 2, 3, 10, 11, 12, 125, 138, 187; and rhetoric, xxi

Civil War, 31, 32, 57; post-Civil War era, 52

Cold War, xxvii, 95; and Christian capitalism, 135, 139; and conservatism, 93, 144; and liberal consensus, 107, 109; post-Cold War climate, 148; and radicalism, 111, 156; as theological struggle, 96, 102, 103, 115;

Communism: anti-communism, xx, 97, 153; and atheism, xxviii, 96, 156, 163; and dignity of person, 100, 101, 107, 177; forces of, 99; as global specter, 95, 105, 169, 173; as liberal heresy, 104; and liberty under law, 114, 115; and New Deal, 103; and political radicalism, 111, 112, 121, 122; as secular faith, 102, 106

Connolly, William, xviii, 138, 140, 159, 160, 187; and immanent naturalism, 182; and nontheistic reverence, 178, 183, 184

conscience, xxvi, 138, 139, 167; of America, 141; freedom of, xxix, 140, 171; protections of, 168

conservatism, xix, xx; compassionate, 146; Conservative, Inc., 149; fusionism, 97, 103, 125, 134, 135; imaginative, 111; as insurgent force, 107, 147, 150; and laissez-faire, 52; libertarian, xxvii, 52, 98, 99, 104, 111, 112, 140; of Lochner Era, 53; and Middle American Radicals (MARs), 150, 151; and Moral Majority, 137, 144; as movement, xxviii, 93, 96, 101, 102, 122; neoconservatism, 110, 125; and the New Right, 108, 109, 110, 113, 135, 137, 141, 144; and organicism, 30; paleoconservatism, xxviii, 139, 146, 147, 148, 157; performative tradition of, 145; pragmatic, 114; in relationship to Federalists and Whigs, 26; of Ronald Reagan, xxviii, 141, 144; traditionalism, xxvi, 111, 151, 176; and Trumpism, 139, 141

consumer culture, xxvii, 62, 63, 64, 68, 81; and salvation, 65, 89, 92

corporation: and affirmative biopolitics, 185; as alien, 26, 37, 40, 45, 149; body, 47; and Christian theology, 8–11; as civilizing force, 48, 49, 53; and communication, 60, 62, 75; eleemosynary, 17; as enemy of labor, 53; and Fourteenth Amendment, 32–34; and freedom, xiv; and history of political economy, xxiii, 4, 15, 16, 18; and Jacksonian politics, 24, 25; as limit figure, xxvi; as marginalized, 119, 125, 128, 135, 137; and nationalism, 156; as normative model of personhood, xv, 50, 52, 177; as parasite, 11, 44; and the public sphere, 120; and relationship with public, 61, 67, 90; social responsibility, 124; and sovereignty, 138; as shepherd, 65, 68, 76, 78, 89, 90; as soulless, xxvii, 57, 59; as transnational, 148; power of, 39; Progressive critiques of, 56, 63; public v. private, 17; quasi-public, 19–21, 39, 55, 64, 72, 100, 101, 112; and rhetoric, xxv; salvation of, 78; and voice, xxviii, 93, 121, 130, 133, 134; whiteness of, 51

COVID-19 pandemic, 170, 171, 183

Crowell, Henry Parsons: and conservative movement, 97; early life, 69, 71, 79, 92, 93; and evangelical capitalism, xxvii, 63, 68, 92, 93, 96; and Moody Bible Institute (MBI), 73, 74, 75, 78, 154; and stewardship, 77; and theory of constant exposure, 72, 83

D

Dartmouth v. Woodward, 17, 18, 41

Dean, Mitchell, xxii, xxix, 177

deliberation, xxiv; deliberative democracy, 124; deliberative functions of rhetoric, 2; and discourse of evangelical capitalism, 65, 68; and inclusion, 126

Derrida, Jacques, xvii; and anti-naturalism, 182; and the gift, 180, 181

dispositif, xxvi; of Christianity, 8; of personhood, 2, 7. *See also* assemblage

dominium, 6, 7, 98, 113

E

economic theology: alternatives to, 177; of Cold War capitalism, 93; and corporation, 47; and neoliberalism, 98, 158, 175; and paleoconservatism, 148; of personhood, 12; as theoretical perspective, xiv–xvi, xx–xxxvi; and Trumpism, xxix, 155–57, 163, 164, 176. *See also* theology

Eisenhower, Dwight, 91, 105, 106, 107

Enlightenment, xiii, xxvi, 1, 13; and liberalism, 28, 104; values of, 16, 30

entrepreneurs, 19, 56, 143, 144

eschatology, xxix, 97, 161, 171

Esposito, Roberto, xxvi, 2, 3, 6, 8, 12

evangelical capitalism, xxvii, 64, 65, 72–76, 89, 90, 92, 95; and service, 63, 68; and stewardship, 63, 68, 70. *See also* capitalism

F

Field, Stephen J.: conservative jurisprudence, 41; and corporate body, xxvii, 21, 33, 51; and corporate equal protection, 46–49; decision of *In re Ah Fong*, 34; and Jacksonian

persuasion, 26, 27, 31, 32, 52; and laissez faire, 24; and liberty of contract, 34, 39; and political position on Chinese immigration, 35, 37, 38

First National Bank v. Bellotti, xxviii, 130, 131

Foucault, Michel, xvi, xx, xxi, xxii, 2, 64, 185

Fourteenth Amendment: and Chinese exclusion, 37, 44; and corporate personhood, xxvii, 51, 130; and conspiracy theory, 35; and debates over meaning of personhood, 24; equal protection clause, 32, 34, 38–41, 45, 46, 119; and liberty of contract, 48, 50, 131

freedom, xx, 99, 100, 103, 108, 132; of conscience, xxix, 139, 140, 171; of contract, 39; economic, 25, 120, 124; of individual, 143, 145; as practice, 187; religious, xxix, 15, 153, 159, 165, 166; versus slavery in Cold War, 105, 156; of white men, 157. *See also* liberty

Friedman, Benjamin, 12, 14, 15

Friedman, Milton, 99, 122, 125

G

genealogy: as method, xvi, xvii; of governmentality, xxii; of personhood, xxvi

gift, xxx; of charter, 11; and Jacques Derrida, 180, 18; and Marcel Mauss, 179, 180, 181; personhood as, 4, 12, 173, 179, 183, 184, 188; as theory of human relations, 179; wealth as, 69

God, xiii, xxii, 8, 15, 29, 69, 70, 72; Barry Goldwater, 91, 107, 108, 110; Christ, xiv, 8, 69, 79; and corporation, 66; and debt, 182; and divine plan for United States, 171; divine will of, 165; on earth, 100; as ineffable, 68, 91, 104; kingdom of, 75, 76, 164; mortal god of state, 10; and providence, 142, 143, 144; rebuke of, 103; vengeance of, 170; Word of, 140, 152, 154

Gottfried, Paul, 108, 125, 139, 147, 149, 150

Grear, Anna, 13, 179, 184, 185

H

Hayek, Friedrich von, 98, 102, 104, 113, 144, 148

Hobbes, Thomas, 10–12, 44, 120, 149, 182

Hobby Lobby (Burwell v. Hobby Lobby), xv, 135, 137, 138, 140, 159

Hoffman, Ogden, 39, 40, 42, 43

humanism: anti-humanism, 178; liberal, 13; limited, 184; more humane, 175; post-humanism, 3; recuperation of, 177, 178, 179, 185

I

immanence: and bureaucracy, 100; and dominium, 98, 113; and economic praxis, 11; of existence, 177; and governance, xxii, xxvi, 2, 47; and means, 5, 105; and naturalism, 181, 182; and pleasures of the self,

115; and political economy, xiii, xiv, 53, 96; of price system, 144; in relationship to transcendence, xix, xxix, 142, 157, 162; and resistance, 188

In re Tiburcio Parrott, 25, 39, 40, 41, 45

incorporation, xxvii, 19, 29, 52; and the body, 23, 24; liberalization of, 32

individualism: possessive, xxix, xxx, 4, 134, 179; and Chinese labor, 42; classical, 53; corporate, 17; in early Christianity, 8; and Enlightenment, 1, 13; and market liberalization, 11; militant, 154, 155, 163; and neoliberalism, 183, 187; and Progressive reform, 56; ruthless, 169

J

Jackson, Andrew, 18, 27; age of Jackson, 19, 20, 21, 42, 96; Jacksonian democracy, 25, 26, 28, 29; and Jacksonian politics of personhood, 30, 31, 149

Jefferson, Thomas, 28, 30

K

Kearney, Denis, 24, 37, 53; and Workingmen's Party of California (WPC), 25, 36, 38, 40, 44

Kirk, Russell, xxviii, 99, 111, 112, 125, 148

Kotsko, Adam, xxviii, 156, 157

L

laissez-faire, 14, 24, 28, 29, 31; conservatism, 52; constitutionalism,

256 | Index

38, 40; jurisprudence, 52

Leshem, Dotan, 4, 5, 8

liberalism: political liberalism, xiii, xx, 101, 102; and capitalism, xv, xxvi, 11, 96, 115, 135; and civil society, 10, 12; classical, xxi, 59, 132; consensus, 107, 109, 110; contract law, 18; and corporate law, 19; corporate, 109, 123; decline of, 145; and democracy, 122; and economism, 176; and Enlightenment, xxvi, 13, 28; and governance, xxi, xxiii, 51; and individualism, 16, 64; and naturalism, 98; as opposed to democracy, 98, 99, 114; and personhood, 4; and political economy, xiv, 30; and racial difference, 49; as secular religion, 163; and United States, 15

libertarians: and anti-Communism, 102, 125, 148; Christian libertarianism, 93, 104, 144; and conservatism, xix, 52; and corporate liberals, 123; opposition to traditionalists, 98–100, 103, 106, 148; triumph of, 108, 109

liberty, 31, 32, 50, 52, 96, 112, 116; of contract, 33, 34, 39, 48; economic freedom, 56; of individual, 97, 108, 113, 132; of speech, 138; religious, 138, 152, 171; under law, 115. *See also* freedom

life, xxi, 3, 50; beauty of, 183; of corporation, 47; democratic, 181; denial of, 42; as everlasting, 160; fragility of, xxx, 178; gift of, 176, 177, 178, 188; nontheistic reverence for, 178; perpetual life, 9; political

and economic, 14, 67; public, 60, 77, 166; social, 186; uncertainty of, 157; value of, xxx, 2, 176, 179, 184

Locke, John, 12, 13, 14, 15

M

MacPherson, C. B., 11, 12, 13

manifest destiny, xxvii, 25, 27, 28, 30, 48; and political theology, 29

Masterpiece Cake Shop v. Colorado Civil Rights Commission, 159, 172

materiality, 128; actor-network theory (ANT), xxv; and affect, xxiv; of body, 179; of corporate body, 50; new materialism, xviii, xxiv; sociomateriality, xxiv; of world, 182

Mauss, Marcel, 1, 2, 7, 8; on the gift, 179–81

Mexican American War, 27, 29

modernity: advertisers as apostles of, 59, 65, 66, 68, 84; and biopolitics, xx; and corporation, 89, 91; and industrialism, 48, 63, 78, 79, 96; luxuries of, 64; and political liberalism, 12; and secularization, xiv, 92

N

neoliberalism: and capitalism, 138, 159, 160; and dehumanization, 165, 175, 184, 188; heretical, xxviii, 156, 157, 158; late, xxvi; logics, 178; and moral order, 135; and personhood, 177, 188; as political cosmology, 176; as political identity, xix, 183; racial, 151; rationality of, 187; Reagan-era, xxviii, 143; resistance to, xxv; rhetoric of, xxx; right-wing critics of, 148; rise of, 98, 99, 111; scholarly approaches to, 211n8; theological inheritances of, xxii, xxiii, 139, 144

Nietzsche, Friedrich, xvi, 159

Nixon, Richard, 112, 117, 126, 127, 129

O

oikonomia, xxii, 4, 5; *oikos*, 16

Opitz, Edmund A., 104, 144

order, 100, 101, 124; capitalist, 88; economic, xx, xxiii; geopolitical, 151; moral, 16, 40, 112; natural, 98; political, 110; providential, xxiii, 28, 31; public, 116; social, 67, 96, 109, 154, 158, 159, 186; of things, 160; transcendent, 97

P

personhood, xix; absolute power of slavery, 7; and biopolitics, 2; of Chinese migrants, 42; and *Citizens United*, 137, 138, 140; contractual v. constitutional, 185; corporate personhood, xv, xix, 112, 130–34; dignity of, 97, 101, 104, 106, 107, 177; and economic theology, xxiii; economic theories of, 5, 8, 175; evangelical-capitalist, 160, 161, 162; and Fourteenth Amendment, 32, 34, 40, 50; genealogy of, xvi–xviii, xxvi, 1; as gift, xxx, 4, 12, 173, 176–79, 182–84; hierarchy of, 25, 51, 52; human, xiv, xxiii, xxv, xxix, 2, 13, 100; as instrument of power,

xxvi, 3, 6, 7; as locus of politics, 176; Jacksonian politics of, 30; Justice Field's legal theories of, 27; and marketplace of ideas, 119; metaphorical attributes of, xxvi, 24; metaphysics of, 7, 11; natural persons v. artificial persons, 8, 9, 10, 18, 41, 42, 130, 131; and neoliberalism, 143; nonperson, xxvi, 7; regime of, 49; rhetoric of, xviii, xxv; sacralization of, 178; theories of corporate, 46, 186; and Trumpism, 141, 159

political economy: and atheism, xxii; and biopolitics, xx; of credit, 19; genealogy of, xvi, xxiii, xxvi; modern, 64; and personhood, xix; and producerism, xxvii, 43; as rationality of government, 11; relationship to Christianity, xiii, xiv, xxv; Smithian, 14, 15; and white male autonomy, 30

Powell, Lewis F., Jr., xxviii, 97, 136; and the Civil Rights Movement, 114–16; and diversity, 112, 113, 119, 125, 126, 131–33; and Powell Memo, 111, 117, 120–30, 133; and *Regents v. Bakke*, 117, 118, 126, 132

power: and biopolitics, xx, xxi; corporate, 68, 121, 124, 128, 131; federal, 113, 114, 118; language of, xvi; of language, xvi, xvii; of market economy, xxiii, 53; in modern West, xxv; of neoliberalism, xxiv; ordering, 2; pastoral, 64, 65; of personhood, xxv; as political negotiation, xxix; sovereign, xiv, xx, xxiii, xxvi, 2, 11, 42, 47, 177, 185; state, xxiii, 100, 106;

258 | Index

and will, xvi

private, xxvi, 11; commerce, 17; contract, 18; corporations, 17, 19; life of power, 140; and the market, 98, 113; ownership, 184; property, 100; realm of economic activity, 14, 99; realm of the home, 47, 109; in U.S. liberalism, 15

Progressive Era, xxvii; and anti-corporate sentiment, 56, 58, 60, 63; faith in science, 61, 77; Progressive reformers, 55, 68

property, xxx, 4, 5, 12, 15, 19, 27, 172; artificial, 131; common, 184; corporate, 16–18, 46–49, 185; and corporate speech, 130, 131; and equal protection, 40; private, 34, 43, 100; right to, 39, 41, 42, 50, 179; and slavery, 6

public relations, 87, 88, 89, 92; and corporate moral legitimacy, 63; and femininity, 62; history of, 57, 60, 61; and pastoral power, 64, 83, 90; and publicity, 61, 62, 81, 84, 86

public, xxvi, 11; anxieties, 59; Christianity in, 154, 168, 171; and corporate communications, 57; corporations, 17; discourse, 164; as flock, 65, 68, 76, 88, 89, 90; functions of *oikonomia*, 5; infrastructure, 17; opinion, 60; realm of political life, 14, 166; sphere, 110, 119, 120, 125–32; in U.S. liberalism, 15; welfare, 108

Q

Q-Anon, 141, 163

Quaker Oats, xxvii; and Henry Parsons Crowell, 63, 71; as pioneer of advertising, 58, 68, 72–74, 76

R

Reagan, Ronald, xxviii; and neoliberalism, 138, 139, 144–46, 148; and New Right, 137

ressentiment, 140, 159, 160, 162, 165, 173, 175, 176

rhetoric: of American liberalism, 15, 16, 49; apocalyptic, 175; and biopolitics, 3; and the body, 23, 24; and the catastrophic homology, xxviii, 152, 154, 155; and civil society, xxi; and collective responsibility, 186; and confession, 65; and conservatism, xx, 52, 53, 103, 147; of conspiracy, 157; as constitutive, xvii; and co-optation of identity politics, 151; of corporate personhood, xviii, 25; and criticism, xv, xix; and democracy, xxix, 181; of Denis Kearney, 40; and dignity of the person, 97; and *dispositif*, 2; of diversity, 118, 119; and double bind, 110; and economics, xxiii, xxiv, xxv; and the gift, 180; of human rights, 185; and incorporation, 24; Jacksonian, 31, 42; of John Birch Society, 171; of Justice Field, 34, 47; of Justice Powell, 120, 123, 124, 130, 131, 133, 134; of the labor theory of value, 43; and manifest destiny, 28; of the market, 132; of Middle American Radicals (MARs),

150; and neoliberalism, xxx, 177; and the parables of advertising, 66; and performative tradition of conservatism, 145; and personhood, xxvi, 7; and perverse style, 158, 159; and political action, 187, 188; of political correctness, 149; and politics of personhood, 176; and popular sovereignty, 30; and Progressive reformers, 68; pro-Trump, 154; rhetorical criticism, xv; and rhetorical strategies, 59; and Roman Empire, 5, 6; and Ronald Reagan, 142, 143, 144; and third persona, 128; of service, 63, 78, 82, 87, 90, 92; of Stephen E. Strang, 141, 162–65, 168, 171, 173; of stewardship, 63, 69, 73, 74, 77; of radical conservatives, 106, 153; theological function of, xvi; of traditionalism, 99, 101; of Trumpism, 156, 160, 161, 162, 167, 169, 172; of yellow peril, 44

Roman law, xxvi, 1, 12; Canon, 8; and Empire, 5; of persona, 3, 6, 7

Romney, Mitt, xv, 146, 147

Roosevelt, Franklin Delano: and conservative opposition, 153; and New Deal, 88, 90, 93, 103, 110; and reshaping of American liberalism, xx; and statism, 91, 96, 110, 153

rule of law, xx, 112, 113, 114, 115, 116, 118, 121

S

San Mateo County v. Southern Pacific Railroad, 25, 35, 39, 40, 46, 47; and

The Railroad Tax Cases, 45, 131

Santa Clara County v. Southern Pacific Railroad Co., xxvii, 39, 46, 51, 52

Sawyer, Lorenzo, 39, 40, 45, 48, 49, 50

Schmitt, Carl, xxii, 98, 148

Second National Bank of the United States, 18, 26

secular: Christology, 161; forces, 165, 167; humanism, 160; martyrology, 161; new world order, 163; faith, xxv; secularism, xiii, 76; secularization, xiv, xxii, 9; secularization of personhood, xxvi, xxx, 173, 176, 177, 182; secularization of Protestant values, 66, 77, 78, 149; society, 158; reason, 155

Sellers, Charles, 20, 21, 26

service: and consumer culture, 62, 81, 84; as feminine, 85; and Jesus, 68, 80, 85–88; to public, 82; rhetoric of, 63, 78, 90, 92; and stewardship, 77

Slaughterhouse Cases, 33, 34, 39, 41

slavery, 3, 31; antislavery, 29, 30; freedom v. slavery in Cold War, 105; Roman, 6, 7

Smith, Adam, 12, 14, 15; on corporations, 17; and invisible hand, xxii

social contract, xxvi, 9, 12, 30, 53, 120, 180, 182

soul, xxvi, 8; corporate, xxvii, 55, 68, 88; corporations as soulless, 57; of nation, 95, 163; of Western civilization, 102

stewardship, 43, 69, 70, 73, 74, 78; modernization of, 77

260 | Index

Strang, Stephen E.: and Charisma
Publishing, 141, 162; rhetoric of,
165–69, 171, 173; and Story of Ahab,
164; and Trumpism, 163
Supreme Court, 27, 31, 33; Ninth Circuit,
31, 35, 41

T

Tea Party, 135, 139, 147, 151
Terrett v. Taylor, 17, 18
theology: Antinomianism, 20;
Arminianism, 12, 14, 20, 26;
Calvinism, 12, 28, 70, 76, 79, 154;
Christian, xiv, xv, xix, xxiii, xxv,
xxvi, xxviii, 1, 8, 9, 140, 168, 177;
and Civil Rights Movement, 115, 116;
covenantal, 142, 143; debasement
of, 152, 157; function of discourse,
xvi; Jansenism, 12; liberal, 82, 92;
of manifest destiny, 28, 29; and
personhood, 4; prosperity gospel, 153;
providential, 15, 25, 143, 183; and
religion, xix; theodicy, 14; theological
foundations of state, 10; theological
inheritances of political economy,
xxii, 4, 14; Trinitarian, xxii, 2, 7, 8;
of Trumpism, 156; of victimization,
149. *See also* economic theology
traditionalists, 125; and conservative
fusion, 102, 103, 106; decline of, 108,
109; opposition to libertarianism, 99,
100, 134
transcendence: and Christianity, xiii; and
ends, 5, 105; and imperium, 98, 113;
and language, 101; and liberalism,
xiv; loss of, 100; as plane of existence,

177; relationship to immanence, xix,
xxii, xxix, 142, 157, 162, 181; and
sovereignty, xxiii, 11; and truth, 99;
and values, 96, 115, 148; vantage, 2
Truman, Harry S., 103, 105, 106, 107
Trump, Donald, xv, xxviii, 140, 151, 157,
164, 165, 171; and economic theology,
155, 156, 163; and evangelical
support, 152, 154; and King Cyrus,
163, 167, 168; as martyr, 160, 161;
as redeemer, 141, 142, 158, 166, 167,
170, 173; and secularized Christology,
161; as strongman, 153; Trumpism,
xxviii, 138, 139, 159, 160, 169

U

United States, xviii, xxiii, xxvi;
and American Revolution, 14;
changing political economy of,
19; conservatism in, xix, 52;
Constitution, 17, 18; as global
superpower, 95, 106, 160; God's
divine plan for, 171; law, 16; legal
protections of, 46; and liberalism,
15, 59; markets, 16; and Paris
Agreement, 169; public, 68, 76;
religious awakening in, 163
V
value: economic, 7; of life, xxx, 2, 179,
184; politics of, 3, 4
Veblen, Thorstein, 19, 56
voice, xxvi; corporate, xxviii, 97, 124,
128, 133; diversity of, 119, 132;
elevation of, 120, 137, 130, 134; of
market, 110; voiceless, 121
vulnerability, xxix, 157, 167; embodied,

184, 185; of human estate, 165, 179, 183

W

Weaver, Richard, 99, 100, 102, 113, 134, 148

Weber, Max, xxii, 70, 77

Western civilization, and corporation, 51; cultural inheritances of, 115; decline of, 150; defense of, xxvii, xxviii, 111; racial exclusions of, 159; and theology, 116, 142; as under attack, 96, 97, 102